# Evil Genius in the
# Garden of Eden

# Evil Genius in the Garden of Eden

✦

## How Toxins Make Us Sick and Corporations Profit From Our Illness

*Vic Shayne*

iUniverse, Inc.
New York  Lincoln  Shanghai

# Evil Genius in the Garden of Eden
## How Toxins Make Us Sick and Corporations Profit From Our Illness

iUniverse, Inc.

For information address:
iUniverse, Inc.
2021 Pine Lake Road, Suite 100
Lincoln, NE 68512
www.iuniverse.com

ISBN: 0-595-30686-1

Printed in the United States of America

# Contents

# *Special Recognition*

A great number of people helped me produce this book, shape my opinions, and educate me about toxins, pollutants, corporate evil and sustainability, some of whom I have known personally, and others whose works are worth noting. But first, thanks to my wife, Janice, who first introduced our family to organic foods so we could jump off the merry-go-round of eating typical grocery store foods full of chemicals and other health-defying ingredients. Thanks also to my children: Tasha, for editing this work, and Josh for his eternal help in ironing out computer problems.

Thank you to Ed Begley, Jr., for not only being a talented and entertaining actor, but more importantly (at least to me), a great advocate of, and roll model for, environmentalism, sustainability and independent thinking. Thanks, Ed, for contributing to this book and supporting me in this effort. And thank you to my friend Graham Hill, 21wheels.com, for letting me complain to him over breakfasts about the frustrating reality of worldwide pollution and corporate deception. With Graham, it's wonderful to see a person dedicating his life to sustainable enterprises that serve to uplift all of humanity. Graham contributes to solutions with electric vehicles, sustainable mobility, logical transportation and creative urban planning. He's proof that business can exist in a win-win relationship with a healthy environment.

I especially want to honor one of the most prolific thinkers of our time, Dr. David Suzuki, whose rational thought, integrated approach to life and science, and works on sustainability and ecology, have deeply inspired me throughout the research and writing of this book. Our email exchanges provided me with valuable direction. Dr. Suzuki is one of the few modern scientists who understand that we live in a world of such interconnectedness that we cannot in any way afford to regard pollution and environmental destruction in an impersonal, detached light.

Lastly, thanks to the works of the late great scholar and author Joseph Campbell (*Myths to Live By*), I can retain most of my sanity as I witness the unraveling of our natural world and the suppression of free thought at the hands of evil geniuses whose thirst for power and profit knows no bounds. As we read in Campbell's books, deception, criminality, evil-thinking, war-for-profit, lust for world domination, national ethnocentricity and greed are as old as humankind. But never before in the short history of our world has modern technology been so lethal and available as to present a real and present danger for global destruction.

# Preface

*Science is a useless, destructive, dangerous, dead enterprise*
*unless it is employed with integrity, good conscience,*
*humanity, wisdom, responsibility, and vision in a wholistic contest.*

This book is a collaborative effort involving many individuals and institutions working to make our world a cleaner, safer place by exposing the dangers of toxins in our lives, as well as the culprits responsible for directly and indirectly contributing to the decay of our external and internal environments. Facts and statistics abound to reveal environmental destruction, corporate bad guys controlling our media, toxic lifestyles, useless consumerism, nefarious institutions, and the impact of toxic products and byproducts on the health of our families. When you're finished reading, you'll at least be informed as to the state of the world in which you live; and you'll understand how chemicals are making you, your family and your neighbors sick. And you'll discover, as I have over the course of my research, how certain powerful entities are keeping you and I, the public, from finding out how enormous the problem of toxicity really is. Perhaps even more importantly, you'll be directed toward proactive steps to make changes for the better, with website addresses, positive strides made by enterprising individuals, suggestions for a healthier lifestyle, references for further reading, and ideas to improve life on our finite planet, ultimately uplifting your own personal health! But the greatest message of all to be gleaned is that every living creature and the earth itself is interconnected and interdependent; so, to ignore, or contribute to, environmental destruction is to destroy our own chance for health and happiness.

*"…On the great continent of freedom, freedom of communication is an important province. As with health, only the person who loses it realizes its true value. But one does not suffer from it only on an individual level: in countries and epochs in which communication is impeded, soon all other liberties wither; discussion dies by inanition, ignorance of the opinion of others becomes rampant, imposed opinions triumph."*

—*Primo Levi*
*The Drowned and the Saved*
*Chemist, Author, Auschwitz Survivor*

*"We no longer can afford to allow corporate America to dictate our lifestyle!
We must become sustainable yesterday."*

*—Graham Hill
21 Wheels, LLC*

*"When we ask the question 'Do we have enough time?' or 'How much time do we have?' we have to be specific—how much time for what? Do we have enough time to save the Aral Sea? No, it's dead. Can we save India's rain forests? Probably not, they may have reached the point of no return. Can we save the glaciers in Glacier National Park [in the United States]? Probably not, half of them are gone already and the other half are projected to disappear within the next 30 years. Can we reverse the environmental trends that are slowly undermining the global economy before we face economic decline and collapse of the sort that was experienced by earlier civilizations? I think so, I think we can. But we don't have a lot of time."*

—Lester Brown
*Radio Free Europe, 2002*

# *Foreword*

Volumes have been written over the centuries about the Spirit of America—that special, indomitable quality in the heart of a people who embrace and revere ingenuity and vision—a people living in a land blessed with an unequalled abundance of natural resources from coast to coast. This spirit has given rise to some of the greatest ideas and inventions in the history of man. As we look thoughtfully into our new millennium, this spirit should be our guiding force, leading all of humankind forward while leaving behind old, unfeasible, immature practices that leave in their wake destruction and suffering. We know, for example, as Vic Shayne writes in this book, that—regardless of social class, political affiliation, race, religious preference, gender or level of education—we are all biological beings and that we cannot thrive breathing polluted air, absorbing nuclear waste or finding sustenance in dead, chemicalized foods. The choice to embrace clean energy, to purchase hybrid vehicles, to break away from fossil fuels and nuclear power, and to oppose genetically engineered foods should be made based on our biological realities, not political posturing.

The attitude embodied in the expression "It's just business, nothing personal" has only garnered toxic waste dumps leaching into our drinking water, toxic sludge being used on food crops, air pollution measurable in escalating cancer rates, global warming, and the destruction of ancient cultures in the blink of an eye. Business practices are very personal to us all, as we all must depend upon clean air, soil and water for our survival.

Certainly, in this great land, we need to be leaders, thinking and reasoning like an advanced culture that can now appreciate the need for sustainable and responsible personal and corporate business practices. We can no longer afford to continue on a crash course while exterminating all that is natural in exchange for short-term financial gain. The mark of a great nation is in its progression only when it is balanced with responsibility for its citizens, the world at large, and future generations. To act any other way is to ignore the lessons of history that have placed the value of money over human life.

Although Vic Shayne has written extensively about corporate evil, we need to make it clear that corporations, per se, are not necessarily evil, unless they act without conscience and regard for the common good. If corporate owners and their affiliates believe that the only way to turn a profit is by leaving us a legacy of ecological destruction, then we must refuse them our patronage. Corporations are evil, to use Dr. Shayne's description, when they are so irresponsible as to encourage the populace to purchase vehicles that destroy the air that none of us can do without. They are evil when they create "dead zones" in our oceans from toxic dumping so that the fish we put on our dinner table is laden with dioxins, mercury and other cancer-causing chemicals. Corporations are evil when they are so selfish and short-sighted that our relatives suffer with cancer and other diseases that are directly linked to industrial waste, artificial ingredients pumped into foods, radioactive waste leaking into the groundwater and land, pesticide use and production, and weapons manufacturing. They are also evil when they merely hide their destructive practices by moving their manufacturing and dumping to other countries, destroying the oxygen-producing rainforests, and spilling millions of tons of crude oil into the sea all around the world. Simply put, our small planet cannot afford such abuse; and so many corporations have the choice not to be abusive.

We are at a crossroads in human history. We can succumb to destruction or embrace a realistic, progressive attitude. We currently have the technology to clean up our act. We now have the technology to manufacture vehicles powered by non-polluting fuels. We can produce energy for homes and businesses from wind, water and solar power. We know well that organically grown foods are health promoting, and we know how to grow these foods and that their nutrient-dense ingredients have sustained life here on earth since the beginning of time. And we know that chemicals cause cancer. We must apply all of this knowledge and change our course for the sake of humanity and the preservation of life on this small planet.

How shall we navigate through these crucial years ahead? Vic Shayne presents both problems and solutions. He states that the choices we make as consumers can make a difference in corporate behavior. We must all begin to act and think according to the ideal embodied in the Spirit of America—with wisdom, fore-thought, consideration, generosity and creativity. We have to be conscious that today's actions (and inactions) shape the future of this planet. The information in this book is but a sampling of the complex problems we face as a world community. The blame lies not just on the shoulders of corporate evil, but also on those of us who enable them to perpetrate their injustices as we support them with our buying dollars. Corporations exist for one main purpose—to make money. If we don't like their destructive practices, we can exert our influence by supporting only those companies that act responsibly. Without our patronage, destructive corporations will be forced to change their practices or face extinction in the marketplace.

Our corporate, political, educational and social leaders should be beacons for progress, not perpetrators of the modalities and methods of an ignorant past. Their power should be used to uplift this world, not to destroy it. We need to use our spirit, power and ingenuity to set a world example of creative genius, not evil genius.

*—Ed Begley, Jr.*

# A Little Parental Advice:
# Watch Out for Corporate Bullies!

All corporations are not evil; just the ones that carelessly profit from the loss of health, life, liberties, freedom and human dignity. When human loss and suffering forms the basis of enterprise, or are seen as merely incidental "side effects," the temptation to prolong and create such suffering is too great for too many corporations to pass up. Instead of working to relieve the suffering, evil corporations have learned there is more profit-making potential in becoming part of the problem rather than the solution. Indeed, it seems more money, time and effort is often expended in trying to hide or lie about corporate misdeeds than trying to correct them.

Gigantic, multinational corporations that have risen to power are out of control, taking over the rights of citizens by influencing lawmakers (legally and illegally), buying out family-owned businesses to monopolize industry, taking over federal government administration positions, reshaping agriculture, introducing unproven scientific Frankenfoods that threaten our very biological existence, controlling the media and waging massive public relations and advertising campaigns to twist and invent "reality." They are drunk with power, greed and wealth while our families are dying of cancer, and the environment is being destroyed and dismantled, and our own government "leaders" have chosen to serve their needs rather than the needs of the public. It's outrageous, but true. It's insidious, but it happened so gradually that we have had our rights pulled out from under us just the same. They're fooling us, dividing us, abusing us, cheating us and destroying the future just so they can make a profit and wield power. If we protest, complain or demand to know what they're up to, they defame us, disguise themselves, take us to court as if we the victims are the guilty party, attack protesters and try to put the blame back on us.

Evil geniuses are banking on the fact that most people will think such evil genius is the invention of paranoia and cynicism—unless it is your neighborhood that has been poisoned by their toxic pollution, or your relative who has ended up in jail for opposing them, or your union that has been torn apart, or your mother who has been diagnosed with cancer, or your brother who has been denied a livelihood. If you talk to enough Americans, you'll begin to see that you're not alone. Mega-corporations in this country are out of control and have overstepped their bounds as they exercise and demand more and more power. The only hope we have is to ban together as a strong nation and choose to make purchasing decisions that are nothing but environmental, sane, healthy and sustainable. This is our source of power—our insurance for the future of this civilization—and we must exercise it while we still can.

# A Sick & Suffering World
# Is Good For Business

Book titles are important when the author has tried to convey a single, impressive meaning wrapped up in a catchy phrase to arouse the reader's thinking processes. The title of this book, *Evil Genius in the Garden of Eden*, was created to instill two main themes. First is the notion that our earth is a holy, sacred place, not necessarily in a religious sense, but more of a spiritual sense. The Garden of Eden symbolizes purity, innocence, lushness, fertility and the seeds of unbridled life, freedom and happiness. It is also the birthplace, metaphorically, of the notion that humankind has been imbued with a vision that decisions lead to actions which can be either good or evil. And from this vision of good and evil we must exercise responsibility for ourselves and our world.

The second theme is that of Evil—the entity that forges the long, painful process of destruction, disrepair, loss of innocence and disrespect for the sanctity of the Garden and all its inhabitants. What drives evil but the human passions so aptly outlined in ancient Indian philosophy—greed, anger, power, fear, lust, vanity, and attachment. In this writing, I employ the phrase "Evil Genius" to convey the notion that those corporate and political entities destroying our planet and our lives—our Garden of Eden—are not stupid, insane or whimsical characters. Their harmful, careless, reckless activities are not by way of accident or coincidence. Rather, the evil geniuses are intelligent, calculating, manipulative and ingenious in their planning and methodologies. They create suffering and fear by their words and deeds for the expressed purpose of making huge profits and controlling magnificent industries, governments, peoples, and myriad institutions responsible for anchoring our civilization. As a byproduct of their blind greed, evil geniuses have realized that a sick and suffering world is good for business. Thus, they have successfully employed sophisticated psychological techniques, honed by experts in human behavior, to capitalize on our passions. They have turned us, like robots, into insatiable spenders, consumers, wasters and even paranoids afraid of losing those things that they have convinced us we must possess. By creating fears in us via their advertising and PR (public relations) campaigns, then using our fears to manipulate us, the evil geniuses have eroded our values, our spirit, our relationships, our sense of self, our integrity, and—perhaps worst of all—our trust in the power of nature right here in our withering and neglected Garden of Eden. Whether this was their ultimate goal—to erode our humanity and drive us to extinction—is anybody's guess, but the fact remains that this is the result of their nefarious activities.

The evil geniuses are so adept at what they do—so effective—that most of us do not even notice we are not thinking and acting naturally and entirely of our own accord. If this sounds like science fiction, consider how motivated the millions of members of the modern world are by fear. Fear makes money. If you're afraid of getting sick and dying, you buy insurance and spend fortunes on drugs, multivitamins and medical doctors. If you're afraid of aging or not looking like a super model, you buy cosmetics, hair dyes, face lifts and breast implants. If you're afraid of smelling like a human being, you buy cologne and deodorizers. If we're afraid of germs and bacteria, we get vaccinations and spray our food supply and homes with deadly chemicals. When you're afraid of missing out on the fun, you spend your money on elaborate vacations and off-road vehicles that destroy the environment. If you're afraid of being out of fashion, you spend lots of money on clothes. If you're afraid of God striking you dead or not letting you into the afterlife, you spend your hard-earned money on politicians backing religious extremism. If you are afraid of muggers you spend money on guns and bullets and alarm systems. If you're afraid of other nations stealing your precious oil, you support warfare, military spending and imperialism. If you're afraid of your life and scared of being bored or overly stressed-out, you'll spend your money on drugs and alcohol. The list of fears are endless—as endless as the marketing ideas of the evil geniuses that keep our fears alive. Filled with all of these fears, we're running in a thousand different directions trying to quell them with artificial solutions that are conveniently provided by the corporations owned by the evil geniuses.

When we ask the difficult and puzzling question: Why do we have so many environmental problems—toxic air, water and land and sick and dying people—then we have to wake up to the fact that we got to this place of mass destruction and decay due to our decaying attitudes. We just don't think naturally any longer here in the modern world. We waste first and ask questions (maybe) later—too much later. We are trained and manipulated by the experts not to think responsibly as we use products and services that defy natural logic. We ignore our own words of wisdom we bestow upon our children: "Plan for the future; your impetuous actions today may come back to haunt you in the long run."

We are not just physically ailing here in the fading Garden of Eden. We are mentally, emotionally and spiritually ill—afflicted with unhealthy attitudes that we have allowed to seep into our consciences in a steady stream of propaganda to the point wherein our ideas are not our own. After all, who among us would dump toxic chemicals into his backyard stream and kill or poison the fish he plans to eat for supper? We wouldn't let our cars run in a closed garage because we know how deadly the emissions are, yet OUTSIDE of our garage we accept the same act as perfectly okay. And we wouldn't cover our faces in toxic grease, except when it takes the form of makeup, moisturizers, sun screen, shaving cream or soaps.

Getting people to wake up and recognize that we have an immense problem here is a difficult and nearly impossible task, given the power, persistence and creativity of the evil geniuses who keep us in fear and a state of always wanting more, more, more. Thus, our environmental problems are not outside. They are inside, emanating from our attitudes and deviation from all that is natural. This basic truth about the origins of our problems begs us to examine the complexity of life and why environmental cleanup is not such an easy task unless we first go to work exposing and challenging the evil geniuses.

## WE AND OUR PROBLEMS ARE COMPLEX

There is no simple solution that can be employed to halt and reverse the contribution to, and continuation and ravages of, our sick and toxic environment, because life is *complex* and *dynamic*. Each problem we face—whether it's the state of our personal health or the health of the environment—is actually an intricately woven network of factors that has somehow developed into a unique "situation." Because life's problems are ever-changing, it becomes difficult to resolve them using static strategies and rules. We can't catch a runaway bull by standing still. Our current environmental situation is a runaway bull, and Nature (including you and I and our families and the animal and plant kingdoms) are the China closet. There's more depth to this analogy. Despite the fact that our chemically altered environment is killing us and causing diseases too numerous to mention, most people are not even aware that there is a raging bull out of control. This brings to the surface another dimension of this complex problem—our national media.

Owned, supported by, and controlled by the evil geniuses, our means of mass communication is part of the problem, not the solution. Other contributors to the problem (i.e., environmental destruction and toxicity) are great and complex systems in their own right, including but not limited to: the modern medical system, the chemical manufacturing industry, the educational system and, above all, the marketing and public relations puppeteers who have perfected a means by which modern society can be controlled, manipulated and consciously altered to accept as well as overlook that which is killing us. Owing to these major media players, our world is sadly and dangerously out of balance. Yet, like the crack addict killing himself for a chance to feel better, these entities, so intricately involved in activities leading to our world's environmental demise, are drunk with greed and power to the point where they destroy their (and your) own air, water and land for profits. It's insane, but true; unless they are planning to escape to another plantet that the rest of us don't know about, any sane person is hard-pressed to understand their madness.

Because life is "complex," it becomes impossible to unravel our interwoven mesh of problems to simply pinpoint our one greatest concern or the most alarming of our problems. Which is worse, for instance: air you can't breathe or water you cannot drink? Is it preferable to die by suffocation or poisoned drink? We are struggling first with the tremendous task of changing the consciousness of society which has been manipulated by those who have worked so diligently to make us see the world through the skewed eyes of consumerism and wasteful practices. If the populace could begin to recognize that we do indeed have problems and are being "played" by giant corporations pretending to be our friends and protectors, we can start to take our problems more seriously by understanding just how our sick and decaying our environment really is (and to realize that our personal health is directly related to the health of our environment). If we have such a real-ization, maybe we can begin to resolve all of our environmental problems simul-taneously, letting our every thought and action be toward the common good rather than the select few. Is this realistic? Maybe it is if we can employ the same psychological tools for good instead of for the perpetuation of destruction. We need to make PR turn around and go the opposite way.

No doubt we have been duped, played, manipulated, taken advantage of, brainwashed, lied to and cheated by powerful institutions with whom we have entrusted our almighty dollar and sense of self. For our loyalty to their version of the "American" way, we have knowingly and unknowingly traded our improved modern lifestyle and freedom for poisoned lakes and rivers; polluted air; geneti-cally altered food supplies; mass media that does not report most of the impor-tant issues affecting our lives; a superiority complex; a warped sense of nationalism; social isolationism borne of automobiles, suburbs and impatience; radiation and nuclear fall out; fast food and processed food diets devoid of nutri-ent value; toxic soils; pesticides that kill people and bugs without discrimination;

the torture and inhumane treatment of the animals we eat and the ones going extinct in far off lands; isolationism that keeps us from relating to other human beings as "real" and valuable; callous disregard for life and the natural process; and mass death and disease blamed on genetics and germs rather than environmental toxicity.

It is difficult for most people to accept the fact that they have been tricked and manipulated, because our defense mechanisms—our egos—don't want to admit that they can be overridden and circumvented by an advertising wizard on Wall Street. So, for now, the masses of our "modern society" remain in a state of denial—denying that our world is run by huge corporations that are destroying us both environmentally and personally, causing diseases, wars, human suffering and wrong-thinking. We cannot deny the stress and suffering, but people are afraid to admit that their lives are not their own. Helplessness is scary.

To keep us from discovering the magnitude of their destruction, the powers-that-be continue to control us by feeding our addictions. Yes, we do have serious addictions! They keep us addicted to television, entertainment that explodes and mutilates, toys, plush surroundings, fast and fancy automobiles, computerized lifestyles, fast food, malls and everything electronic and artificially stimulating. While we are lulled into a sense of euphoria from all these modern things, our natural surroundings are falling apart. Our world's food supply has been overtaken by a handful of corporations, our rain forests (in the U.S. too, not just in the Amazon) are disappearing, nuclear waste and other chemical wastes are polluting every river and water source in the world, our air is unfit for human lungs, our cancer rate continues to skyrocket from the ingestion of chemicals, and our population growth is out of control.

If you think about it, you will understand why I call those who have designed and implemented this mindset of consumerism and destruction "Evil Geniuses." It is both evil and ingenious to have devised effective methods to control the minds and activities of our population—to keep us in a state of artificial ecstasy—so that corporate giants can continue to make more and more money and garner more and more power. The fact that our environment and the health of our loved ones is sacrificed for this power- and profit-drive is of no concern to the powers-that-be. Your family's health and welfare is worth the sacrifice (yours, not theirs) to feed their greed. Aside from the heartbreak of watching your mother or sister die of cancer is the reality that these greedy power brokers have put us on a collision course with destruction. To paraphrase environmentalist Dr. David Suzuki, we live in a finite world, yet we are driven to live lifestyles based on infinite consumption. There is no way this can work, if only from a logistical standpoint. We cannot afford to continue to act and think as if there is no limit to destruction.

Something has to change; the first of which is our consciousness—our recognition that we have a serious problem and we cannot rely on our corporate overlords, government agencies, industry "experts," or institutions to be our saviors, because they are actually part of the problem. We need to seek our own solutions. Fast.

The amount of information available on environmental destruction and toxicity is overwhelming. There are many other books and magazines that more adequately report the statistics and accounts of how pollution continues to impact our health, and I highly recommend them all. While this book highlights a few of these cases, its main objective is to give you an idea WHY we have a problem by examining the underpinnings that hardly anyone discusses—certainly not today's mass media. If we fail to understand the reality and intent of the evil geniuses behind the multi-billion-dollar corporate propaganda machine and the chemical producers, then we can never attack this problem at its roots. Further, whereas other books and resources treat environmentalism as a global, nonspecific outdoor pollution problem, it is my intention to show that this is a very personal problem, as it impacts our health, lifestyles and emotions. World pollution begins with you and I.

If you've ever had a sick child, you know in your heart that you'd be willing to do anything it takes to stop your child from hurting. We must now look at our environment as a fragile child suffering before our eyes. As caretakers for our world, we must become a part of the solution and no longer part of the problem. Ignorance of the laws of nature is no excuse for allowing and enabling our own demise to occur.

Each of us must now come to realize that our environment and our bodies, minds, spirits and emotions are inseparable parts of the complex and dynamic whole that is life itself. As a world civilization, we are sick and dying, and we must do something to reverse the disease of mind, body and environment.

# Walking on Water:
# Now Anybody Can Do It

*If Jesus walked on the surface of the Mississippi River[1] today,
it wouldn't have been such a miraculous event.*

*—author*

*"If Jesus came back and saw what was being done in his name,
he would never stop throwing up."*

*—Woody Allen, Hannah & Her Sisters*

There are so many environmental disasters and chemical threats at home and in the workplace, and such strong, ongoing and massive corporate destruction of our environment that the subject is absolutely physically, mentally and emotionally overwhelming. There is no place to start and there is no end in sight. Each day, millions of tons of deadly chemicals are billowing into our skies, being poured into lakes, streams and oceans, and soaking into the earth. More than 100,000 people die each year from prescription drug use.[2] Corporations and gov-

---

1.  "The Mississippi River ranks first in the nation as the most polluted river. Of the 1.5 billion pounds of toxics reported discharged directly to all U. S. waters between 1990 and 1994, close to half (702 million pounds), went directly into the Mississippi. This figure represents more than twice the amount of all other U. S. waters combined." (Mississippi River Ranks First as Nation's Most Polluted River," 2002,/illinois.sierraclub.org/PiasaPalisades/mississi

2.  "Adverse Drug Reactions May Cause Over 100,000 Deaths Among Hospitalized Patients Each Year," (*JAMA*. 1998;279:1200-1205) [http://www.ama-assn.org/sci-pubs/sci-news/1998/snr0415.htm] *Science News Update* Apr 15, 1998. Also see: [http://www.aetna.com/public_policy_issues/patientsafety.htm] "Adverse reactions to prescription drugs are a major cause of death in the U.S. An estimated 106,000 hospital patients die each year from adverse reactions, making adverse drug reactions the fourth most frequent cause of death. (*Money* 12/98; study from *JAMA* 4/98)"

ernments contributing to this destruction are more interested in making profits than preserving and encouraging health and life on our planet. They intend to be rich and powerful even if it means that you, they or their children can no longer breathe, drink or eat. In a word, it's insanity. The vast compilation of information on environmental destruction, corporate cover-ups, lies to the citizens of the world, skewed research, pollution and chemical destroyers is depressing to think about. It's even more sad and hopeless that our leaders are failing miserably to protect and defend us. Rather, they are co-conspirators—willing collaborators—teaming up with corporate killers rather than the citizens to whom they pretend to be responsible.

Environmentalist Robert F. Kennedy Jr. writes:

> George W. Bush will go down in history as America's worst environmental president. In a ferocious three-year attack, the Bush administration has initiated more than 200 major rollbacks of America's environmental laws, weakening the protection of our country's air, water, public lands and wildlife. Cloaked in meticulously crafted language designed to deceive the public, the administration intends to eliminate the nation's most important environmental laws by the end of the year [2003]. Under the guidance of Republican pollster Frank Luntz, the Bush White House has actively hidden its anti-environmental program behind deceptive rhetoric, telegenic spokespeople, secrecy and the intimidation of scientists and bureaucrats.[3]

Kennedy's article, published in *Rolling Stone*, is well worth the reading, despite your political affiliation. It shows the failure of our modern leaders to protect our lives and our futures. Kennedy shares with us these horrendous facts on Bush's record:

- For the first time since the passage of the Clean Water Act in 1970, America's water-pollution levels are rising, according to the Environmental Protection Agency. Our estuaries are dramatically more polluted than they were just four years ago. 218 million of us now live with ten miles of a polluted water body unsafe for drinking, fishing, swimming or boating.

- The White House has proposed new air-pollution limits that allow twice as much sulfur dioxide and three times more mercury emissions than if the Clean Air Act were left alone and fully implemented. The Centers for Disease Control says one in twelve American women of childbearing age has

---

3.   Kennedy, Jr., Robert F., *Rolling Stone* magazine, December 11, 2003, Issue 937, p. 180-181

unsafe mercury levels in her body, putting more than 320,000 newborns at risk annually.

- The local fish in twenty-eight states, along seventy-one percent of the coastline in the lower forty-eight states and in eighty-two percent of estuaries are too dangerous to eat regularly. The Great Lakes and their connecting streams are under fish-consumption advisories. Instead of cracking down on polluters, the Bush administration is letting power plants release more emissions into these bodies of water.

- The pace of Superfund cleanups had declined by more than fifty percent since Bush took office. The program is bankrupt; Bush wants taxpayers, not polluters, to pay for cleanups. Twenty-five percent of Americans live within four miles of a Superfund site.

- The oceans are emptying of fish, with most large oceanic populations having collapsed to ten percent of 1950 levels. Marine policies endorsed by the Bush White House are also permanently destroying habitats.[4]

Now that I've cheered you up by bringing you this one (out of many) dark cloud, I don't want you to blame me, because I didn't cause the problem. I drive a fuel-efficient vehicle, I recycle, I eat organic foods and I care about my fellow human being. I also see through the lies and greed spewing from the mouths of politicians and corporate leaders. Now I want you to join me in examining the realities of chemical toxicity, political enablers and corporate killers and their public relations professionals hired to make everybody think the world is a rosy, cozy place in which to live as long as we do not discover the truth.

There are endless arguments about air, water and land pollution! Yet, look closely at who's saying what. ALL of the opposition to strict pollution control measures is launched by polluters and their supporters (employees, scientists on their payroll, employees who have been brainwashed to believe their lies, and politicians on the take). The only people saying that toxins in our food and environment are perfectly safe are the people creating the toxins. That's right. Nobody in his/her right mind would put up a fight about getting rid of pollutants other than chemical manufacturers, automobile manufacturers, toxic waste creators, corporate-backed scientists, the nuclear industry or other perpetrators of this global problem. Nobody.

Republican pollster Frank Luntz told his fellow Republicans, "You need to continue to make the lack of scientific certainty a primary issue by becoming even more active in recruiting experts sympathetic to your view."[5] There you have

---

4.    ibid.

it—the politician's solution—find a way lie to the public because power and money is more important than health and our future.

## WHO AMONG US IS BIOLOGICALLY DESIGNED TO BREATHE CARBON MONOXIDE?

If we were to take a cross section of the country's population—a fireman, a college professor, a banker, a billionaire oil man, a tobacco lobbyist, an environmentalist, a doctor, a sailor, a baker, a lawyer, a politician and a mother of four—and put them all in one room and pump in a load of car and truck exhaust, who do you think would testify that they like the odor and air quality, and can breathe just fine? Actually, this was one of the ways the Nazis found to murder thousands of people in the 1940s. Everyone died from the exhaust; not a single one of them was able to breathe and survive. If you tried the same experiment today, each person in that room, even for a few minutes, would all get sick. All of them would cough, gag and turn green; and if they didn't eventually find clean air, all would die. We all need clean air to breathe and remain healthy. This is an undeniable biological necessity despite whether you're an asthmatic or a corporate scientist claiming that it's perfectly okay to stick your face next to the exhaust pipe of a diesel truck.

WE ALL AGREE that pollution destroys life and makes it impossible to live in a state of health. The only ones telling us otherwise are the companies responsible for creating pollution—those among us who are making our air unbreathable and our waters unfit for marine life. It's us against them, and they are winning. Why are they winning? Because they are using their billions of dollars to muscle their way into our lives, refusing to clean up their acts, denying their responsibility for cancer and disease, hiding their activities, shipping their waste across the world, fooling the public in their television commercials, paying off scientists to claim that their toxic waste is safe and often beneficial, and just plain lying in many other ways. They control the major media in this country by supporting them with their advertising dollars to promote nuclear energy, automobile purchasing, chemical manufacturing and a throwaway mentality. Meanwhile our air, which WE ALL NEED to be able to live and breathe, is becoming too deadly in which to thrive. Our soils are drenched with deadly chemicals from pesticides to synthetic fertilizers and toxic sludge. Our once-pristine rivers, streams, lakes and ocean are becoming dead zones where nothing can live. Maybe this is not fully apparent to people living in big cities who never visit rivers and streams,

---

5.    ibid, p. 184

but for those of us who have witnessed the changes, it's frightening and sickening. As a test of truth, take three containers with you on a field trip. Fill one up from your tap water (unfiltered), another from a lake, and the third from a river of your choice. Then take them for an independent water analysis where quality water filters are sold. Surprise!

Since we, as human beings, REQUIRE air, water and soil for our very existence, when these are all polluted, we will perish. There is no argument or debate here. It's a matter of biology, not merely an opinion: We cannot breathe truck exhaust instead of pure air. We cannot eat plants with no nutritional value. If you don't believe me, go stand in the middle of a busy intersection at the peak traffic hour and see how difficult it is to breathe. Our poor air quality is multiplying by leaps and bounds. Every day, unless you live in the middle of nowhere in the South Pacific, you are slowly getting sick from car, truck, airplane and industry exhaust. There's no doubt about this.

A host of authors and speakers have pontificated about spirituality and the delicate balance of life on this planet and stewardship and so forth. Often such talk is viewed as silly "new age" rhetoric. But if we look past the lofty philosophy and deep into the scientific facts, there is no doubt that we as human beings have our very existence tied to the health of the planet on which we live. To think otherwise is to be ignorant. Ignorance kills.

Because we are so entwined with the health of our environment and planet, to ignore pollution, toxic dumping and throwaway, wasteful attitudes, is to commit cosmic suicide. Irresponsibility is killing us as it destroys our environment, taking away our ability drink pure water, breathe pure air and eat pure food. Author/scientist David Suzuki, in *The Sacred Balance: Rediscovering Our Place in Nature*, explains,

> In such an interdependent universe human beings hold enormous responsibility; each individual is accountable, and every action has repercussions that reverberate far beyond the moment. Past, present and future form a continuum in which each generation inherits a world shaped by the actions of its forebears and holds it in trust for all the generations to come. Many world views endow human beings with an even more awesome task: they are the caretakers of the entire system, responsible for keeping the stars on their courses and the living world intact. In this way, many early people who created world views constructed a way of life that was truly ecologically sustainable, fulfilling and just.[6]

---

6. Suzuki, David, *The Sacred Balance: Rediscovering Our Place in Nature*, Greystone Books, Vancouver, BC, 1997, page 12

Now that we know what we are dealing with—we the human beings who need to breathe air against the corporations that are chemical, institutional polluters pretending to be our friends—we can do something about this and hand our world over to our children with a brighter prognosis for the future. First we have to understand the extent of our global problem, then we must hold ourselves up as responsible for, and capable of, our state of health—which also means the health of our planet. We have thus far created, allowed and promulgated a destructive approach to living; now we must adopt a new view of understanding and sustainability.

Of course, the subject of toxins is vast. This is true not only due to the complexity of problems caused by human-made chemicals and toxic waste, but also due to the fact that toxic chemicals are everywhere and in great numbers and they are intermixing and interacting in our environment. Let us open our eyes to the enormity of the problem on its many levels—personally, locally, and globally, as well as measures to avoid, prevent and change the influence of deadly chemicals on our families' lives. We need to reestablish in our own minds and our national psyche that which has become lost as we have far too long immersed ourselves in an orgy of scientific theories and tunnel vision. It's time once again to look at the whole picture and realize that without responsibility, science and business enterprises are more destructive than constructive. We have to turn our thoughts to what we know is instinctively right for us, our families, our country and the environment, ignoring the massive assault of media messages issuing from corporations pretending to be our friends and defaming those among us who dare to wake up in defiance and say: "How do your business practices impact my family's health and happiness?"

# Who Are The Evil Geniuses?

In every James Bond film there is an evil genius—the multibillionaire who has plans to take over the world or destroy it, or both. He isn't stupid, nor is he particularly blatantly crazy-acting like Jerry Lewis, Adam Sandler or a television evangelist with a bad toupee. No, he's cold, calculating and intelligent. But despite motion picture stereotypes, the real evil genius is not a sickly character sitting in a chrome-plated chair in front of an electronic map of the world and breathing out of an oxygen tank. Instead he's a man of the world in a custom-made suit on his way to dinner from New York to Paris on his private jet. But he is definitely a warped figure in his own right, seeing only his own desires and dreams, out of touch with the needs of "ordinary" people, and there's nothing more important to him than his selfish goals. He wants world domination and to stamp out all competition just like James Bond's Dr. No, Goldfinger and Austin Power's Dr. Evil. You may see a mom on television crying tears of joy when her son calls home on Mother's Day, but you should know that behind this image is the corporation headed by a heartless Dr. Evil luring you and millions of others toward your phone to make a three-dollar call across the country. If he has to make you laugh or cry by viewing his commercial, then it's worth the price to secure your business.

The scariest thing about Dr. Evil is that he is not fictional. Sure, he's characterized in movies and novels as an eccentric embodiment of hellish ideas, but the real evil genius sits in a yacht off the south of France, or jet-sets with his ultra-rich friends in some cafe in Venice as the rest of us choke on the pollution spewing from one of his many careless factories dotting the globe. He sips Champagne and eats meals that cost more than most people spend on food in a month as his corporate board of directors come up with marketing ideas and products that do more than just arouse the senses of modern man—they also destroy the environment and cause deadly diseases from their toxic by products. His public relations consultants concoct and carry out covert media campaigns to send our sons to war so he can make another million dollars an hour selling grieving parents gasoline refined from captured oil that eventually produces an enervating smog over every city in the world. The life of your son or daughter, mother or father, sister or brother does not matter to Dr. Evil, because, for as long as it lasts, he's breathing the sea air from his yacht as it glides through the South Pacific where there is still some blue, clear water beneath his boat.

The evil geniuses of this world destroy life and cause suffering in the course of doing "business as usual" for their wealth-building enterprises while concomitantly having their corporate power brokers (the people who run the day-to-day operations) hire public relations and marketing firms from Wall Street to crank out propaganda so we will buy their bill of goods. And should someone stand in their way, the propaganda machine works the opposite way too, defaming all the opposing parties who are screaming out, "Hey! Wait a minute. Your enterprises gave my husband and sister cancer. You made a toxic cesspool out of our nearby lake. You're polluting the air and cutting down all of the trees then running TV commercials extolling how virtuous you are." And as of late, your message—your pain—will never be heard, because the evil genius owns the television station as well. Your message would simply be bad for (his) business.

Yes, the evil geniuses (who seem like "really nice guys" were you ever to meet them by accident—and it *would* have to be merely by accident for them to rub elbows with the likes of you) hire propaganda experts (who are millionaires as well) with giant public relations firms to work on their behalf to convince the public that Greenpeace, environmentalists and health food consumers are crackpots, nuts, quacks, tree huggers, wacos, wackos, alarmists and antiAmerican antagonists. If you discover the connection between the corporate powers and their mass manipulation, you are branded a believer in conspiracies, as if that is a bad thing. "You think everything is a conspiracy. You are a pessimist." These are the insults they create to intimidate people from pursuing the truth about how they are being manipulated, poisoned, lied to and cheated. Corporate PR soldiers work on the principle that, if you can't disprove criticism (because there are volumes of data proving corporate wrongdoings), then at least you can defame the victims so nobody will listen to them. Hire a team of scientists to say that environmentalists are crazy (never mind the fact that environmentalists have Nobel scientists on their team). Speaking of calling environmentalists antiAmerican, we have to conveniently overlook the fact that the evil geniuses do much of their business outside of America and have mastered the art of offshore banking and globalized business.

All of this defamation is for one purpose only—so that the evil geniuses can continue to make boatloads of money without opposition from annoying mothers whose children cannot breathe or turn yellow due to the amount of poisons spewing from factories operating in defiance of the laws of nature and the common sense of humankind. Evil geniuses are spoiled rich kids who don't want anyone to stand up and say, "You are destroying our environment and making us sick. You are producing toxic waste that cannot be disposed of." The Dr. Evils of this world are used to getting what they want because they are very powerful. Corporate crime fighting attorney William Lerach explains, "'Their whole life has been fighting and overcoming people who say no, you can't do it, don't do it, it's illegal. These guys say, 'To hell with you, we're doing it, we're getting it done, nobody can stop me.' And when they get to the top, nobody dares stop them.' What these animal spirits need is 'adult supervision.'"[1]

When you are an evil genius, everyone else is dispensable, second rate and of inferior stock. After all, who else can have the ear of the president or prime minister any moment of the day or night? Who else can sneeze at the wrong (or right) time and send a shock wave through the world's stock markets? Who else can make billions of dollars and pay no taxes yet make all of the demands they want? Who else can manufacture the truth then have it aired in the mass media for all to hear? And who else has enough financial resources to fund research at major universities and publish the skewed data as if it were an unbiased finding?

I say that we can compromise. We can restore our Garden of Eden, returning it to a beautiful, lush environment and have modern conveniences at the same time. The rich boys may keep their yachts (running on solar and hydro power, of course), polo tournaments, casino gambling in Monte Carlo, and $500 T-shirts so long as they can make their fortunes without destroying the rest of us. After all, there's nothing wrong with making a lot of money and living the *dolce vita* as the result of your hard work and ingenuity.

Undeniably, the technology for safe, sustainable and environmentally friendly manufacturing and farming is now available. All we have to do is to get the big boys to behave themselves and make the switch. **The only way we can convince them to do this, as consumers of their products, is to speak with our buying dollars.** Support what is good for us and our planet (the air we need to breathe) by only purchasing earth- and human-friendly products. Say "no" to genetically engineered foods, nuclear power, the entire oil industry, chemical pesticides, synthetic fertilizers, toxic chemicals and a corporate-owned media. Say "yes" to the

---

1.    Greider, William, "Is This America's Top Corporate Crime Fighter?—William Lerach's Legal Crusade Against Enron and Infectious Greed," The Nation, August 5/12, 2002

corporations that are improving the world and we inhabitants who are sick (literally and figuratively) of increasing cancer and disease rates caused by toxic production, toxic wastes and toxic dumping. Dr. Evil needs to retool his weapons into plowshares and convert to sustainable enterprises, because, like it or not, he's destroying his own air, land and sea as well. Surely this must be apparent to him while he's snorkeling off the coast of Greece where the marine life has diminished in health and numbers! And he better be careful, because the incidences of shark attacks off the coasts of the Mediterranean have increased dramatically over the past few years. These killer fish have to come closer to shore for their food source, as the numbers of fish in the deep blue sea are being wiped out due to corporate fishing enterprises and deadly pollution. On second thought, maybe Dr. Evil doesn't worry about such things, believing that sharks don't eat their own kind.

# Everybody's Talkin' 'Bout Toxins

*The health-harming effects of chemicals depend upon their quantity, timing, duration, pattern of exposure and properties. Some chemicals kill cells or tissues in the body; others attack the genetic material in a cell's nucleus, damaging the DNA. This can lead to gene mutations, setting in motion a sequence of events leading to cancer, birth defects, developmental or reproductive disorders.*
*Cancer-causing chemicals are called **carcinogens**; those causing birth defects are **teratogens**. Chemicals that damage the reproductive system or normal development of the fetus, infant, or child are called **developmental/reproductive toxicants**. Other chemicals, **endocrine disrupters,** interfere with normal hormone function. Toxic chemicals cause a long list of health problems, including damage to the lungs, liver, kidney, bones, blood, brain, nerves, and the reproductive system...*[1]

Everybody's talking about toxins these days. Detox diets, detox books and detox supplements have become as much of a mainstay of the natural health care movement as weight loss programs and flu remedies. This is not a fad. It's an awakening. There is growing fear that we, as citizens of the modern, "civilized" world, are becoming overwhelmed and inundated with toxins—poisonous substances—that are in our environment, foods we eat and even the supplements and drugs we ingest. Controlled in their news coverage by huge corporations, the major media in the United States has all but ignored and covered up the most significant and life- and health-threatening problem we have ever faced—chemical saturation. If this were not true, maybe we all would have been properly bombarded with a fantastically important message from the world's top scientists trying to tell us we are headed for disaster owing to environmental destruction. Did you hear this scientists' warning the nightly news? Me neither. But they DID warn us...

---

1.    chemicalbodyburden.org

In 1992, 1,700 of the world's respected scientists, including the majority of Nobel laureates in the sciences, issued a statement so direct and powerful that you would certainly think our major media would have published it without a second thought. Hey, isn't our media supposed to keep us informed of major events that affect EVERYONE on the planet?? It was called "World Scientists' Warning to Humanity," and it was far more important than the news reported in the same year that included professional sports scores, new car sales' figures, the release of the Disney film "Aladdin" and the popular movie "Wayne's World," the number of gold medals won by athlete Carl Lewis or the fact that President George Bush didn't particularly like the taste of broccoli. In case you missed it, our world's leading scientists, spearheaded by the late Henry Kendall, former chair of the Union of Concerned Scientists' board of directors, had this to proclaim in November, 1992:

### Introduction

Human beings and the natural world are on a collision course. Human activities inflict harsh and often irreversible damage on the environment and on critical resources. If not checked, many of our current practices put at serious risk the future that we wish for human society and the plant and animal kingdoms, and may so alter the living world that it will be unable to sustain life in the manner that we know. Fundamental changes are urgent if we are to avoid the collision our present course will bring about.

### The Environment

The environment is suffering critical stress:

**The Atmosphere.** Stratospheric ozone depletion threatens us with enhanced ultraviolet radiation at the earth's surface, which can be damaging or lethal to many life forms. Air pollution near ground level, and acid precipitation, are already causing widespread injury to humans, forests, and crops.

**Water Resources.** Heedless exploitation of depletable ground water supplies endangers food production and other essential human systems. Heavy demands on the world's surface waters have resulted in serious shortages in some 80 countries, containing 40 percent of the world's population. Pollution of rivers, lakes, and ground water further limits the supply.

**Oceans.** Destructive pressure on the oceans is severe, particularly in the coastal regions which produce most of the world's food fish. The total marine catch is now at or above the estimated maximum sustainable yield. Some fisheries have already shown signs of collapse. Rivers carrying heavy burdens of eroded soil into the seas also carry industrial, municipal, agricultural, and livestock waste—some of it toxic.

**Soil.** Loss of soil productivity, which is causing extensive land abandonment, is a widespread byproduct of current practices in agriculture and animal husbandry. Since 1945, 11 percent of the earth's vegetated surface has been degraded—an area larger than India and China combined—and per capita food production in many parts of the world is decreasing.

**Forests.** Tropical rain forests, as well as tropical and temperate dry forests, are being destroyed rapidly. At present rates, some critical forest types will be gone in a few years, and most of the tropical rain forest will be gone before the end of the next century. With them will go large numbers of plant and animal species.

**Living Species.** The irreversible loss of species, which by 2100 may reach one-third of all species now living, is especially serious. We are losing the potential they hold for providing medicinal and other benefits, and the contribution that genetic diversity of life forms gives to the robustness of the world's biological systems and to the astonishing beauty of the earth itself. Much of this damage is irreversible on a scale of centuries, or permanent. Other processes appear to pose additional threats. Increasing levels of gases in the atmosphere from human activities, including carbon dioxide released from fossil fuel burning and from deforestation, may alter climate on a global scale. Predictions of global warming are still uncertain—with projected effects ranging from tolerable to very severe—but the potential risks are very great.

Our massive tampering with the world's interdependent web of life—coupled with the environmental damage inflicted by deforestation, species loss, and climate change—could trigger widespread adverse effects, including unpredictable collapses of critical biological systems whose interactions and dynamics we only imperfectly understand.

Uncertainty over the extent of these effects cannot excuse complacency or delay in facing the threats.

## Population

The earth is finite. Its ability to absorb wastes and destructive effluent is finite. Its ability to provide food and energy is finite. Its ability to provide for growing numbers of people is finite. And we are fast approaching many of the earth's limits. Current economic practices which damage the environment, in both developed and underdeveloped nations, cannot be continued without the risk that vital global systems will be damaged beyond repair.

Pressures resulting from unrestrained population growth put demands on the natural world that can overwhelm any efforts to achieve a sustainable future. If we are to halt the destruction of our environment, we must accept limits to that growth. A World Bank estimate indicates that world population will not stabilize at less than 12.4 billion, while the United Nations concludes that the eventual total could reach 14 billion, a near tripling of today's 5.4 billion. But, even at this moment, one person in five lives in absolute poverty without enough to eat, and one in ten suffers serious malnutrition.

No more than one or a few decades remain before the chance to avert the threats we now confront will be lost and the prospects for humanity immeasurably diminished.

## Warning

We the undersigned, senior members of the world's scientific community, hereby warn all humanity of what lies ahead. A great change in our stewardship of the earth and the life on it is required, if vast human misery is to be avoided and our global home on this planet is not to be irretrievably mutilated.

## What We Must Do

Five inextricably linked areas must be addressed simultaneously:

- **We must bring environmentally damaging activities under control to restore and protect the integrity of the earth's systems we depend on.**

  We must, for example, move away from fossil fuels to more benign, inexhaustible energy sources to cut greenhouse gas emissions and the pollution of our air and water. Priority must be given to the development of energy sources matched to Third World needs—small-scale and relatively easy to implement.

  We must halt deforestation, injury to and loss of agricultural land, and the loss of terrestrial and marine plant and animal species.

- **We must manage resources crucial to human welfare more effectively.**

  We must give high priority to efficient use of energy, water, and other materials, including expansion of conservation and recycling.

- **We must stabilize population.**

  This will be possible only if all nations recognize that it requires improved social and economic conditions, and the adoption of effective, voluntary family planning.

- **We must reduce and eventually eliminate poverty.**

- **We must ensure sexual equality, and guarantee women control over their own reproductive decisions.**

## Developed Nations Must Act Now

The developed nations are the largest polluters in the world today. They must greatly reduce their over-consumption, if we are to reduce pressures on resources and the global environment. The developed nations have the obligation to provide aid and support to developing nations, because only the developed nations have the financial resources and the technical skills for these tasks.

Acting on this recognition is not altruism, but enlightened self-interest: whether industrialized or not, we all have but one lifeboat. No nation can escape from injury when global biological systems are damaged. No nation can escape from conflicts over increasingly scarce resources. In addition, environmental and economic instabilities will cause mass migrations with incalculable consequences for developed and undeveloped nations alike.

Developing nations must realize that environmental damage is one of the gravest threats they face, and that attempts to blunt it will be overwhelmed if their populations go unchecked. The greatest peril is to become trapped in spirals of environmental decline, poverty, and unrest, leading to social, economic, and environmental collapse.

Success in this global endeavor will require a great reduction in violence and war. Resources now devoted to the preparation and conduct of war—amounting to over $1 trillion annually—will be badly needed in the new tasks and should be diverted to the new challenges.

A new ethic is required—a new attitude towards discharging our responsibility for caring for ourselves and for the earth. We must recognize the earth's limited capacity to provide for us. We must recognize its fragility. We must no longer allow it to be ravaged. This ethic must motivate a great movement, convincing reluctant leaders and reluctant governments and reluctant peoples themselves to effect the needed changes.

The scientists issuing this warning hope that our message will reach and affect people everywhere. We need the help of many.

- We require the help of the world community of scientists—natural, social, economic, and political.

- We require the help of the world's business and industrial leaders.

- We require the help of the world's religious leaders.

- We require the help of the world's peoples.

**We call on all to join us in this task.**[2]

---

2.    Union of Concerned Scientists website: ucsusa.org, 2002

Essentially, our top scientists—the ones who actually give a damn—have warned the world that disaster is imminent due to pollution, over-population, chemical production, and other end products and byproducts of senseless, irresponsible behavior. These scientists told us we have to do something about this now or we've all had it. What's been done since the warning? Look out your window, down the street, around your neighborhood and out on the highway. Do you see any fewer buildings, strip malls, automobile traffic, airplanes or smoke stacks? Me neither. Thanks to the media's noncompliance and industry's lack of concern for your family's health, we're all ignoring our scientists' warning. I guess scientists should only be listened to when they're promoting drugs, chemicals, weapons of mass destruction, computers and deadly pesticides! As American's we're proud to say that we have the best scientists the world has ever produced. But this is a double-standard, because when they take their research and warn us about an impending disaster, we conveniently ignore them.

## HOW DID WE GET SO FAR AFIELD?

Our world wasn't always a polluted, toxic-drenched place in which to live. If there was pollution at all, it was usually isolated in big cities, mining areas and natural gas outlets. Corporate greed changed all that. In the 1940s and '50s scientists for big corporations began to dream about "better living through chemicals." Their dream was to change the face of modern life with chemicals concoctions from DDT to plastics. Now this dream is a nightmare for the reset of us, because the chemicals created by corporate scientists have found their way into our cells and the tissues of all living creatures on earth. Now we are suffering immeasurably from chemical invention and infusion driven by a blind desire to appease the lust for profits.

> The chemical landscape created as a result of intensive and continuing chemical use during the 20th century has been internalized. Because the chemicals found within our bodies are not labeled with return addresses, it is difficult to identify where they come from.
>
> For example, almost all of the dioxin found inside your body got there from eating contaminated food. However, it may have originated in a local medical waste incinerator or it may have been created by a distant, chlorine-based, paper manufacturing plant located thousands of miles from your home. Whatever its source, somewhere it entered the food chain and made its way into the food you ate. Similarly, a pesticide found inside your body may have come from pesticide spraying done at a local school, in your garden or kitchen, or it may have arrived on foodstuffs grown with pesticides in the U.S. or abroad. Its origin will be difficult to identify.[3]

Still, the mainstream media—owned, operated and influenced by certain corporations and individuals and families richer than most of the countries on earth—refuse to acknowledge the negative impact of toxic chemicals and avoid at all costs any responsibility associated with keeping the public informed about health dangers.

Journalist Dianne Dumonowski, co-author of the book *Our Stolen Future* explains, "The chemical revolution to improve life has been in full swing since World War II. The unforeseen result has been global contamination, which has altered the chemical make-up of life itself. Compounds that mimic hormones are disrupting reproductive and developmental processes. Male sperm counts have dropped as much as fifty percent in recent decades, while women have experienced dramatic increases in hormone-related cancers. Ironically, the future of human life may actually be threatened."[4] This is just the tip of the iceberg.

With communities in all corners of America engaged in lawsuits against chemical producers, toxic waste dumpers, oil spillers and nuclear waste disposers, the cry for regulation and justice can be heard mainly through alternative media and word of mouth. A small town in Alabama is suing Monsanto for causing cancer by dumping waste into the waterways, there's a whole region in Louisiana nicknamed "cancer alley," and global warming is so bad that (p)resident George W. Bush's administration has made it a priority to hide.

In his 2003 article, "Crimes Against Nature," Robert Kennedy Jr. writes:

> There is no scientific debate in which the White House has cooked the books more than that of global warming. In the past two years the Bush administration has altered, suppressed or attempted to discredit close to a dozen major reports on the subject. These include a ten-year peer-reviewed study by the International Panel on Climate Change, commissioned by the president's father in 1993 in his own efforts to dodge what was already a virtual scientific consensus blaming industrial emissions for global warming.
>
> After disavowing the Kyoto Protocol, the Bush administration commissioned the federal government's National Academy of Sciences to find holes in the IPCC analysis. But this ploy backfired. The NAS not only confirmed the existence of global warming and its connection to industrial greenhouse gases, it also predicted that the effects of climate change would be worse than previously believed, estimating that global temperatures will rise between 2–5 and 10.4 degrees by 2100.[5]

---

3.   chemicalbodyburden.org, 2002
4.   Dumanoski, Dianne, "Hormonal Havoc: Your Body and the Chemical Experiment," national broadcast, April 8, 2000, alternativeradio.org

Many doctors today are making their living specializing in a new field related to "chemical sensitivities," while others are challenging the idea that too many incidences of flu, colds and cancer are caused by bacteria and viruses rather than chemical toxicity. Multiple chemical sensitivities (MCS) physician Ann McCampbell, M.D., demands not only the recognition of how terrible the toll on human health is, but also that illness from exposure to chemicals is a valid and escalating problem even as chemical manufacturers and polluters refuse to acknowledge the deadly impact of their actions. She writes:

> Despite the chemical industry's disinformation campaign…and its influence over doctors, lawyers, judges, and government, incremental progress is being made with respect to MCS [multiple chemical sensitivities]. This is a testament to the strength, courage, dedication, and sheer numbers of people with MCS. In fact, there are so many people becoming chemically sensitive that attempts to ignore or silence them are ultimately doomed to fail. But even though it is just a matter of time before MCS gets the recognition it deserves, each day it is delayed prolongs the suffering of millions of people with MCS and puts millions more at risk of developing it. It is, therefore, essential that medicine, government, and society begin to look past the industry disinformation campaign and see what is really going on. That is, see that patients, citizens, clients, neighbors, and family members are increasingly becoming disabled with this serious physical illness and that the chemical industry's anti-MCS campaign is solely motivated by its desire to preserve profits.[6]

## HOW DARE WE SAY THAT A MAJOR CAUSE OF CANCER IS FROM CHEMICAL PRODUCTION AND POLLUTION?

Millions of dollars each year are poured into cancer research in the United States and elsewhere around the world. Yet cancer continues to increase without any signs of making a dent in curative measures or prevention. Clinician Ray Strand, M.D. writes:

> In spite of the tremendous amount of money spent on cancer research and treatment, cancer remains the second leading cause of death in the United States. There were 537,000 cancer deaths in 1995 and 1.3 million new cases projected to be diagnosed in 1996. Unlike heart disease, there has been a

---

5.    Kennedy, Jr., Robert F., *Rolling Stone* magazine, December 11, 2003, Issue 937, p. 187

6.    McCampbell, M.D.

steady increase in the number of deaths caused by cancer over the past 30 years. We have spent over 22 billion dollars in cancer research over the past 25 years, only to see absolutely no decrease in the relative number of people dying from cancer. The greatest advancements in cancer treatment have developed because of earlier diagnoses of certain cancers. Everyone agrees we need to look at primary prevention of the development of cancer, since treatment is usually not very effective.[7]

Where is cancer research money going? And who is backing the research? (See the chapter, "Have We Lost Our Minds & Media to Corporate Science?") With all of the geniuses running around this country in lab coats and goggles, you would think there would be some inkling of hope that the fight against cancer would be coming to a head. No such luck, because they are all looking in the wrong places. Is this purposefully? While Joe Scientist takes a break from his cancer research, puts down his beakers and test tubes and walks outside for a smoke and a bag of cheese puffs, he says to himself, "Golly, I love science!" As he sits on the rooftop drinking his Coke, watching black, yellow and orange smoke spew out of a nearby incinerator (designed by some other scientist) and the trucks and cars down below on the street make billowy clouds of gray exhaust, Joe Scientist understands that his job is to somehow prove that cancer is caused by genetics, viruses and bacteria. Of course, he ignores the plain fact that escalating and widespread cancer rates are not a historically genetic fault of the human race, because cavemen didn't worry about it. No, Joe Scientist just does his job because he's NOT paid to discover the truth. His paycheck is underwritten by some unseen corporation that owns his company's company. He's paid to do what he is told and look for genetic and viral causes of cancer despite the fact that the smog from below is choking the Cheetos out of him. The results of Joe's work will enable two great outcomes to happen for his company: First, they can make millions or billions of dollars from the invention of a new drug to treat cancer; and second, they can continue to mislead the public from the truth in order to assure the first outcome. The truth? Yes, that the same company paying Joe and producing cancer drugs CAUSES cancer because the company produces the cancerous chemicals used in pesticides, drugs, cleaning products, weapons manufacture, transportation, building materials and so on. This is a vicious cycle that results in making billions on both ends of the spectrum. But since Joe's immediate concern

---

7.     Strand, M.D., Ray, "Specific Diseases and Case Studies," www.bionutrition.org, 2002

is his paycheck, he does as he is told; unless his conscience overrides his analytical mind—a rarity that occasionally takes place.

Why do we not even come close to cancer prevention? Because to expose the fact that cancer is caused mostly by toxins in the environment and in our food chain is to expose the fact that the huge corporations are evil. That would be very bad for their business. But Joe Scientist will never find out because he's just doing his job, looking in all the wrong places so that some day the local news media can call on him in his white lab coat, with his Ph.D. degree hanging on the wall behind him, and announce to the tired and sick public that the cure for cancer is right around the corner thanks to the fantastic genetic research he and his team of geniuses are doing for the benefit of mankind. But to keep up this work, Joe and the news reporter will encourage you to send in your dollars to support his important almost-discoveries and his theories and to support the cancer association. It's a very clever system—you might call it evil genius—but we are all growing tired of it because it apparently just isn't working! Cancer is real, it's ugly and it's killing our family members off day by day. And big corporations are causing it.

## WAKE UP CALL

Can we all wake up and smell the real roses (not the plastic ones sold at Wal-Mart)? Can we begin to see the scope of chemical toxicity in our environment, bathroom medicine chests, food supply, kitchen pantries, restaurants, and medications?

Now you can put down this book and take a break by sitting in a lotus position to ponder the evils practiced by too many companies and their reckless, careless, insensitive owners, managers, spokespeople, board members, shareholders and public relations experts—making huge profits at the expense of our families' lives and health. In your clear state of meditative thought, you'll get a glimpse of the impact pollution is having on the earth, our ONLY home. When you come back to reality after your meditation, you can seek out measures you can take to protect yourself, improve the earth, save your family and become proactive in making life livable by making healthy choices. But until you recognize the evil genius, you might as well continue to dwell with your head in the clouds.

The human body is not meant to ingest human-made toxins—chemicals that are not native to life on earth. Despite the fact that our minds are manipulated to ignore this fact, our bodies know this and they respond by revolting. The symptoms of this revolt include sickness, suffering and death. In fact, many of the symptoms that today's doctors refer to as a "cold" or "flu" are in actuality due to toxins that are in our bodies. Such symptoms include headaches, bone aches, chills, fever, skin eruptions, hormonal irregularities, cold sweats and cancer.

More and more of us are waking up to the gravity of this truth. Now you'll know for sure.

# Pollution Is A
# Worldwide Problem

We live in a polluted world. In this modern era, because of our great population density worldwide, our interaction with people across the planet and unrestricted travel to every nook and cranny of the globe, pollution, toxic dumping and environmental harm is a worldwide problem. It is not restricted only to one area. If a radioactive cloud forms over China, we will realize its effects in New York. When there is a nuclear reactor that melts down in Russia, all of Europe will feel the fallout. Each time your lawnmower and automobile spews exhaust into the air, the ozone layer is destroyed, contributing to global warming, not localized warming. When a cruise ship or barge dumps its toxic waste into the ocean off the coast of Italy, the entire ocean is affected all the way to South Florida and the North Pole.

There are volumes of examples of the worldwide impact of toxic waste production and chemical spills, as corporations spread their wings across the globe. Even the television set in your living room in Anywhere, USA, can be related to cancer in Anywhere, Earth. *Earth Island Journal* magazine reported:

> Chemicals involved in the manufacture of TVs and semiconductors at the former RCA facility in the county of Taoyuan, northern Taiwan leaked into soil and groundwater around the plant. Former plant workers are now blaming the pollution for 1000 cases of cancer including 20 deaths, and numerous stillborn children in the area around the plant. The workers told their tale to a gathering in San Jose, California in May [2002] in an attempt to educate US companies about some of their actions abroad, and to force the polluters to make restitution.[1]

In countless cases, we see large, international corporations move their manufacturing plants to foreign countries to avoid taxes, procure cheap labor and—often topping the list of advantages to this practice—to avoid having to comply with strict environmental laws. Such actions keep environmental destruction out of

---

1. Earth Island Journal, Autumn 2002, p.18

the media and away from public scrutiny when at all possible. In plain language, huge corporations move their manufacturing plants to places where they will receive little resistance for their deadly practices. This is perhaps the first admission/confession that such corporations are fully aware of their contribution to pollution and disease on a global level. But sometimes their nefarious activities are just too big to go unnoticed.

Such was the case in Bhopal, India, in 1984 when a Union Carbide factory leaked poisonous, lethal gas, killing "as many as 7,500 people immediately and is [still] causing tens of thousands of people in the area to suffer severe medical problems...The abandoned factory remains, with toxic waste and pesticide residue strewn about the property. The groundwater in the area is still contaminated.[2] "The leak of deadly methyl isocyanate, or MIC, gas took place on Dec. 3 1984, shortly after midnight, after water somehow entered a storage tank and triggered a chemical chain reaction. Pressure soon rose so high that the MIC gas rushed out of the tank's safety valve, a Union Carbide report concluded; a pressure gauge wasn't operating at the time. Wind carried the gas into residential areas of Bhopal, killing people without warning. Those who left their homes and tried to flee on foot only got exposed more."[3]

What do you think happened to the company employees and managers connected to the death and human suffering in this incident in Bhopal? Do you think anyone was made to stand trial for his actions? You don't think the parties involved were just able to walk away from the horror their company created, do you? Think again. Until recently (2002), Warren Anderson, CEO of Union Carbide at the time of the disaster, was nowhere to be found as the Indian government has searched almost two decades for his whereabouts. But Greenpeace found him. Anderson was eventually discovered living the life of luxury at his home in Bridgehampton, New York. Although he is wanted in India to face charges of culpable homicide in the deaths of 20,000 people since the disaster, Anderson has been successfully hiding in the U.S. since 1984 following the chemical explosion that resulted in life long suffering for almost 120,000 survivors. "If Greenpeace can track down India's most wanted, why haven't the U.S. authorities extradited him? Our government has been swift to pretend to react to

2.  "Greenpeace Points Spotlight at Potential Bhopal—Type Disaster at Dow Plants in the U.S.—17th Anniversary of Deadly Chemical Spill in Bhopal, India—Environmentalists Demand Justice for Victims and Action to Prevent Another Disaster," Greenpeace, USA, Dec. 31, 2000

3.  Pearl, Danny, "Effects of Union Carbide Gas Leak, Linger Only in Lives of Its Victims," February 2001

the financial crimes of Enron and WorldCom, [pointing the finger at certain individuals at the upper levels]. Anderson is charged with the deaths of thousands of Indians; shouldn't this be a priority?"[4]

"On the night of the disaster, when an explosion at Union Carbide's pesticide plant caused 40 tons of lethal gas to seep into the city of Bhopal, six safety measures designed to prevent a gas leak had either malfunctioned, were turned off or were otherwise inadequate. In addition, the safety siren, intended to alert the community should an incident occur at the plant, was turned off. Union Carbide responded to the disaster by paying survivors inadequate compensation and abandoning the plant, leaving tons of dangerous toxic chemicals strewn around the site and the people of Bhopal with a toxic legacy that is still causing injury today. In 2001, the company shed its name by merging with Dow Chemical."[5]

How is it possible for someone—some multi-billion dollar, multi-national corporation—to get away with causing 20,000 deaths and countless suffering without appearing in front of judicial officials? By a comparison, for much lesser "crimes," look at the big ordeal (and rightly so) that drivers causing accidental motorist deaths are put through! Or how about the way abused wives are thrown into jail for killing their spouses in self defense. Is justice really justice when it comes to multinational, politically influential corporations and their leaders? No, there is a different set of rules for the rich and powerful. They get away with homicide! Maybe Ralph Nader hit the nail on the head when he commented, "To see a corporate crook in jail is about as rare as the Australian dodo."[6] The last time I checked, the dodo was still extinct.

## TOXIC WASTE: ARE YOU WILLING TO GIVE PERMISSION TO DUMP IT IN YOUR BACK YARD?

Like a teenage fashion trend, the idea of exporting toxic waste became all the rage by the 1980s. Greenpeace reports:

> In the late 1980s Greenpeace researchers discovered a pattern of waste shipments from richer industrialized nations to poorer, less industrialized ones. Initially the preferred dumping grounds for toxic wastes was Africa. After scandals in the late 1980s, that shifted to Latin America and Eastern Europe.

---

4. "Wanted CEO Found Living in Luxury in the Hamptons: Greenpeace Calls for Arrest of Former Union Carbide CEO," www.greenpeaceusa.org/features/anderson_found, 2002

5. ibid

6. NOW with Bill Moyers, PBS, Aug 9, 2002

Currently, Asia is the last dumping ground for waste from the West. As waste disposal became more stringently regulated and more expensive in the North, waste generators and brokers thought up hundreds of schemes to send these wastes to the developing world, sometimes disguising their plans as humanitarian aid or environmentally beneficial recycling. Most of these schemes died once made public, but many cases of waste exports did occur. Toxic incinerator ash from Philadelphia was dumped on a beach in Haiti. PCBs from Italy wound up on a farm in Koko, Nigeria. Obsolete pesticides from Germany ended up in Albania. The path of toxic waste trade was the path of least resistance.

After the scandals of the late 1980s and early 1990s involving this exploitative trade in wastes, most of these schemes began incorporating some form of recycling to justify them. Some of these "recyclable" wastes were never recycled, like some 10,000 barrels of U.S.-generated mercury wastes which sit in a warehouse in South Africa. Even where recycling did take place, the process often caused devastating toxic contamination of workers and surrounding communities. Examples include the recovery of lead from car batteries, and zinc from galvanizing ash.[7]

Another example of a far-reaching environmental disaster was the massive oil spill at the hands of an Exxon tanker called Valdez in 1989 off the northwest coast of North America. The immediate effects caused the death of countless sea creatures, birds and wildlife onshore. But this was just the beginning. A group called the Survivors of the Exxon Valdez Oil Spill issues this sobering statement:

We are the 40,000-plus victims of the 1989 Exxon Valdez oil spill: the fishers and Native Americans upon whose lives and livelihoods the spill wreaked havoc. Today, a full ten years later, we continue to suffer economically and emotionally—and it's because of Exxon's nonstop misconduct in handling the spill.

In 1994, we won a verdict against Exxon in one of the most famous trials in American history. In May 1999, the U.S. Court of Appeals for the Ninth Circuit heard Exxon's appeal. The latest news from the Ninth Circuit can be read here.

All these years, meanwhile, an unrepentant Exxon has paid us nothing.

About two-thirds of us victims are from Alaska. But thousands of us are from every other state in the nation. So how could the spill have affected people from the South, West, Midwest and East? Until the spill, we fishers from the continental United States would travel to Alaska to make our living during the fishing season. We'd then return to our home states. And that's where we

---

7.    "International Trade in Wastes," Greenpeace, http://archive.greenpeace.org/search.shtml, 2002

are today: neighbors of yours, still hurting. Given Exxon's continued refusal to make us whole, the economic boom of the 1990s has passed us by.

Our financial losses, in turn, have led to a number of cases of clinical depression and broken families.

Contrary to Exxon's ongoing campaign of public misinformation, not only are we victims still suffering, but so is our environment. In February 1999, the government reported that only two of the 24 animal species hurt by the spill have recovered. And as the television reports covering the March 24, 1999 tenth anniversary of the spill showed, Exxon's oil remains on the beaches of Alaska today.[8]

There are many, many examples of the breadth and depth of destruction from irresponsible, shortsighted, careless and greed-driven practices the world over. Not only do "toxic events" create problems across the world when they occur, but also for generations to come. Arrogance and the lack of understanding and arrogance of modern, corporate science that fails and refuses to admit to the global and generational impact of today's mistakes, artificial creations and insane experimentation. We all suffer for profit-driven science. One of the most alarming examples is how we are still reeling from the effects of nuclear weapons experiments conducted a half-century ago. CNN reports:

> Radioactive fallout from 1950s above-ground nuclear weapons testing spread farther than researchers previously realized and most increased cancer rates in the United States, according to a scientific report.
>
> "Any person living in the contiguous United States since 1951 has been exposed to radioactive fallout, and all organs and tissues of the body have received some radiation exposure," the Centers for Disease Control and Prevention and the National Cancer Institute said in a progress report prepared for Congress. The report was reviewed by the Institute for Energy and Environmental Research.
>
> The preliminary report—the actual study is not yet complete—has alarmed some members of Congress, including Sen. Tom Harkin, D-Iowa.
>
> CNN's Natalie Pawelski reports on a scientific study of the toxic effects of Cold War nuclear testing, which one senator says contributed to at least 15,000 U.S. cancer deaths. (March 1)
>
> "What we know is maybe the tip of the iceberg here," Harkin said. "We know that there's been upwards of perhaps 15,000 deaths that are attributable to these nuclear tests." Congress received the preliminary report last August.
>
> More than 2,000 nuclear tests have been conducted worldwide since the first nuclear bomb was built in the Manhattan Project in World War II, but

---

8.    Survivors of the Exxon Valdez Oil Spill, 2000, www.jomiller.com/exxonvaldez/

the CDC/NCI study considered only those above-ground tests that took place between 1951 and 1962. The United States and the Soviet Union agreed in 1963 to restrict nuclear tests to underground sites.

"What is surprising and very new is that it has created intense hot spots in the continental United States all the way from California and Washington to Vermont, New Hampshire and North Carolina," said Dr. Arjun Makhijani, president of the IEER.

And yet, the government has yet to formulate a public health response, according to IEER outreach director Lisa Ledwidge, a biologist.[9]

Whether we see it or not, we now live in a world community. This truth is both a blessing and a nightmare at the same time. We are now afforded the luxury of enjoying and partaking in other cultures, imported goods from exotic places, vacations and business trips the world over, and the instantaneous exchange of valuable information across great distances. The nightmare comes from irresponsibility and abuse—when individuals, corporations and nations ignore the value and role of nature and environmental balance. This ignorance and abuse affects us all, including the perpetrators of the abuse.

## WHAT'S SPEWING OUT OF INCINERATORS?

Where does your garbage go? If you live in a big city you may put your garbage out on the curb once or twice a week and wave hello to the garbage collectors as they roar down the street making a collection. Or maybe you just take your garbage to the end of the hall, drop it in a chute and never look back. Regardless, the nation's garbage is going *somewhere* to be *handled*, not disposed of. It mostly either piles up in a mountain of collective garbage or is burned in an incinerator. Sometimes it's a combination of both methods. When garbage sits in a landfill it emits toxic gases and seeps into the ground, destroying the soil and leeching into the ground water. A garbage dump may render toxic a lake, reservoir, stream or creek many miles away. Just because you don't see it, it doesn't mean it's not poisoning you. As the old saying goes, "Ignorance of the law is no excuse." In this case we are speaking of the laws of nature, gravity, biology, chemistry and toxicology.

In every town incinerators are emitting black smoke by the tons. When I was a boy, I practiced little league football in a lush green park adjacent to one of these incinerators. We all agreed—players, parents and coaches—that the incinerator really stunk. But what we didn't know, because nobody was talking about it in

---

9. "Study: 1950s nuclear fallout worse than thought," March 1, 2002

those days, is that incinerators are generators of some of the most destructive toxic fumes. They smell bad because they are spewing poisonous substances. Topping the list of toxic byproducts of incineration are mercury, lead and dioxin. It's a toss-up as to which of the many toxins pose the most threat to life, but dioxin as of late has caught the attention of environmental scientists.

Dioxin is a byproduct of incinerated chlorine-based chemicals and is considered by scientists as one of the most toxic of all known chemicals. Dioxin is known as a persistent substance. It is stored, and remains, in the tissues of plants and animals. "EPA (Environmental Protection Agency) officials...admit that the EPA has no standards to address the immense risks posed by food chain contamination from incinerators emitting dioxin."[10] In essence, dioxin, as well as other chemical poisons, do not only poison people, animals and plants directly exposed to it, but is also passed on to consumers as they eat the plants and animals that are toxic.

> Despite this information, incineration has rapidly proliferated throughout the country as the "profitable answer" for disposal of the nation's stockpile of toxic waste and garbage. In fact, incineration does not destroy the waste, it transforms it. Dioxin, lead, mercury, PCBs and other air emissions from incinerator smokestacks cannot be adequately contained even with the most advanced equipment. These poisons are widely dispersed, and like acid rain, result in uncontrolled pollution of the surrounding water, soil, and farmland.
>
> The dangers of these bio-cumulative chemicals multiply dramatically as they are absorbed up through the food chain, from soil and water to plant and animal life to humans. In the case of dioxin, it takes seven years for your body to eliminate half of the dioxin in your system.[11]

## THE SOLUTION: LET'S STOP BEING SUICIDAL

Each of us must stop using toxic products and products that create toxic residues when discarded. We need to cease our financial support (with our spending dollars) of corporations that create products and waste that are not environmentally friendly. We must stop purchasing and using products that create dangerous, toxic waste during manufacture. As a small planet, already overtaxed by population and toxic waste, we must either do this or face annihilation at the hands of

---

10.  Harrison, Esq., Mick G. *GOVERNMENT ACCOUNTABILITY PROJECT,* "Poisoning Ourselves: The Impact of Incineration on Food and Human Health, An Executive Summary," Project Censored, 1994, September 1994

11.  ibid

greed and ignorance. We must appreciate our relationship to the earth and atmosphere as a means to understanding ourselves and our needs as biological beings requiring pure water, soil and air for nourishment, disease prevention, healing and happiness.

As consumers we all have a choice as to which products and services we want to support, depending on their total impact on our environment—the world around us that provides our air, land and water. Using any environmentally destructive product is suicidal.

## *HERE'S WHAT YOU CAN DO TO BEGIN TO RECOGNIZE THE ENORMITY OF POLLUTION IN YOUR OWN NEIGHBORHOOD:*

- Go online and type in your zip code to determine how polluted your neighborhood and city is: www.scorecard.org

- Go online to see what impact a nuclear reactor disaster would have on you and your family in your zip code: www.greenpeaceusa.org/nuclear/locator.htm

- Buy products that do not harm the earth (these are listed further on in this book)

# Turning Heads by
# Twisting Toxic Truths

In the 1990s a new term—"spin doctor"—came onto the American scene. Spinning is associated with a concept that is as old as the hills, as in "putting a new spin on it." Spin doctors in the arenas of politics, industry and economics take great pride in their ability to twist the truth and influence public opinion. They are professional truth-twisters with no apparent conscience or bounds of ethics. To put a new or different spin on an idea means to sell the idea in a different light, most often because if you represent the idea as-is, it will not be well-accepted. Those who are successful at spinning are known as spin doctors and can successfully make an evil genius, shady politician or industry giant and his dubious activities look good in the public eye. If a spin doctor is adept enough he or she can even change the public's opinion of war, conquest, corporate wrong-doings or political deceit. Talented spin doctors can make bad things seem good, and good things seem bad. Much of their success lies in the ability to take the public's mind off of the negative and place its attention on something else.

To sell the public on nuclear energy, for instance, spin doctors working for power companies need to sell the benefits of cheaper energy and forget about the catastrophes that may (and do) result from nuclear meltdowns, storage of spent radioactive rods and accidents related to the industry. Spin doctors can also make the public awe-inspired over the wonders of chemicals while simultaneously downplaying the horrific toll these same substances have on our health and environment. Spin doctors who are the "best" at their trade are evil geniuses.

As of late, this ilk of evil geniuses has been hammering away at making the American public buy the nonsense that big, polluting, self-centered, self-serving industry and a host of political enablers really care about the citizens of the United States and the rest of the world. If they can get us to believe they are serving us and are on our side, then they can continue to get away with their health-defying policies. So far their evil plan is working and their bank accounts are bulging as proof of their success.

### The un-American Spin

Did you ever notice that the term "unAmerican" periodically permeates the popular culture and media in the United States? The funny thing is that the term unAmerican is used in the same way a thief calls an innocent bystander a thief just to get the attention off himself. Dr. Bernard Jensen, a pioneer in the natural health care movement, used to say that when you point a finger at someone you have four fingers pointing back at yourself. This was his way of saying that people in glass houses shouldn't throw stones. During the infamous McCarthy Era in this country (mid 1950s), Senator Joe McCarthy, a self-righteous, intimidating man who won his reputation as a fearless tail gunner in World War II, spearheaded one of the ugliest periods in American history. McCarthy jailed and ruined the lives of thousands of Americans by accusing them of unAmerican activities, participating in communist conspiracies and acting in unAmerican ways, then making these citizens try in vain to prove their innocence, turn against their friends and co-workers and sign confessions. In the land of the free and home of the brave, where the U.S. Constitution theoretically provides that all citizens are innocent until proven guilty, McCarthy challenged the Law and successfully carried out witch hunts against Americans who were exercising their rights to freedom of speech, freedom of the press and freedom of expression. And the rest of Congress, the media, the FBI and even the presidency, went along.

Following McCarthy's reign in Congress, after countless people committed suicides to avenge their ruined livelihoods and reputations, McCarthy's diligent anti-American campaign at last faded out. In its wake, though, Americans in high profile positions, including actors, movie directors, writers, philosophers, politicians, religious leaders and teachers, decided that such a monstrous campaign should never happen again in this land of democracy and free speech. People should be allowed to speak their minds, and freedom and justice should prevail above all. McCarthy scared the American public—rich and poor alike—not only because he was a Congressman out of control, conducting his own private war according to his own interpretation of American values, but even more so because of the ugly idea that truth and freedom could be stifled in the United States of America. All he had to do was put a new spin on the idea of what is considered American. Sadly, McCarthy didn't take his terror tactics with him into the grave.

Here we are, fifty years later, and the term unAmerican has again risen to the forefront. It is again being used by people in power who want to divert public opinion away from their own shady, greedy, unhealthy activities. Following the events of September 11, 2002, after terrorists crashed two passenger planes into

New York City's World Trade Towers, the United States fell into a panic and frenzy. Scared, embarrassed and violated, the national psyche—in a state of shock and fear—was seeking a way to rebound and regain its face. That's when the nationalistic fervor began to swell, with people all across the country hanging American flags out of their windows, on the roofs of their cars, in the rear windows of their SUVs, in schools and in work places. The president and vice president (who are financially married to the weapons and oil industries and keep their monies in offshore bank accounts to avoid taxation) jumped on the nationalistic movement and declared war on terrorism. They also declared war on American civil liberties. Many believe the Administration's newfound fervor was an excuse to seize power in the Middle East to build oil pipelines and ensure the flow of the black gold through otherwise hostile territories.

So fervent was the sentiment against foes of America following 9/11 that the powers-that-be decided to jump on the wave of emotions and prove to the public how devoutly American they could be. "Pro-American" advertising campaigns shamelessly appeared on television within a week of the September 11th tragedy. Shamelessly? Yes, they were shameless because **a feigned, misguided pro-American sentiment was used to sell American-destroying products**. Re-read this last sentence because it defies logic! Even the Super Bowl became a forum for a worldwide spectacle of nationalism, complete with flags, fireworks, military jet fly-overs, speeches and a guest appearance by military personnel and the president's father.

After the tragedy of September 11, 2001, we had a chance to see who the major opportunists were in this country—huge corporations playing with our minds and capitalizing upon our pain and vulnerability. They tossed around the words "hero" and "brave," riding on the laurels of rescue workers who lost their lives in a very real and heroic American fashion. But what did the corporations do to piggyback on the heroic actions of others? Those companies running their ads behind the pro-American banner had four fingers pointing back at themselves. Automobile companies, in their slick TV ads, proclaimed their pro-American mission for all the nation to see. How ironic, because auto manufacturers lead the way in the destruction of America's environment via exhaust emissions, contributing to global warming, lung cancer, and a host of other illnesses. We also saw pro-American ads funded by computer manufacturers whose lead-filled products pollute our rivers and streams; and pro-American ads from gasoline/oil companies whose destruction is so infamous it hardly bears repeating.

Unlike the crude politics of the McCarthy Era, politicians and big corporations today use different, more subtle tactics. Instead of grilling their opponents on national television in front of a Congressional hearing for being unAmerican, the powers-that-be seek to suck up all the emotional sentiment for themselves, allying their companies and goals with the "American Way" (whatever that is). Now appearing on the television screen we see ads by automakers, oil companies and even the White House telling us how pro-American they are. Their actions speak otherwise, yet they are hidden from public scrutiny; but their voices are heard loud and clear as they work behind the scene to squelch the voices of millions of opposing Americans who see through their deceit.

This is a shameless capitalization on the delicate and wounded emotional state of Americans. As we are being hypnotized by the drone of our television sets and creature comforts we have to somehow fight off our drowsiness and open our eyes to see that...

## *IT IS unAMERICAN TO CONDUCT THESE ACTIVITIES:*

- The proliferated and senseless use of oil and gasoline, especially in light of complaints that the Middle East nations are profiting off Americans and ruining our lives. If you drive a gas-guzzling vehicle, you are part of the problem even if you are screaming at the top of your lungs that you hate the oil barons who are yanking your pocketbook. Oil companies and automobile manufacturers who run advertisements saying they are pro-American are really unAmerican because they are keeping us hooked on a fuel source that only serves to line their own pockets. They make billions of dollars off the American public and are keeping us dependent on foreign oil. This is pro-Corporation, and unAmerican. Don't let their flag-waving ads fool you.

- The destruction of our beautiful environment. We watch television ads of cars, trucks, vans and other vehicles tearing through America's pristine wilderness. The advertisements show us how fun it is to drive through forests, streams and dirt roads—all very unAmerican activities when you think about it. One of the greatest treasures of America is the richness of our scenic areas—trees, mountains, rivers, valleys, desserts and coasts. When you drive a sports utility vehicle (SUV) through this beautiful landscape, off-road, you are destroying America now and for generations. To promote this type of behavior is as unAmerican as you can get.

- Making your fortune at the expense of the American people's health and welfare, especially while you are acting as a paid servant of the public. Consider the fact that there is a steady stream of pro-American advertising and public relations out of the White House as I write these words. But if we take a closer look, it is rather obvious that politicians, who are supposed to be representing the interests of the American people, are engaged in a serious conflict of interest. They are selling out the American public for their personal money-making agendas. Public "servants" in the presidential administration and Congress make millions of dollars from oil, pharmaceutical, chemical, weapons and energy industry profits.[1] Each of these industries are destroying your America by dumping deadly, cancer-causing chemicals into the air, land and sea, including nuclear waste and fallout. Our "leaders" are destroying the American landscape, natural resources, lives and futures while pretending through their pro-American rhetoric that they are working hard for us. The interests of Americans are secondary to their profit-making schemes.

- Contributing to global warming. Automobile, factory and household spray emissions are causing global warming by destroying the ozone layer in our atmosphere. To have a presidential administration that denies and hides this truth despite what the top scientists in America have proven, is an unAmerican reality. For any presidential administration to promote the further destruction of the ozone layer, leading to climate changes and natural disasters, is unAmerican and selfish. The president visits the sites of the most destructive and widespread fires this nation has ever seen and, with a straight and earnest expression, tells people to buck up, have courage and press on in the American way. All the while, he promotes the use, manufacture and proliferation of ozone-destroying technologies, because, among other reasons, he is financially invested in them.

---

1.    "In today's White House, former polluters make environmental policy." The cast of characters include vice president Richard Cheney, former CEO of Halliburton, the oil-services giant; head of the White House Energy Task Force; James Stevel Griles, Deputy Interior Secretary, a former oil and mining lobbyist who still meets with former clients about strip mining and methane drilling; Spencer Abraham, Energy Secretary, led the charge to scuttle fuel-efficiency standards for SUVs and created incentives to buy gas guzzlers; Andrew Card, White House Chief of Staff, former GM lobbyist. Days after the Bush inauguration, Card froze Clinton-era proposed rules; Gale Norton, Interior Secretary, Former lead-industry lobbyist, presented altered report stating Arctic drilling would not harm caribou; James Connaughton, Chairman, Coucil of Environmental Quality, a former utility lobbyist who advises Bush to ease pollution controls and ignore global warming; Rebecca Watson, Assistant Interior Secretary, once a lawyer for mining and drilling firms, now approves rule changes that benefit her old clients; and Bennett Raley, Assistant Interior Secretary, an ex- "property rights" advocate who caused a massive salmon kill in Oregon by diverting water for irrigation. Kennedy, Jr., Robert F., *Rolling Stone* magazine, December 11, 2003, Issue 937, p. 183.

## *THE NEXT TIME YOU HEAR PRO-AMERICAN RHETORIC ON ADS AND IN THE MEDIA, TAKE THESE STEPS:*

• Question whether the companies or persons making pro-American claims have an ulterior motive and are really fooling the public.

• Watch the ad with the sound off and let your eyes tell you what the images are saying. Is it really fun to drive your car through a stream and in the pristine American wilderness and destroy the ecosystem? Is it really a wise act to pollute our own drinking water as we drive a four-wheel-drive SUV through a mountain creek? We should act like responsible adults, ESPE-CIALLY because the oil and car companies and their political puppets are not. They are encouraging us to destroy our own lands. With a smile and a song they're giving us a loaded gun pointed at ourselves and encouraging us to pull the trigger!

• Find out whether your president, vice-president, cabinet members or congressional leaders make their money from their intimate connections in companies that are known for the unAmerican activities of destroying the environment, using up our natural resources, causing wars, killing our relatives with cancerous chemicals, broadening the hole in the ozone layer or abusing the American system. This background information is easy to find, but the problem is few people are willing to investigate for themselves.

### *What is unAmerican?*

UnAmerican activities are actions that are destroying the lives and environment of Americans (and the world). The most pressing issues we face are environmental concerns and the destruction of life on earth by chemical toxins. The balance of nature has been upset by the greed of humankind. Now that we recognize this fact and we absolutely now have alternative, cleaner, friendlier technologies, there is absolutely no reason to support unAmerican politicians and un-American corporations.

# Have We Lost Our
# Minds & Media
# To Corporate Science?

"Corporate Science"—now here's an oxymoron, conflict of interest and snow-job all wrapped up into a convenient little ball! How can science be linked to corporate interests and still be called "science"? It cannot. It should just be called "propaganda." By definition, science is supposed to be unbiased and meticulous in its fact-finding, methodology and record-keeping, as well as independent, curious and revealing. This hardly describes most of today's so-called science. In this modern era, science is biased beyond popular comprehension. This may come as quite a shock to the millions of us who have come to respect scientists for their presumed integrity, independence, intelligence and diligence. Are these old and jaded images of scientists realistic today?

Scientists are paid to do their jobs. If they work for big corporations, including drug and chemical manufacturers, they are paid to prove that their corporations are doing good things for the world and to sell substances that work successfully. I said "successfully," not healthfully. Scientists are not paid by corporations for proving that the chemicals they are producing are bad for the environment or threatening to life and health. Instead of working to benefit society, corporate scientists are loyal only to their corporate bosses. After all, what motivation would a big corporation have to pay scientists out of their profits merely to benefit the world? Would you put a scientist on your payroll—give him $150,000 and a company car—just to have him improve the value of life here in America? Not if there wasn't an ulterior motive. Think about this, because it makes all the difference. Scientific findings are used to further the financial gains of companies, not to uplift life on earth, even though TV commercials show us dedicated men and women in white lab coats inventing a new way to use plastic. Oops! They forgot to tell us that plastics outgas and toxic pollutants sit in landfills for thousands of years and poison our families while they're sleeping at night. The companies making certain drugs fail to tell the rest of us that side effects of their industry include cancer of the uterus and breast—details you may want to know before popping a pill that some scientist invented to keep you from having babies, ward off menopause or make cows produce more milk to go with your cereal.

## CHEMICAL WARFARE ON AMERICA

During World War I, chemicals such as mustard gas were used as weapons. The effects were so horrendous and frightening that, following the war, all "civilized" nations agreed to never use chemical weapons for warfare again. Rules of war? Interesting. Did we really learn our lessons on how terrible chemicals can be when they attack a human being? Apparently not. What about the use of Agent Orange in Viet Nam? The chemical manufacturers instead learned to hide and minimize the truth about the dangers of chemicals while playing up their "scientifically proven" benefits. Hide the truth from the public. Throughout the decades, people owning, using, promoting and manufacturing chemicals have had the blood and suffering of countless men, women and children on their hands.

For half a century, the chemical industry has waged a high-stakes, high-priced public relations war against the American public. The industry has used every trick in the PR business with polling, focus groups, news media outreach, propaganda materials such as videos, pamphlets and speakers' programs, paid advertising, promotion of pro-industry scientific experts and research, and most of all, "greenwashing"—PR campaigns that hype chemical makers' "environmental commitment" while hiding the truth about how they poison the populace with toxins.

Chemical makers understand that if you have a dangerous, deadly and environment-destroying product, you have to work EXTREMELY HARD to push people to accept the "benefits." You have to wow them into thinking that a bottle of Windex is better than water, vinegar and elbow grease. You have to make people think that their bed sheets must smell like fresh lemons, even if it takes a synthetic mixture of chemicals to achieve this goal. It's a lot of work, but if you are hell-bent on making huge profits, somebody's gotta do it!

## WORKING HARD TO MAKE US BELIEVE IN MAGIC

There are two main types of hazardous chemicals that destroy our health: chemicals made purposefully as end products (for example, plastics and bug sprays), and chemicals that are byproducts (waste) of industry (for example, dioxin and plastic gases). In both cases, if the production of dangerous chemicals are the foundation for your personal wealth and success, you better have some evil geniuses working for you to cover up the fact that you are ruining people's lives. You have to hire scientists, public relations experts, marketing whizzes and even secretaries who can look Michael Moore in the face and say, "Get those cameras out of here and get out of our offices. Mr. Big is not here today, he's in the South of France with Mr. CEO. I mean…well, I mean, he's in a meeting right now."

It's not easy to make chemical waste and unsafe substances accepted by the general public. This is mainly because people are adverse to chemicals. Artificial ingredients and poisons make us sick, so the chemical industry must work very hard to create public acceptance. One way to do this is by repeatedly downplaying, ignoring, hiding and minimizing adverse health effects, death, suffering and environmental damage caused by unnatural compounds. Chemical companies use PR firms to "show" and "teach" America how wonderful their products are, focusing on the concocted benefits rather than the tragedies. They spend millions to accomplish this sinister goal:

> EWG [Environmental Working Group] analysis of internal industry documents shows that from 1952 to 1996 the Chemical Manufacturers Association [CMA] (now known as the "American Chemistry Council") spent an **estimated** $185 million to shape public opinion (inflation adjusted dollars)….
>
> These figures don't include the PR and ad campaigns of major CMA member companies such as DuPont, Dow Chemical and General Electric, who spend millions each year on their own; CMA's political lobbying and "grassroots" outreach programs; and the industry's sizable political contributions. According to OpenSecrets.org these contributions reached a total of $38 million to federal candidates from 1990 to 2000.
>
> The Chemical Industry Archives reveal for the first time not only the size of the CMA's PR effort but its scope, and the industry's determination to win the public opinion war at any cost. The documents paint a portrait of an industry whose objective is to polish its image and increase its profits without due regard for the consequences to public health and the environment.[1]

Chemical manufacturers ignore cancer rates in children while hammering the public with information about how they make life wonderful for American housewives—the same housewives—mothers—whose children all over the world are suffering to death from exposure to lead, dioxin, pesticides, nitrate, arsenic, formaldehyde, mercury, PCBs and hundreds of other substances. The chemical industry works diligently to "inform" women about the wonders of chemicals,

---

1.    "Polling, PR and propaganda: How the chemical industry creates 'Public Perception'", Environmental Working Group, 2002

how a can of room deodorant can mask even the worse effects of gastroenteritis, and how germs can be killed dead by spraying the bejeezus out of every counter, corner and crook of your house until you are breathing chemicals through your skin. Women are the primary targets of ads selling chemicals. Chemical industry spokespeople tell us why:

> The chemical industry very badly needs the support of this specialized and numerous group...On a systematic and programmed basis we should tell them how our research and products have made their lives easier and more enjoyable, how we have helped them in their domestic tasks...It is not hard to visualize how readily our food additive publications can be converted into program materials for women's clubs...The loyalty of women can help us tremendously if they understand the facts about food additives, labeling, water pollution and even plant safety.[2]

"Facts"? But they're not giving all the facts. They're leaving out the facts that chemicals are killing children. Wouldn't this "specialized group" of mothers *want* this fact?

## SELLING YOUR CHILDREN

Maybe chemical companies figure that if women can see how wonderful chemicals are, they will overlook the fact that their children are dying of cancer and suffering from asthma. How stupid do they think women are? By the way, mothers, you should know that while you are at work or not at home to tune in on your television set to the wonders of chemicals in action, there's a really good chance that your children are getting an unhealthy dose of propaganda at school. Exposure through television and the classroom, it is hoped, will be enough to cancel out your awareness that environmental toxins are senselessly taking the lives of children from China to California.

### Children are Dying & Suffering for Corporate Profit

Corporations spend more than a half billion dollars per year on school "education." Lifetime Learning Systems, representing corporate interests, has a way of (to quote their words), "reaching and teaching kids" while they're not at home watching corporate ads on television.[3] Lifetime Learning Systems, a division of

---

2.   ibid, Environmental Working Group,
      http://www.chemicalindustryarchives.org/dirtysecrets/PR/3.asp
3.   lifetimelearningsystems.com

*Weekly Reader*, claims to reach 52 million children while in school. This way our children can learn corporate PR along with math, science and English literature. They all meld into one learning experience. The company boasts: "Lifetime Learning Systems, founded in 1978, was the first company to create sponsored educational materials that are printed and distributed free to teachers. The distribution can be either nationwide or highly targeted within the Pre-K to grade 12 universe. Our clients include major corporations, trade associations, not-for-profits and government agencies."[4]

According to Sharon Beder, author of *Global Spin—The Corporate Assault on Environmentalism*, "The great advantage of embedding corporate messages in sponsored learning materials over more direct means of advertising is that any residual skepticism with which conventional advertisements might be treated disappears altogether when it comes to advertisements and public relations material secreted within school lessons. As one writer points out: 'Imagine—your target market not only reads your ads—they get tested on them.' One kit put out by Teacher Support Software, which is used in many kindergartens in Texas, includes test questions such as 'Taco Bell has [blank] and burritos.'"[5]

It's hard to turn down money for our under-funded school systems—from universities to kindergartens (especially since the Bush administration continues to cut funding for schools).[6] The financial dilemma alone creates an open door for corporations to enter the once-sacred classroom.

Take Coca Cola, for example, who cleverly created the Coca-Cola Scholars Foundation. What a way to get your name in schools across America! The Coca-Cola company, which does not manufacture or sell a product that is health-promoting by any stretch of the imagination, not only sells their sugar-loaded beverage in vending machines along with brightly packaged, chemically concocted junk snacks, has made their way into the school system as a company that just wants to help your child pay for a better education. The Coca-Cola Scholars Program, according to the company's sales brochure, "stepped to the forefront of corporate support for higher education through the creation in 1986 of the Coca-Cola Scholars Foundation, Inc. A joint effort of Coca-Cola Bottlers and The Coca-Cola Company, it is the largest business-supported scholarship program of its kind, signifying the same commitment to leadership and excellence that enables Coca-Cola to maintain international preeminence year after year in the

4.    ibid
5.    Beder, Sharon, *Global Spin—The Corporate Assault on Environmentalism*, Chelsea Green Publishing Company, Vermont, page 167

beverage industry."[7] Good for them. But is this good for your children? It may be good for our doctors, dentists and pharmaceutical companies, but is it good for your children to think so highly of such a company? Coca-Cola tells us that "Bottlers envisioned a program that would make an enduring contribution to our nation's future, and one accessible to the widest range of students possible. Selection is therefore based on a balanced consideration of leadership, character, achievement and commitment, both inside and outside the classroom."[8] What kind of leadership, commitment and character does this corporation display, anyway? Is it a prime example of leadership, commitment and character to encourage

---

6.  Congressman George Miller, 7th District, California (Bush Administration Cuts Public School Funding to Pay for New Private School Voucher Scheme; Proposed budget includes provisions Republicans promised against; Monday, February 3, 2003) writes: WASHINGTON—Representative George Miller (D-CA), the senior Democrat on the House Education and the Workforce Committee, today castigated the Bush Administration for reneging on its promise to properly fund education.

In the budget draft delivered to Congress today, the Bush Administration cut hundreds of millions of dollars in public school funding in order to pay for its new, private school voucher plan. Republicans have always asserted that their private voucher plan would not come at the expense of public school programs.

"Once again, the Bush Administration has proved that maintaining its commitment to the conservative Republican agenda is more important than keeping its promise to American children," said Miller. "President Bush's 2004 budget fails to pay for critical provisions of the No Child Left Behind Act—the cornerstone education reform act."

The Bush budget slashes funding for after-school programs by $400 million; that means that many programs will be shut down and thousands of children denied participation in programs that provide critical supervision and instruction. The Bush budget deeply cuts vocational education by $300 million, which is 25% of the entire program's budget at a time when young people need vocational skills to find good jobs. And it provides no increase for Pell grants, America's premier higher education program for the nation's neediest college students, or the crucial Head Start program.

"Our nation's public schools do not deserve to be cut at the expense of private school vouchers," concluded Miller. "Our public school children do not deserve to suffer because of a demand by the Republicans to defund public education."

The Bush budget contains $300 million for private school vouchers, a proposal explicitly rejected by the Congress and by the public.

our already sugar-logged youth to drink Coca-Cola? No, but they get away with their invasive PR campaign year after year without challenge.

## MELDING CORPORATE MESSAGES
## WITH EDUCATIONAL CURRICULA

By melding corporate messages with educational curricula, a blur is formed between disinformation, misinformation, facts and skewed information. By crowding out the non-corporate voices of independent scientists, environmental groups, concerned parents, citizens' watch groups and others without commercial ulterior motives, the corporate foothold in the classroom represents a form of censorship so insidious that even teachers rarely notice their presence and effects.

Sharon Beder (Global Spin) explains, "In most cases, the so-called educational materials give students a distorted picture of environmental issues and other problems, social choices and tradeoffs. They present a corporate view as 'fact' and report the results of corporate-funded studies without saying who financed them. They often fail to 'acknowledge the sponsor's own financial interest, or to disclose conditions and information that affect the accuracy of what they teach.' There is not really any competition from non-corporate views, because environmental groups and others don't have the funding that is necessary to develop and distribute such an array of professionally produced materials and distribute them widely. And teachers do not have the resources or knowledge to balance the material with differing points of view."[9]

Non-corporate groups clearly do not have the clout over school boards and politicians to push their way into the classroom. The best course of action would be to simply **deny all corporate access to public educational institutions**, because corporate goals do not include education, but rather *corporate* education (also known as propaganda) for the ulterior motive of retaining customers, creating more customers, ensuring future customers, and harvesting public support for corporate activities and agendas. Allowing corporate propaganda in our school systems is a form of mental child abuse, preying upon our children in an environment that is supposed to be safe from the outside world. It is also an affront to parents who are given no means of counteracting or debating corporate messages.

---

7.    Coca-Cola Scholars Foundation brochure, P.O. Box 442, Atlanta, Georgia 30301, 2002

8.    ibid

9.    ibid, pages 167-168

Even nationalism can be skewed the corporate way when an American flag is strategically set beside a corporate logo.

## POISONING THEIR MINDS AND BODIES

In case you don't have the time or sympathy to explain the wonders of chemical poisons to your children, the chemical industry is doing this for you, behind your back in their tireless promotion to students from ages four to twenty-four. Only they tend to leave out the important details that your children need to know.

> For decades, the chemical industry has sponsored awards programs for students and teachers. By 1997, CMA [Chemical Manufacturers Association] was scheduled to spend $105,000 on awards for "teachers at the junior high and elementary school level." Regardless of the industry's motives for rewarding teachers, it is safe to assume that any teacher who receives an award from CMA will be more willing to consider its views. The industry knows this, and has moved to exploit its access.
>
> In a 1997 memo, the industry's communications strategists recommended spending nearly $300,000 to produce ChemEcology, "a publication covering the health, safety and environmental quality activities of the industry, including how industry products contribute to the quality of life." The proposal boasts that 80,000 teachers and students read ChemEcology every month.[10]

Public education has long held an image—perhaps far too ideal—of objectivity, with students supposedly studying in an atmosphere out of the reach of commercialism. This is just not so. Many parents are appalled to find out that their sons and daughters are literally deluged with propaganda in the very place where learning is supposed to be a sacred activity. Chemical companies and other corporate giants have successfully made inroads with teachers—the centers of influence who can reach out to hundreds of thousands of children nationwide once impressed as agents (often unwittingly) for big industry. Veteran school teacher John Borowski described the powerful influences and presence of major corporations at the National Science Teachers Convention, April 2000, Orlando, Florida:

> When I started teaching 20 years ago, I could never have imagined such a perverse display: industries and their front groups trying to justify everything from deforestation to extinction of species. Worse yet, they were targeting

---

10. "Reading, Writing and Indoctrination: How the Chemical Industry Infiltrates Schools," Environmental Working Group, 2002, Chemical Industry Archives

America's teachers and, ultimately, our children. Corporate America has dug its claws into one of the last refuges of commercial-free space left in our society: public schools. One of the pillars of our democracy, public education, is now for sale:

- The coal industry's Greening Earth Society passed out videos and teachers' guides to the "fallacies" of global warming that mocked environmental concerns.

- Weyerhaeuser boasted of the recovery of Mt. St. Helens, as if this somehow justified clear-cutting.

- The "Temperate Forest Foundation" offered a video titled "The Dynamic Forest." In this shrill presentation, insects and fire hurt forests, but industry provides the needed remedies–with the help of chain saws.

- The American Farm Bureau, avowed enemies of environmental education, propositioned teachers to reconsider the dangers of chemical biocides.

They were selling lies, and the teachers were buying—quickly filling their bags with curricula as corrosive as the pesticides that the Farm Bureau promotes.[11]

## CONFUSING THE ISSUE

Chemical companies want you to think of righteous scientists and shapers of the future when you think of the word "science." They want us to confuse this respectable image of a scientist with their sinister activities. It's a clever tactic, as the general public is constantly reminded that this nation has reached greatness thanks to the efforts of scientists such as Edison, Firestone, Einstein and Pasteur. While you are wallowing in this noble idea, the chemical manufacturers want you to know that they are the leaders in today's science, carrying on the brave and world-saving, world-improving work of their predecessors. Chemicals, including drugs and nuclear waste, are the end result of scientific effort. By piggybacking on the ideal image of science, chemical makers are trying to win your good graces. Don't let them, because they are wolves in sheep's clothing (not natural wool, but a mixture of rayon and nylon).

---

11.  Borowski, John F., "Targeting Children: Industry's Campaign to Redefine Environmental Education", Center for Media & Democracy, PR Watch, Volume 7, Number 2, 2001

## THIRD-PARTY, CORPORATE-SPONSORED FRONT GROUPS

A few decades ago, American industries realized that they could not address the public directly with their self-proclaimed, life-enhancing products because they would be laughed right off the platform. Mothers and others are no dummies and are not likely to believe a chemical company or major industrial polluter who is trying to tell them that they are engaged in the greatest work known to humankind. These industry leaders put their heads together (which didn't hurt because their brains are smaller due to the fact that the conscience portion has been missing since birth). They came up with an evil-genius idea: to create a third-party association made to look like an independent authority singing their praises. Let me repeat this since it's an extremely important secret to let out of the bag. Industry leaders have concocted a host of associations that are made to look independent of the industries that support and influence them. These associations, in turn, crank out all kinds of propaganda, from newspaper articles to television reports, and from educational school materials to speakers' bureaus all for one purpose—to promote the industries' activities in the most positive of lights. They even make their own slick, professional videos that they supply to the media for airing on the nightly news. Every major industry now has an "independent" (wink, wink) association to sing its praises—from the nuclear power industry to fast food restaurant chains.

The chemical industry (Manufacturing Chemists' Association) set up a respectable-sounding group called the Education Activities Committee that has on its agenda the goal of promoting the benefits of science and scientific studies. By reading the association's documents, it becomes clear that the ulterior motive is to endear youngsters to chemical manufacturers and their activities. By making chemical use acceptable (and fun!), there can be greater acceptance for environmental destruction, pollution, escalating cancer rates, allergies, skin diseases and untold human suffering.

In 1972, the Manufacturing Chemists' Association's Education Activities Committee added a new aim: "to promote through the educational system public understanding of the chemical industry" that formally stated: "Our contact with elementary school education is minimal. Yet it is in these early years of schooling that lasting attitudes are formed toward industry and careers in it. An industry newsletter to elementary school teachers is on the drawing boards. We currently study the potential audience, content and impact of such an effort."[12]

---

12.   ibid

Imagine that. In our school systems, while we think little Jason and Jennifer are learning about how Washington crossed the Delaware, they are also getting an unhealthy dose of chemical soup taught by willing teachers using industry-sponsored "educational" [i.e., propaganda] materials.

> By 1990, the industry had become still bolder in its efforts to infiltrate school curriculums. [sic] That year, CMA's Public Outreach Committee introduced its outreach plan for educators and students by saying: "Education is a key route toward improving public perception over the long term." The committee concludes with a request for more than $420,000 annually for outreach to teachers and students—almost four times the largest sum earmarked for any audience except the general public.
>
> In 1996, CMA's Communications Committee gathered to plot new strategies. The recommendations of a working group on education made some startling recommendations:
>
> - A "survey of young children (6th-8th grade)" to help the industry "define success"
>
> - "Site school partnerships/Adopt-a-school"
>
> - "Research what kids watch (pop media) that impacts students…via influencers" such as "Internet/games, cartoons/TV shows, sports/music figures," and "textbooks."

Chemical manufacturers and others who use (abuse?) our school systems for their self-promotion and self-aggrandizement are wont to defend their activities with the argument that this is the American way! Free enterprise and all that. What's wrong with it? For one thing, we must ask ourselves if our schools are the proper environment for corporate-slanted information, and whether our teachers should be used as sales agents for corporate propaganda. We should always object when opposing points of view are either not heard or are scoffed at. Are parents given a choice to expose their children to industry PR? Who is going to present the truth about the horrors of chemicals when they cause cancer, asthma, lung disease and other illnesses, and lay waste to our children's environment? Children are supposed to be learning about the benefits of democracy and fairness, but how fair is a system wherein only one side of industry is represented—the side backed by the most money and power? Who says chemicals are great? Or safe? What voice is present to counter manufacturers' claims with evidence of toxicity and their inherent dangers? Chemical companies sell by insidious means while teachers, administrators and politicians let them get away with it.

## HERE'S SOME SOUND ADVICE FROM A TEACHER
## TO PARENTS

Our schools should not be the playgrounds for corporate propaganda-pushers who want to push their way into our children's minds with false, twisted, one-sided and destructive messages that it's okay to poison our waterways and air, that it's okay to pollute the air with exhaust and cutting down our forests is not going to cause disease and widespread destruction of life on this planet. Children should learn the truth, not the covered-up version of what is going on in this world at the hands of big business. Environmental science teacher John Borowski advises:

> Parents must assume the role of front-line warriors in this winnable war. They must demand that any curricula, [sic] provided by corporate sources be reviewed, just like the process by which textbooks are reviewed prior to adoption. They must challenge their local boards of education to keep their local schools free of commercial influences. They must ask their children to share the materials they receive at school. Corporate predators in education are no different than those who peddle tobacco to our children. They must bear the scorn of society and be stopped in their tracks.
>
> Most importantly, we must highlight the wonders of true environmental education. Thousands of incredible teachers are working every day to enlighten their students. They need funding, and it is incumbent upon society to see that schools don't have to go begging to industry.
>
> And teachers must begin to comprehend what I call the "teachable moment": that indelible instance when data and caring and insight all merge as one, representing all that is good about ecological sciences in public schools. This moment does not require a slick video, fancy equipment or corporate money with strings attached. All it takes is students and teachers, exploring the natural world together.
>
> I have seen children connect to their natural world through discussing *A Sand County Almanac* in the classroom, hiking in the giant cedars of Opal Creek, and identifying invertebrates in our majestic tidal pools. This year alone, I have watched more than two dozen seniors choose environmental topics for their senior projects. Three young men are examining the possible breaching of the Snake River dams. Another young Hispanic man is painting a large mural on our school which depicts the trees of Opal Creek.
>
> Children care about the world and its beauty which is our common heritage. They expect adults to lead, to represent their best interests, and to protect them from exploitative commercial influences. The battle to make America safe for childhood is a battle worth fighting.[13]

---

13. Borowski

## A CORPORATION BY ANY OTHER NAME IS STILL
## DESTROYING THE EARTH AND MAKING YOU PAY FOR IT

Names are important, which is why since the turn of the last century corporations have worked so hard to build name recognition. Throughout the world we recognize names such as Nike, Coca Cola, DuPont, General Motors, General Mills, Kellogg's, McDonald's and Gerber's. Names stick in the minds of consumers and are, if all goes as planned, subconsciously related to value, dependability and even nationalistic flavor. It takes a lot of clever planning and implementation to create name recognition, which is why corporations hire top-gun public relations and advertising firms to do the job. In recent times, however, there has been, in the field of name-building, an intensive PR campaign designed to make even the most destructive companies look honorable. It all begins with a name change that the public will accept as friendlier, more environmental and down-home. Old company and association names are being changed to further fool the public. This only proves that companies know they are up to no good and that they need to deceive the public to carry on their destructive activities. Companies that promote, use and manufacture cancer-causing, disease-making and environment-destroying chemicals (including food chemicals) have been reborn under newer names.

Julie Kay, *Mother Jones* magazine, September 2002, explains, "It's been that kind of a year for corporate America—the kind when CEOs take the Fifth, when PR people seriously consider switching careers, when the only thing that will scrub a company's name clean is…a new name. Philip Morris made headlines last spring by rechristening itself Altria—a name that, according to the company, is meant to echo not 'altruism,' but the Latin âltus, or 'high.' Andersen Consulting renamed itself Accenture a while back. Pricewaterhouse Cooper's consulting arm will soon do business as Monday…and Enron is looking for a new name. Such makeovers have a long history, though they do seem to be increasing in popularity: One consulting firm estimates that of the 3,000 plus corporate name changes last year, an unusually high number appear to be motivated not by technicalities such as mergers and acquisitions, but by image concerns."[14]

It's hard to keep up with all the name-changing these days, but here are some examples:

ChemLawn/ChemGreen has changed names to TruGreen LandCare

---

14.   Kay, Julie, "The Company Formerly Known As," *Mother Jones*, September 2002

Tricon Global Restaurants has changed to Yumi Brands

Agricultural Insecticide & Fungicide is now CropLife America

Benton Oil & Gas Company is now Harvest Natural Resources

Nuclear Engineering has become U.S. Ecology

Monsanto Specialty Chemicals is now Solutia

Although changing names is not necessarily an indictment of any criminal activity or wrong-doing, it is still undeniable that many name changes are performed as a means of misleading the public or hiding from a sordid past and the consequences of ill-repute.

By their names, we can hardly tell any more what many companies really do and really stand for. This brings us to more closely examine big corporations that are jumping into the health care/natural foods business. Are they for real, or just capitalizing on a new market niche? Jeffrey Hollender, president of Seventh Generation (healthy products) explains:

> ...many of the homegrown companies and sustainable food businesses we think we're supporting with our natural food purchases are increasingly turning out to be the very same megamultinational corporations we're trying to avoid in the first place.
>
> Anyone who doesn't think that we're in a record-breaking economic era of merger mania and dramatic corporate consolidation just hasn't been paying much attention. No matter where you look, bigger companies are eating smaller companies for breakfast and emerging at lunchtime bigger and hungrier still. In industry after industry, the countless companies that once provided diversity and competition in the American economic landscape have been reduced to a mere handful of monoliths with odd hybrid names like AOL Time Warner and Disney Capital Cities ABC.
>
> Given the incredible appetite businesses have for their smaller brethren these days, and the fact that executives often seem to prefer to increase their market share by buying up existing brands rather than growing their own, it's no surprise that the trend eventually spread to natural foods...
>
> Once, of course, natural foods were an obscure niche product. They were good for maybe a chuckle or two at traditional food company board meetings, but little else as far as the major players were concerned. Now, however, Corporate America couldn't be more interested in gobbling up the companies that are seen by many as the last bastion of healthy independence in an increasingly unsustainable food system. After all, as more and more Americans discover the sordid truth about just what's in their dinner and just how that dinner was

made, natural foods are experiencing the kind of growth rates most analysts drool over.

That's why [at the time of this writing, 2002] a brand like Santa Cruz Organic is now owned by J.M Smucker and standbys like Odwalla Juices, Fresh Samantha and Mad River Sodas are all owned today by Coca Cola.

And that's just the tip of the whole foods iceberg. Earth's Best baby foods are now a jointly owned subsidiary of Hains and Heinz. White Wave and Silk soy beverages are made by industry giant Dean Foods. Worthington's vegetarian meat substitutes are really Kellogg's vegetarian meat substitutes. (And Kellogg's now owns the Kashi cereal brand, too.) Multinational monster Unilever ate Ben & Jerry's ice cream in one chunk. Small Planet Foods was devoured by General Mills. Balance Bar and Boca Burger by Kraft. Powerbar by Nestle. Lightlife by ConAgra. Stonyfield Farms by Dannon. Even pioneering Cascadian Farms got swallowed up by General Mills.

It's an epidemic, all right. In total, according to Adams, Harkness & Hill, a leading industry analyst, there were over 60 transactions involving the sale of a natural product company between January 2000 and March 2002...On the one hand, you can clearly make a case that consumers are being hoodwinked to a certain extent. Whereas we could once be reasonably certain that buying natural food brands cast an important economic vote for an appropriately scaled sustainable food system, likely served as a guarantee of higher quality and perhaps even healthier food, and supported independent Mom & Pop producers working for change, today that implicit assurance is hardly guaranteed. In fact, it's now possible to fill an entire grocery cart at your local natural foods store and never send a dime to the people or places you once felt so good about supporting. On the contrary, from a holistic perspective, that cart of food may not be much different than a cart of food from a regular supermarket.

...[On the other hand], it could be that the selling out of natural food brands and the ideals they represent via their absorption into enormous multinational companies isn't a corruption at all but rather simply the beginning of the large-scale transformation to a universally sustainable food system that we've been waiting for.

We'll see. My own jury is still out on this issue, and I will remain deeply concerned about the trend until these corporate giants can prove their heart is in the right place by supporting and maintaining the mission, vision, and ideals of the natural food companies they acquire...In the meantime, caveat emptor. Don't take natural food brands for granted. Read their labels carefully even though in most cases parent company references will not appear. Scrutinize ingredients. Make sure the natural foods you buy maintain their better standards regardless of who owns them. Research this ownership on the internet to see whether or not it's a brand you want to support, a chore that's becoming unfortunately unavoidable.[15]

As always, we have to invoke the *caveat emptor* (buyer beware) approach to any company that has been bought out or absorbed and used to be founded upon an independent, good-hearted, altruistic and natural approach to food manufacturing. Because many dangerous—even cancer-causing—ingredients are routinely omitted from food product labels, we have to sincerely ask whether we can really trust a giant food manufacturer to be selectively pure in terms of its new acquisition. In other words, if a multinational, multibillion-dollar food producer—well-known for creating junk food filled with health-defying chemicals—buys up a Mom and Pop organic foods company, why would they not just continue to do business as usual and infuse their new company with the same chemicals they use in the rest of their products? If giant food corporations, known for genetically engineered ingredients, artificial and chemical additives and processing, bought out all of the smaller, trustworthy, pure, organic brands, they would have no reason (other than their conscience, which is undeniably non-existent) to cheat and poison the public. Would you really still be able to trust Mom and Pop Organic Brand if it was now owned by Kraft foods, a subsidiary of Phillip Morris Tobacco? *Merely buying out an organic food company does not infuse the mother company with a sense of conscience!*

## ACTION TO TAKE:

- Take the advice of Jeffrey Hollender, Seventh Generation: "Ask questions and demand honesty. Things are not necessarily what they seem these days and you can be sure there will be more to come on this subject. In the meantime, until natural whole foods, sustainable methods, and holistic ideals predominate in the food system and the marketplace, it's the wise consumer who looks before they eat. [sic]"[16]

- Become involved and informed. Find out who is behind the "educational" materials and programs at your children's schools. Keep asking questions until you get to the bottom of it! Your children's lives depend on your strength and power.

- Subscribe to some of the responsible, respectable alternative media to keep abreast of corporate activities and how corporations are trying to get away with murder and other nefarious activities under the guise of free enterprise. Read *Mother Jones, The Nation, E Environmental magazine, Earth*

---

15.   Hollender, Jeffrey, "Unnatural Selection: Who's Really Making Natural Products?," *NonToxic Times*, Seventh Generation, Aug. 2002

16.   ibid

*Island Journal, Utne Reader,* and the yearly book *Censored* (
projectcensored.org).

- Read books by Noam Chomsky

- Stop watching the nightly news, because most of it is PR anyway.

- Demand that your school system presents the other side of the issue—the dangers of chemicals, from outgassing to skin exposure. There are many resources for this—resources backed by reputable independent scientists with mounds of research and studies.

- Make teachers and school administrators understand that you love your children and want the best for their health, even if they don't care enough about your children to teach them the dangers of chemical poisoning.

- Bring in articles, book covers, book marks and reading materials on how to make your children's future brighter without dangerous, toxic chemicals;

- Bring your own materials into your children's schools with statistics on dangerous chemicals, photos of victims and personal stories. Your side should be heard above the corporate voices that have infested our school systems nationwide.

- Go with your children to the websites **chemicalindustryarchives.org.** and scorecard.org. Read all of the articles and study the impact of chemicals on your family's health.

- Write letters to your Congressional representatives and tell them you are against having your children die of cancer just so the chemical industry can make huge profits.

- Use alternatives to synthetic chemicals. There are plenty of these now. Here are some internet sources:

   http://www.safe2use.com/data/links/alternatives.htm

   http://www.nutritionresearchcenter.org

   http://www.emagazine.com/marketplace

   http://www.eonproducts.com

   http://www.safe2use.com

   http://www.aubrey—organics.com

   http://www.naturalhomeproducts.com

http://www.americanatural.com

http://www.toxint.com/index.html

http://www.ecowise.com

http://www.happyhippie.com

http://www.seventhgeneration.com

- Go to your nearest health food store and shop for home and personal care products that do not contain poisonous chemicals. If you can't find a health food store in your area, find one online.

## *VALID RESEARCH OR FOLLOWING ORDERS?*

Corporations and politicians "prove" the benefits of their products and services with so-called research. Scientists are not what they used to be. We may be envisioning Einstein and Edison, but too many of today's scientists are EMPLOYEES of major industry hired to prove the benefits of the industry's products and services. They are not hired to go out on their own and make genuine discoveries. Corporations are not paying for enterprise, freethinking, rationality or unbiased interpretation; they want results so they can take their research and publish it in the media so that people will buy their stuff.

The corporate science with which we are inundated disturbs not only watchdog groups, mothers' groups, environmentalists and health enthusiasts, but many well-meaning scientists as well. Corporate manipulation and abuse of scientists is so rampant that many independent scientists are fighting back, as evidenced in this Kellogg's example:

> Scientists associated with the American Council on Science and Health (ACSH) today deplored attempts by some American corporations to manipulate scientific findings by withholding funding when research results displease them.
>
> Citing a recent and blatant example involving the Kellogg's Corporate Citizens Fund, ACSH President Dr. Elizabeth Whelan, in a letter to Kellogg CEO Arnold G. Langbo, wrote, "It is apparent to us at ACSH that Kellogg terminated our support because we did not choose to bow to Kellogg's party line that fiber is a health panacea for preventing, among other things, colon cancer."
>
> The missive to Kellogg from ACSH was prompted by a letter from Kellogg informing the council that the company was cutting off its support because ACSH was not assisting the company in its "continuing endeavors to bring public health messages to the consumer."

"Kellogg's 'public health' message," said Dr. Whelan, "must be based on their business objectives rather than on the sort of peer-reviewed, sound scientific methodology that we use at ACSH."

ACSH scientists are troubled by the fact that corporations now are attempting—boldly—to manipulate science to improve their sales. Dr. Whelan also noted that "certain sinister elements in corporate America think they can influence the sacred scientific method with their dollars. But such tactics, she added, "cannot and will not be tolerated."[17]

Unless they can get away with it!

## SCIENTISTS ARE JUST PEOPLE LIKE YOU AND I, EXCEPT FOR THEIR FUNNY CLOTHES

Scientists are paid employees with spouses, families, mortgages, car payments, egos and relative problems just like the rest of us. They work for money and their work is not necessarily filled with uplifting experiences or awe-inspiring discoveries. When scientists dare, as they do on occasion, to buck the system and defy the corporate intention, trouble brews. Many scientists over the years have lost their jobs and research grants for honestly concluding that they disagree with the intentions of their bosses, or they find that their corporate employers are being dishonest, deceitful or biased. Or they discover dangers outweigh benefits. After losing their jobs, these brave but unlucky souls are then defamed to the greatest degree so that they become public laughing stocks and are no longer credible.

Even if a doctor, researcher or scientist is not an employee of a big corporation, he/she still stands to feel the wrath of the corporate giant who stands to lose money based on a discovery that opposes the corporate-wealth design. With their powerful ties to the media, corporations publicly bash these scientists over and over again, and in many instances, over the course of many years. Among the unfortunates is Dr. Peter Duesberg, one of the world's leading virologists, who dared to say that there is no evidence to prove that HIV causes AIDS and that the pharmaceutical company that invented the so-called anti-AIDS virus drug AZT is making billions of dollars despite the unsubstantiated AIDS-HIV connection. Dr. D. lost his grant, his job and his reputation for his stance. You can read his fascinating personal account in his book, "Inventing the AIDS Virus."

Another scientist, pediatrician Herbert Needleman, MD, also met with industry wrath when he discovered in the 1950s that lead from industry was poisoning

---

17.   American Council on Science and Health, "Scientists Lash Out at Corporate Attempts to Manipulate Science," New York, NY—March 6, 1998

children and affecting brain function. Today, "everybody" knows about the dangers of lead. But when Dr. Needleman first exposed these dangers, his threat to industry sparked a decades-long string of defamations, lawsuits and corporate bullying. His motive was to save the health of children. Industry's motives were to make profits at almost any expense. Dr. Needleman was in the way.

## *Who is Dr. Needleman?*

Dr. Herbert Needleman is a distinguished researcher who, after having determined the developmental implications of excessive exposure to lead, played a key role in the fivefold reduction in the prevalence of lead poisoning in American children. In 1979 he mounted the first large-scale study of intelligence and behavior in children with no outward signs of lead poisoning. He followed these children into adulthood, showing that lead exposure is associated with increased risk for failure to graduate from high school and for reading disabilities. His work was instrumental in the decisions made by the Environmental Protection Agency to mandate the removal of lead from gasoline and by the Consumer Product Safety Commission to ban lead from interior paints. Additionally, Dr. Needleman's studies prompted the Department of Housing and Urban Development to remove lead from thousands of housing units across the country. He founded the Alliance to End Childhood Lead Poisoning, an education and advocacy organization with which he continues to work to reduce the hazards of lead-based paint in many inner city homes. For his extraordinary contributions to the understanding and prevention of childhood lead poisoning, Dr. Needleman received the Heinz Award in the Environment in 1995. Currently a professor of pediatrics and child psychiatry at the University of Pittsburgh Medical Center, Dr. Needleman has been a consultant to the Environmental Protection Agency, the Centers for Disease Control and Prevention, the Office of Housing and Urban Development, and to state and local governments, including the Commonwealth of Pennsylvania lead program. He is a member of the Institute of Medicine at the National Academy of Sciences, and co-authored *Raising Children Toxic Free* with Dr. Phil Landrigan and Mary Landrigan, M.P.A. Dr. Needleman earned his M.D. from the University of Pennsylvania and trained in psychiatry at Temple University Health Sciences Center.[18]

For all of his service to humankind and our environment, Dr. Needleman was attacked repeatedly by lead-using/lead-producing industries, hauled into court, defamed in the media and made to undergo years of abuse. Even after successfully

---

18. Kids & Chemicals Researchers, PBS Special hosted by Bill Moyers, 2002, www.pbs.org/now/science/doctors.html

defending his reputation and scientific research, and saving lives of children by campaigning against lead paint, Needleman continues to be the target of industry. You would think this defamation would have ended now that "everyone knows" that lead is poisonous to children, but this is not the case. Dr. Needleman crossed the powers-that-be, and is paying a lifetime of harassment for his campaign to get lead out of paints, children's toys and other products.

## HERE'S WHAT TO DO THE NEXT TIME YOU SEE A TELEVISION COMMERCIAL TOUTING THE WORK OF DEDICATED SCIENTISTS IN WHITE LAB COATS

- Laugh at your screen, realizing that it's just corporate propaganda.

- Understand that you're watching a slick ad produced by a highly paid ad agency with professional actors.

- Don't believe anything you hear until you first verify the claims with an independent research team of scientists.

- Change the channel.

- Write a letter to the ad sponsor and tell them to stop insulting your intelligence.

- Cancel your cable service and go outside to play.

## FIND OUT HOW SCIENTISTS & UNIVERSITIES & CORPORATIONS ARE INTERMARRIED...

The Integrity in Science Database, www.cspinet.org/integrity/database.html, is a good resource to show you which scientists are funded by which corporations. You can use your own common sense to decide whether corporate funding influences scientific "research" and "findings." This database is supported by The Center for Science in the Public Interest (CSPI) to (in their words) "provide information about the corporate ties of scientists, academics, and non-profit organizations in the fields of nutrition, environment, toxicology, and medicine. The aim of the database is to encourage transparency in the conduct, oversight, and reporting of science and to make information available to the public. We believe that disclosure of financial and other potentially biasing ties is an important mechanism of accountability and that a democratic public is best served by the free flow of information."[19] You can log onto this website and type in the name of your favorite university, such as Harvard, Yale, Princeton or UCLA and see the connection between corporate dollars and our esteemed researchers. This will open your eyes if your mind is open. It will also show you that today's research is not so independent as we are led to believe.

When you go online to **http://www.cspinet.org/integrity/database.html**, just type in the name of your favorite corporation such as Monsanto, Unilever, Dow or Nestle and you will soon discover how these giants fund today's university scientists.

Another great feature of this online research is that you can find out just how "for-profit" nonprofit organizations really are. When nonprofit organizations endorse for-profit corporations, there is something shady going on. The net result is that you have to ask yourself "Can I trust any charity that is linked to corporate interests that affect the charity's 'scientific findings' or news releases? How believable is it when, on the nightly news, the anchorman reads off a story that begins, 'The American Heart Association today reported that _____...?" Take the American Cancer Society, for example:

> According to a story in the *New York Times*, "The American Cancer Society...endorsed Florida orange juice..." (8/13/97)...An editorial in the *New England Journal of Medicine* stated: "And why should the American Cancer Society [ACS] endorse only SmithKline Beecham's antismoking products?" Jerome P. Kassirer & Marcia Angell (9/4/97, p. 700) See also, *Los Angeles Times* (8/13/97). The ACS, however, denies that its actions are endorsements. Rather, it characterizes such transactions as a license for the "nonexclusive use of its logo on Florida orange juice and SmithKline Beecham's antismoking products" in "exchange for monetary grants and other considerations used for the fight against cancer." (e-mail to CSPI from William J. Dalton, Chief Counsel, ACS, 5/30/01) The ACS's "Cancer Facts & Figures-1998" acknowledges on the front and back cover "a generous grant" by Glaxo Wellcome drug company. According to *Advertising Age*, the ACS was involved in a deal with General Mills to include information on packages of Wheaties (1/17/00; p. 54).[20]

The next time you work for, or donate to, an association or charity, you should understand who you are supporting. Associations prey on the emotions of relatives whose family members have suffered from disease. Persuading people to give

---

19. cspinet.org online

20. NonProfit Organizations Ties to Industry, Center for Science in the Public Interest, www.cspinet.org/integrity/corp_funding.html, 2002

their hard-earned money and heartfelt commitment is a shameful act when the charity is actually a mouthpiece for corporations looking for bigger profits and more power—in some instances the same corporations whose business practices are causing the diseases they're pretending to be interested in curing. What could be more despicable than to capitalize on the death of your child, brother or mother? This is cold-hearted commercialism. When association volunteers come to your door asking for donations, don't give them any money. Check out their corporate ties first. Find out whether this group is out to help the public find a cure for diabetes, heart disease, lung disease, cancer, etc., or is an industry mouthpiece. The number of drug companies tied to the American Diabetes Association, for example, is alarming:

The following is a list of corporate contributors in 2002:

Contributors of $750,000:

- Abbott Laboratories

- Aventis Pharmaceuticals

- BD Consumer Healthcare

- Bristol-Myers Squibb Company

- Eli Lilly and Company

- GlaxoSmithKline

- Lifescan, Inc., a Johnson & Johnson company

- Medtronic MiniMed

- Merck & Co., Inc.

- Novartis Pharmaceuticals Corporation

- Novo Nordisk Pharmaceuticals

- Pfizer Inc

- Takeda Pharmaceuticals North America, Inc.

Benning Corporate Sponsors:

- Abbott Laboratories, Inc., MediSense Products

- Bayer Corporation

- Kraft Foods

- Roche Diagnostics Corporation

Platinum Sponsors:

- Abbott Laboratories, Ross Product Division (Glucerna)

- AstraZeneca

- Dermik Laboratories, Inc.

- J.M. Smucker Company

- Merisant U.S., Inc. (Equal Sweetener)

- Olivio Premium Products

- Tenet Healthcare Foundation

- TheraSense, Inc.

- Wyeth Pharmaceuticals

Diamond Sponsors:

- Archway Cookies, LLC

- Coolbrands International, Inc. (Eskimo Pie)

- CVS/pharmacy

- Ebony Magazine

- Equidyne Systems, Inc.

- General Mills, Inc. (Fiber One)

- Good Neighbor Pharmacy

- Health Care Products

- Health Magazine

- Hermundslie Foundation

- KOS Pharmaceuticals, Inc.

- MBNA

- Murray Sugar Free Cookies

- Ocean Spray Cranberries, Inc.

- Orhto-McNeil Pharmaceutical, Inc.

- People Weekly Magazine

- Rite Aid Pharmacy

- Roche Pharmaceuticals

- Roundy's Inc.

- Schering Plough Healthcare Products, Inc.

- Specialty Brands of America (Cary's Sugar Free Cookies)

- The Procter & Gamble Company

- Voortman Cookies Limited

- Yahoo![21]

What about the American Heart Association? Heart disease is one of the leading causes of death in the United States, giving this charity a huge market share of financial supporters. Here's a sampling of their corporate sponsors:

> American Heart Association was paid $450,000 by the Florida grapefruit growers for exclusive grapefruit use of the association's heart-healthy endorsement. (*Philadelphia Inquirer*, 5/7/97)
>
> American Heart Association has received $1.1 million (and an annual renewal potential of about $300,000) from food manufacturers as license fees to use the "heart check mark." (*Philadelphia Inquirer*, 5/7/97)
>
> AHA charges $2,500 (plus a yearly renewal charge of $650) for a company to put the association's heart-check symbol on a package. Florida Dept. of Citrus paid $450,000 for exclusive promotion and advertising contract from 1994 until early 1997. The National Cattlemen's Beef Association paid $25,000 for its arrangement with the AHA to promote lean cuts of beef. For an agreement with ConAgra in 1992-93, the AHA received $3,500,000 for a

---

21.  ibid

TV program on nutrition. For companies that want an exclusive agreement with the AHA like that of the Florida citrus growers, the cost is $55,000 a quarter or $200,000 a year. Without exclusivity the cost is $25,000 a quarter or $90,000 a year. (*New York Times*, 10/22/97)

National Livestock and Meat Board gave $189,000 to the AHA to sponsor the HeartRide cycling series. AHA says the program will help ensure that people don't think that AHA recommends abstaining from meat. (*IEG Sponsorship Report*)

Merck is spending $400,000 to finance an AHA program teaching 40,000 doctors to treat cholesterol according to guidelines. (*Wall Street Journal*, 6/14/98)

American Heart Association has endorsed only Bayer aspirin. (*NEJM* 9/4/97, p. 700) According to Kramer Laboratories, Inc. (Miami), "Bayer, as we understand it, contributes over $500,000 a year to the American Heart Association." (Letter to AHA, 9/23/96) Web site is sponsored by Pfizer, Campbell, ConAgra (Healthy Choice), and Hoechst (Tufts Nutrition Navigator web site).[22]

Next, consider the American Dietetic Association (ADA), consisting of thousands of dietitian-members across America. This group has tried for many years to outlaw all practitioners of nutrition except for registered dietitians under the pretense that non-dietitians are unqualified to give health advice. That's right, the ADA is pushing for a monopoly to practice nutrition. You may speculate, by their huge corporate sponsors, that the reason why they are crying for a monopoly is so that only one voice is heard in the health care industry—the voice telling us that organic foods are not really so good for us, margarine is a healthy food, beef is an important staple of the diet, sugar is safe, and that today's fast foods and processed foods are actually nutritious, among other things. Dietitians also apparently see nothing wrong with serving up McDonald's fast food right there in the hospital either. That's right, McDonald's restaurants can be found at many hospitals around the country. In Childrens Hospital San Diego, right there in blue and white on their website, you'll find that, "Located just inside the Rose Pavilion, McDonald's offers an express service and is open from 8 a.m. to 8 p.m. daily."[23] Or how about hospitals partnering with McDonald's Restaurants across America and beyond? Grand River Hospital in Ontario, Canada, announces on their website, "*Help Grand River Hospital & McDonald's Restaurants of K-W & Elmira fund the Children's Waiting Room in the new Emergency Services Department:* Join our local efforts on November 20th on the Worldwide McHappy Day

22.   ibid
23.   www.chsd.org/body.cfm?id=962#mcdonald's

2002 when $1.00 from every Big Mac, Breakfast Bagel and Happy Meal goes to this worthwhile cause."[24] Need another example? How about Children's Memorial Hospital excited to tell you that "A full-service McDonald's Restaurant is located on the lower level of the hospital. McDonald's is open Monday-Friday 6 a.m.-10 p.m. and on Saturday and Sunday 7 a.m.-7 p.m."[25] One more: Northside Hospital in Atlanta is proud to announce in its visitor information, "If your family or friends bring you food, please check with your nurse to be sure your doctor has written orders for these items. A member of the Food and Nutrition Services Department is available daily to assist you with your dietary needs. If you have questions concerning your diet, meal service or other special requests, please ask your nurse to contact the Food and Nutrition Services Department...*Patient and Family Dining Options*—Friends and family may dine at McDonald's or our Morrison's Cafeteria on the first floor of the hospital. To hear the Morrison's menu for the day, call extension 3350."[26] On one hand the hospital is so concerned with meeting the dietary needs of their patients while on the other they recommend fast food as an option.

Is McDonald's food so wholesome and nutritious that dietitians approve of it as "good nutrition"? Do they really consider fried potatoes, grilled meat and sugar-filled soda nutritious? Apparently, they don't mind letting people eat this kind of stuff as long as they're making money. Something is seriously wrong with this picture. People in the business of trying to heal their patients (dietitians) shouldn't be allying themselves with corporations in the business of making them sick by offering foul-nutrition devoid of nutrient value and loaded with chemicals, refined sugars, refined salts, MSG, caffeine, altered fats, preservatives artificial flavorings, food dyes and a host of other chemical ingredients. The University of Michigan Health System reports:

> A trip to the hospital usually means either you or someone you know is in poor health and needs immediate medical attention. And when it's time to go home, most likely, your doctor will give you a list of do's and don'ts, including eat a healthy diet and make sure to exercise. So, when you see your favorite fast food restaurant inside the hospital that just told you to eat healthy, you may be getting a mixed message—a message it appears many of the nation's top health institutions are sending.
>
> In a research letter published in the June 12 issue of the *Journal of the American Medical Association*, researchers at the University of Michigan

---

24.   www.grhf.org/events.asp
25.   www.childrensmemorial.org/parents/admitted/room.asp
26.   www.northside.com/patient/foodservices/foodservices.htm

Health System and Ann Arbor VA Medical Center found 38 percent of the nation's top health institutions had regional or national fast food franchises on their main medical campuses. It's a statistic that is alarming to the authors of the letter.

"Obesity is rising at an alarming rate in the United States, with nearly 18 percent of adult Americans now considered obese. High-calorie diets, due in part to fast food, are partially to blame," says Peter Cram, M.D., lead author of the letter and lecturer in the internal medicine department at UMHS. "However, fast food restaurants continue to pop up across the country and hospitals appear to be no exception."

The researchers performed a telephone survey of 16 facilities listed as "Honor Roll" hospitals by the 2001 *US News & World Report* ranking of "America's Best Hospitals". Six of the 16 "Honor Roll" hospitals were found to have fast food restaurants, with four facilities contracting with 2 chains simultaneously. Survey results:

Among the six with fast food chains includes the University of Michigan Health System, an observation that, says co-author Brahmajee Nallamothu, MD, inspired their research.

"I always found it odd that as a health institution we had a fast food chain in our facility, and I wondered if other top hospitals also did," says Nallamothu. "But through my research I found the UMHS food services department works hard to make sure the fast food chain offers healthy choices. In fact, the restaurant specifically marks the healthy food items on its menu."

Mark Fendrick, MD, a co-author of the letter as well as co-director of the Consortium for Health Outcomes, Innovation, Cost Effectiveness Studies or CHOICES at UMHS, points out hospitals are businesses and they have certain needs they need to address.

"I realize these hospitals need to address important economic issues such as customer satisfaction, employee retention, and financial viability, and I believe fast food restaurants in hospitals offer patients and their families a sense of comfort," says Fendrick, also associate professor of health management and policy at the UM School of Public Health. "However, if hospitals and the medical profession are to remain respected leaders in health promotion, we should re-visit the idea of serving fast food in the very place that we care for our most seriously ill."

The fast food debate echoes another recent issue that faced hospitals, says senior author Sanjay Saint, MD, a research scientist at the Ann Arbor VA Medial Center and director of the UMHS Patient Safety Enhancement Program. "Hospitals should serve as an example for health conscious behavior. Forbidding smoking from American medical centers was a crucial first step. Perhaps encouraging healthy dietary intake will be a second," he says.[27]

### *Here are a few more hospitals and their fast food connections:*

| Hospital | Fast Food Restaurant(s) |
|---|---|
| Johns Hopkins | Subway |
| Cleveland Clinic | McDonald's, Pizza Hut |
| UCLA Medical Center | El Pollo Loco, Numero Uno Pizza |
| Duke Univ. Medical Center | Hardy's, Domino's |
| Barnes-Jewish Hospital (St. Louis) | Burger King, Sbarro |
| Univ. of Michigan Health System | Wendy's |

(Note: U-M's MFit nutritionists [dietitians?] worked with Wendy's to mark healthy food choices on the menu.)[28]

Let's get real here, if you want healthy foods, you don't go to fast food restaurants. You go to health food stores carrying organically grown, natural, whole, real foods devoid of synthetic ingredients and pesticide residues. Looking for healthy foods at a fast food restaurant is like trying to find a gram of objectivity at a political convention.

Although there are many good-hearted, well-meaning and capable dietitians (I know a couple personally), they belong to an association that is about as industry-driven as imaginable. The ADA refuses to take a stand against most chemicals in foods even when they are scientifically proven to be carcinogenic, disease-causing and dangerous to human health. With their corporate spouses, dietitians' hands are tied from engaging in an honest approach to human health lest they step on the toes of their benefactors. It is difficult for me to forget that dietitians in one of the most respected hospitals in Miami, Florida, in the year 2002, served my father frosted flakes, jam, milk and coffee for breakfast while in the intensive care unit after undergoing cardiac bypass surgery. Anyone with even an inkling of knowledge of the most basic principles of Nutrition knows how health-defying this kind of diet is. In fact, these foods could even prove deadly to a patient following bypass surgery. The foods served up to my father by registered dietitians

---

27.  "Nation's leading hospitals serving up fast food: *U-M researchers find 38 percent of top hospitals in U.S. have fast food franchises on-site,*" *University of Michigan Health System,* *http://www.med.umich.edu/opm/newspage/2002/fastfood.htm,* June 12, 2002

28.  ibid.

are nonfoods, loaded with refined sugars, chemicals, dyes, caffeine and toxins, but the hospital dietitians are apparently not concerned with such things. And these people want a monopoly on practicing nutrition?

The American Dietetic Association (ADA) is the same group that has inundated our school system, cafeterias, hospitals, medical clinics, and home health centers with their corporate-tainted messages about food pyramids and fat free diets that have since been busted for their industry favoritism. After all, when the dairy industry gives you a big juicy check, suddenly you begin to recommend that everybody has to have their daily requirement of processed, pasteurized and synthetically "enriched" cheese, milk and cottage cheese. Forget the fact that, if it's not organically grown, it contains pesticide residues, steroids, hormones and antibiotics. The ADA flatly refuses to admit the dangers of refined sugar, pesticides, too much red meat in the diet, altered oils, and artificial sweeteners. But how can they?

> The American Dietetic Association [ADA] has received funding from numerous companies and receives underwriting for "fact sheets" on topics related to the companies' products. Major ($100,000+) donors include: Kellogg, Kraft Foods, Weight Watchers International, Campbell Soup, National Dairy Council, Nestle USA, Ross Products Division of Abbott Labs, Sandoz, Coca-Cola, Florida Department of Citrus, General Mills, Henry J. Kaiser Family Foundation, Monsanto, Nabisco, Procter & Gamble, Uncle Ben's, Wyeth-Ayerst Labs. (Nov-Dec 1996 *ADA Courier*)
>
> ADA and DuPont have an agreement that enables ADA to place nutrition information on the web site http://www.webmd.com/. Dupont is an investor in WebMD. (ADA Press Release, 10/16/00)
>
> Co-produced, with funding from the ConAgra Foundation, a packet of information on food safety titled "Home Food Safety: It's in Your Hands." (Funding disclosed on packet, Nov. 1999)
>
> Published a "Biotechnology Resource Kit," which was funded by the Council for Biotechnology Information." (ADA "Dear Member" letter; 2000)
>
> The American Dietetic Association has announced that it will be seeking to endorse food products (Nov.-Dec. 1997 *ADA Courier*).
>
> ADA and American Pharmaceutical Association (pharmacists) announced a joint consumer-education program on supplements; it is funded by Monsanto [the genetic engineering corporation] Life Sciences Company (press release, 11/8/99).
>
> In fiscal year 2000, the following companies contributed $10,000 or more: BASF Corp., Bristol Myers/Squibb, California Avocado Company, The Catfish Institute, ConAgra Foods, DMI Management, EcoLab, Galaxy Nutritional Foods, Gerber Products Company, Kellogg, Knoll Pharmaceuticals, Lipton, Mars, Inc., Mead Johnson Nutritionals, McNeil Consumer Products

Company, Monsanto, National Cattlemen's Beef Association, National Dairy Council, National Fisheries Institute, National Pasta Association, The Peanut Institute, Potato Board, Procter & Gamble, Roche Pharmaceuticals, Ross Products Division, Abbott Laboratories, Viactiv, Worthington Foods. (ADA/ ADAF 2000 Annual Report, http://www.eatright.org/; November 11, 2000)[29]

Too many of today's associations are serving the interests of corporations rather than families in need. The public, meanwhile, is being bamboozled, because this tie to corporate interests is not made public in the media. Maybe because the media is controlled by these same corporations? If anything, the bedfellows—your local hospital and some national fast food corporation as buddies—are portrayed as a fine example of companies working together for the good of your hometown in a fun and enthusiastic manner.

Associations such as the ADA, Cancer Society, Heart Association, Chemical Manufacturers and the rest are incestuously related to huge corporations involved in enterprises that are killing our families. They "prove" their "worth" with "research" backed by the newest evil genius invention of the 20th Century—"corporate" science.

Corporate science? I don't think so. There is no credibility in the media reports involving the work and findings of associations married to corporate interests. News from these sources should be ignored and regarded as PR—propaganda at its apex.

If you still think that automobile pollution, chlorinated swimming pools, fluoridated drinking water, synthetic fertilizers, food additives, fast foods, pesticides and lawn sprays are safe, effective, health-promoting and beneficial, then the corporate public relations machine has been successful in their efforts to keep you from the awful truth about how these things are killing people and destroying our planet. Our children's future is tainted by corporate greed—greed that is tactfully hidden behind an opaque veil of propaganda.

---

29. ibid

# Defaming the Victims

*If you cannot argue the case on its facts, or if someone is accusing you of foul play,*
*then you have to defame the victims, the messengers*
*and anyone else associated with their point-of-view to keep the facts*
*from being publicly known and accepted. If you make the victim look like a fool*
*or a hysteric, then you may keep her from harming you with the truth*
*or exposing you as a criminal.*

To fully understand the degree to which poisonous, toxic substances permeate our lives and adversely affect our health, first look at the politics of scientific research, corporate business and government. Unless we do this, we risk taking the subject out of context. Corporate politics—BIG MONEY—affects scientific research. This is why we have a continual stream of conflicting research "findings," wherein one team of scientists proves the benefits of a given substance while another team of experts proves that the same substance creates death and disease. Are we saying that scientists are "bought off?" Sometimes. But most of the time, scientists, who are human beings like the rest of us, are devoted to appeasing their bosses. If you are a scientist hired to prove there are benefits to irradiating foods or spraying crops with chemical fertilizers, then you do your job. If you don't, you are fired and some other scientist on the payroll takes your place. This is how business works. If you are a major drug manufacturer and you want medical doctors to write prescriptions for your new drug, then you hire scientists to prove that your new drug is wonderful, beneficial and as safe as possible.

Never mind that prescription drugs are far more dangerous that imagined. "The cost associated with negative therapeutic outcomes resulting from drug therapy is estimated to be between $30.1 billion and $136.8 billion a year, according to an article in the October 9 issue of the AMA's *Archives of Internal Medicine*."[1]

---

1. Science News Update for the week of October 4, 1995, American Medical Association Science News

Adverse reactions to prescription drugs are a major cause of death in the U.S. An estimated 106,000 hospital patients die each year from adverse reactions, making adverse drug reactions the fourth most frequent cause of death. (*Money* 12/98; study from *JAMA* 4/98)" Where it was also pointed out: "An Institute of Medicine report in 1999 estimated that 1 million or more hospital patients each year are injured from medical errors and that nearly 100,000 die as a result of medical mistakes. A 2001 study in the *Journal of the American Medical Association* estimated that between 5,000 and 15,000 deaths annually are due to medical mistakes in hospitals."[2]

If corporate-paid scientists do not support their corporate financiers with "discoveries," then corporations (drug companies, chemical manufacturers, oil companies, etc.) cannot move forward with their sales, and they lose billions of dollars in revenue.

If you are a public relations firm hired by a major oil company to show that oil is the greatest fuel source, then certainly you will not report to the media how deadly automobile pollution is, or how many deadly traffic accidents occur every day. Just doing your job—even though you know you are party to mass destruction of lives—is synonymous with not having—or exercising—a conscience.

## DEFAMING THE VICTIMS

Victims of corporate greed and toxic poisoning are bad for business. It's hard to sell a lot of artificial sweetener or MSG when people are complaining that they can't stop throwing up and their headaches are so bad that suicide seems a logical remedy.

Victims get a lot of public sympathy and make corporations look bad for poisoning their families and forcing them from their homes. Victims are the "little people" who are too small to fight back against major chemical companies. You and I are the victims of chemical spills, air pollution, oil spills, nuclear radiation

---

2.    "U.S. Recreational Drug Deaths," US Drug War FAQlet (c) 1998–2002 Michael Hess  Volume 1, No. 1, http://bbsnews.net/drug-deaths.html; Drug-Related Morbidity and Mortality: A Cost-of-Illness Model, Jeffrey A. Johnson, MSc, J. Lyle Bootman, PhD (Arch Intern Med. 1995;155:1942–1948) [http://www.ama-assn.org/sci-pubs/sci-news/1995/snr1004.htm#oi40876] Archives of Internal Medicine Abstracts—Oct. 9, 1995 (c) AMA 1995 ; Adverse Drug Reactions May Cause Over 100,000 Deaths Among Hospitalized Patients Each Year (JAMA. 1998;279:1200-1205) [http://www.ama-assn.org/sci-pubs/sci-news/1998/snr0415. htm] Science News Update Apr 15, 1998; Also see: http://www.aetna.com/public_policy_issues/patientsafety.htm"

in the atmosphere, global warming and dead zones in the oceans where nothing can live due to pollution. Victims are bad for business and they must be squelched if you are a chemical polluter. There's only one way to treat a victim if you are being accused of giving her children cancer, and that is to defame her. Take away her dignity (or what's left of it), make her seem like a complainer and a nut case. Make her look bad by confusing her in court and dredging up irrelevant, personal history on the witness stand. It's mean, it's disgusting, and it works for corporations whose backs are against the wall. Hey! It's only business, right?

If you can be a proactive business—and you know that your chemical dumping and production are killing people—you will use your work ethic to smash the victims under your jackboots before they even realize they've been poisoned—or maybe right afterward—and you are the reason for the suffering of their families. Take the case of Karen Silkwood who had an axe to grind with a big plutonium company she intended to accuse of endangering people's lives. She died quite mysteriously and "coincidentally"…

> Karen Silkwood died on November 13, 1974 in a fatal one-car crash. Since then, her story has achieved worldwide fame as the subject of many books, magazine and newspaper articles, and even a major motion picture. Silkwood was a chemical technician at the Kerr-McGee's plutonium fuels production plant in Crescent, Oklahoma, and a member of the Oil, Chemical, and Atomic Workers' Union. She was also an activist who was critical of plant safety. During the week prior to her death, Silkwood was reportedly gathering evidence for the Union to support her claim that Kerr-McGee was negligent in maintaining plant safety, and at the same time, was involved in a number of unexplained exposures to plutonium. The circumstances of her death have been the subject of great speculation…
>
> The saga of Karen Silkwood continued for years after her death. Her estate filed a civil suit against Kerr-McGee for alleged inadequate health and safety program that led to Silkwood's exposure. The first trial ended in 1979, with the jury awarding the estate of Silkwood $10.5 million for personal injury and punitive damages. This was reversed later by the Federal Court of Appeals, Denver, Colorado, which awarded $5000 for the personal property she lost during the cleanup of her apartment. In 1986, twelve years after Silkwood's death, the suit was headed for retrial when it was finally settled out of court for $1.3 million. The Kerr-McGee nuclear fuel plants closed in 1975.[3]

If you are Huge Chemical Corporation, Inc., you get yourself a big public relations firm and go to work on molding public opinion, beginning with keep-

---

3.    www.pbs.org/wgbh/pages/frontline/shows/reaction/interact/silkwood.html

ing your wrongdoings out of the nightly news. Meanwhile you have to worry that people like Michael Moore or Bill Moyers decide to let the public see what you've been up to in their back yards. Most of all, if your products or byproducts give people cancer, you can blame their cancer on genetics, viruses or anything else, as long as you keep the general public off your back and you keep your "good" reputation from being smeared in the media. You've got to smear before you get smeared—it's the law of the corporate jungle. Blaming cancer victims for their cancer isn't just the way to keep the heat off chemical companies, it's an action based on economic considerations. Writer Peter Laurie explains how this personal focus distorts the politics of cancer prevention:

> Today this approach [blaming victims] is becoming the norm as the welfare state searches for ways to pass the costs of health care back to the individual.
>
> 'Lifestyle need a bit of a change?', asks a recent pamphlet produced by the Canadian Cancer Society. 'Gain control of your body, mind and spirit.' The implication is clear: you chose it; you change it. Despite the holistic overtones, this approach is rooted squarely in the traditional clinical model of medicine, which seeks the causes of disease in the pathology of the individual body rather than in the social context.
>
> There is a lot at stake in this emphasis on individual causes and solutions. For one thing, it ensures that an overwhelming proportion of the money raised to fight cancer goes into research while little is set aside for public education. In Canada, for instance, over half of the $64 million raised last year by the Canadian Cancer Society was allotted to research; a mere 17 per cent was spent on education.
>
> This shift in responsibility to the individual obscures the many environmental hazards that are anything but a matter of individual choice. One study estimates that nearly 90 per cent of the carcinogens we're exposed to outside work (like polychlorinated biphenyls (PCBs) and dioxins) come from toxic chemicals that have seeped into the food chain. And, of course, such additives don't appear on food labels.
>
> 'You can tell if an orange has been dyed, but you can't tell if a glass of milk has PCBs in it,' says Linda Pim, author of two books on food additives. 'In this area, the consumer has absolutely no control.'
>
> The scientific jury is still out on the precise connections between environmental contaminants and cancer rates. During the 1970s the 'carcinogen of the week' phenomenon in the mainstream media only served to confuse the issue. As a result, health activists have more than once been accused of 'cancerphobia'. Establishment cancer institutes like the American Cancer Society tend to adopt a 'look the other way' attitude to pollution, rather than taking controversial positions that might offend the pillars of corporate society.
>
> The victim-blaming syndrome has also spilled over into the factory. There are some fairly bizarre examples. In 1970, for instance, two giant chemical

companies, Dow and DuPont, quietly began routine 'genetic screening' on employees and job applicants in order to determine their vulnerability to hazardous chemicals. According to company doctors, the tests were intended to screen out individuals with 'defective' genes. The assumption was that if you got ill on the job, it was 'your' genes and not 'their' chemicals that were at fault.[4]

## Cranking Up the Propaganda Machine

In a capitalistic enterprise, money is everything. So is good public relations (another word for propaganda). Propaganda is the dissemination and selling of your ideas to an audience without representing the other side of the issue. When it gets aggressive, as in the big industry and political fields, then propaganda efforts also include a heavy dose of defamation—making your adversaries and competitors look stupid, uneducated, crooked, sleazy, untrustworthy, not credible, undesirable, uneducated, sneaky, unreliable, unqualified and crazy. If you are a processed food manufacturer, for example, you call natural food consumers nasty names like health nuts, hippies, granola heads and rabbit food eaters. If you are engaged in destroying wildlife and the ecology, you call environmentalists tree huggers. Your public relations agency is paid large amounts of your profits to work hard to make the words "environmentalist" and "environmentalism" dirty, crazy and downright un-American. If you successfully bombard the media with this defamation, when it comes time to hear the woeful stories of environmental disasters, the public will be predisposed to thinking that environmentalists are a bunch of radicals and crackpots using scare tactics and irrational behavior to keep you from having a shiny new automobile that gets only 12 miles per gallon while your son is being shot at overseas to protect oil pipelines to keep your car running and your president and his administration rich. You won't even be thinking that the war and the oil aren't even necessary anymore because we have the technology for alternative means of energy production!

Public relations firms, scientific researchers and the giant hazardous chemical-producing industries are very often engaged in disgraceful enterprises that allow money to dictate their words and deeds. Conscience flies out the window when there is a profit motive, and the more you defame your opposition, the better chance you have of getting people to believe your propaganda. As we move through our daily lives trying to make a good living for our families and find happiness, the forces of propaganda and corporate greed forge ahead. When we come

---

4.    Laurie, Peter, "A smouldering problem," www.newint.org/issue198/fault, New Internationalist, Issue 198, August 1989

home exhausted at the end of the day and turn on the television, we are too tired to do much else besides absorb the one-sided messages like sponges as they issue forth in unimaginable volumes from these corporate voices. This is what they are hoping for, anyway, and this is what the public enables them to accomplish. We are too busy with our lives and personal struggles to check out the real facts, question the motives of the media and the corporations, find out if scientific researchers are working for truth or for money, or listen to the opposing point-of-view in alternative media. Well, guess what—our environmental issues are now personal.

## FIND A NEW SOURCE FOR YOUR NEWS TO PROTECT YOUR FAMILY

At this point, maybe you are still confused as to what propaganda and the corporate voice has to do with toxins and our health. The answer is "everything." Most of what we believe about the effects of toxins in our environment comes from one of three sources: personal experience (including word of mouth), personal research, or what we receive through the media. If you only get your information from major newspapers, television networks and radio, then you are getting mostly the corporate point-of-view. We do not hear good things on the major media about Greenpeace, Earth Island Institute, Environmental Working Group, Public Citizen, or Global Response, to name but a few environmental organizations. Relatively speaking, we hear very little of the educated, informed, alternative voices of Ralph Nader, Noam Chomsky, Molly Ivins, Jim Hightower, Al Franken or Howard Zinn. In fact, most people in this nation do not even really know who these people are or what they truly advocate. If our citizens did listen, without also accepting the corporate defamation of these individuals, they would realize the great degree to which corporate activities are damaging and anti-American in their scope.

UnAmerican? Isn't this the nationalistic battle cry? If we are to be free, we must be objective and come to realize that there is no greater unAmerican activity than the goings-on by corporations and politicians within our own borders, pretending to care about us. Thomas Jefferson said, "I hope we shall crush in its birth the aristocracy of our monied corporations which dare already to challenge our government to a trial by strength, and bid defiance to the laws of our country." So far, the corporations are winning the challenge.

For the automobile, oil and nuclear industries to destroy our beautiful environment, our land, sea and air, is undeniably antiAmerican. We must have air, water and earth in the purest form possible in order to thrive in health, and these corporations are destroying these supporting entities without conscience. Men and women in smart business suits are stealing our children's futures with the stroke of a fountain pen. Our elected officials are enabling them to carry on with minimal challenge. While they are busy causing asthma, cancer, emphysema, heart disease, birth defects, hormonal irregularities, and infertility—and while you're grieving over the loss of a loved one—big industry is telling the public through the mass media that those who oppose their activities are crazy "tree huggers" who are trying to take away your fun.

## SUPPRESSING ALTERNATIVES & INVENTING THE LIBERAL MEDIA LIE

The world's largest, most powerful energy corporations are dedicated to suppressing alternative forms of energy that do not destroy our planet. Why? Because solar, wind and water power are too competitive, representing cheaper, cleaner and more efficient alternatives. These technologies are all possible now; they are not futuristic, yet they are not fostered, promoted or discussed in our media because of the corporate stranglehold on our political, government and industrial institutions. The media, owned by giant corporations and supported (with advertising dollars) by huge industries, do not readily allow opposing points of view, even though the powers-that-be continue to perpetuate the BLATANT LIE that the media is liberal. Nonsense. Don't you wonder why we rarely hear in the major U.S. media about the clean, efficient and wonderful benefits of non-polluting, environmental-friendly electric cars, hydrogen automobiles, wind power sources and even bicycles?

Thousands of Americans are involved in these successful, alternative enterprises. Instead we are bombarded with stories on oil, terrorists threatening to take away our oil, new automobile models and the airlines industry. We do not hear about the efficiency of taking mass transit—trains, buses or trams. Television commercials show sexy automobiles with young happy couples or rugged men tearing up the American wilderness in trucks and ATVs (all-terrain vehicles). Pollution in the media is rarely spoken of, and when it is, the finger is pointed at car owners, and NEVER at car manufacturers, the airlines industry, or energy and oil producers. Chemical manufacturers and industrial farmers are not blamed for the mass incidences of cancer, death and destruction they create—killing our mothers, fathers, brothers and sisters. In this day and age, not one of us has eluded the suffering and pain and death of cancer. Either we have had it, or one of our relatives has had it. A liberal media would report the social and environmental ills around the clock. This just doesn't happen.

## *VOTE WITH YOUR DOLLARS*

We can't afford to think that the only way to make a change in the United States, and to stop the destruction of greedy corporations is by protesting, writing letters and campaigning. While all these are helpful, they are not the *only* way to make a difference. There is an easier, faster, more direct, safer way to make your position loud and clear. In case you don't read any more of this book, I will divulge **the secret to all change** in the United States of America—land of the fee, home of the shopping mall—a way to protect and defend American rights and our environment for generations to come, and a way to stop the pollution, wars and cancer-causing enterprises of big industry. All we have to do is band together as consumers, refusing to buy the products and services of corporations who destroy our lives, our planet and our general health. Stop buying your local newspaper and disconnect your television cable. Write letters to the advertisers on television and tell them you are no longer going to buy their products, whether it's SUVs, video games, drugs, insurance or whatever. And don't make it an idle threat. Carry through with your decision not to buy until our media begins once again to represent our interests. When thousands or millions of us do this, the message will be sent that we are mad as hell and aren't going to take it anymore.

By refusing to buy from destructive companies, while supporting pro-sustainability, pro-health and pro-American companies, you can make a difference immediately. That's all there is to it. In America, **your buying dollar is king**—more powerful than big business—for it is the foundation of modern economy, government, politics and lifestyle. Once you become aware of how toxins are killing us and making you and your relatives suffer, you can make purchasing decisions that support the ideal American way of life instead of the pocketbooks of industrial giants pretending to have your best interests at heart. And you can send a quick message to their paid-off political friends with the same motion it takes to zip your wallet closed.

# Television Just Kills Me

What do we hear on the nightly news about cancer? Every few years we hear the SAME OLD STORY—"Researchers believe they are on the verge of finding the cure to cancer—a medical breakthrough...blah, blah, blah." Each of these stories is always related to a drug, a virus and gene, completely ignoring the causes of cancer that are already known and absolutely avoidable (exposure to chemicals in our food and environment). Why? Because **those who cause the most cancer are also those who support, control and own the media**—chemical manufacturers, huge corporate farmers, automobile manufacturers, power companies and oil companies. It has also been stated by a few brave souls that many of the corporations *causing cancer* are the owners of drug manufacturers and medical systems involved in *treating cancer*. Is this evil genius or what? It's like having someone pay you to be his body guard after you attack him. The war against cancer remains an unfunny joke, as long as the perpetrators of this disease are the same ones who are invested with finding a cure and "treating" the sick.

One of the more notorious forms of cancer—breast cancer—has experts looking in all the wrong places. They're blaming short-term breast-feeding among mothers,[1] genetic predisposition, brassiere-wearing and a lack of exercise, to name some creative excuses. While these may have some potential semblance of reality as causative factors, placing the blame on toxic chemicals still meets with the greatest resistance, despite mounting evidence. The most media-ignored culprits are toxins and non-foods in the diet and a polluted environment that disrupts healthy cellular function. Cancer-causing factors include birth control pills, drugs, pesticides, and chemical waste, to name a few. Prevention, as seen by drug and chemical companies, is an admission of guilt, so in the meantime, women continue to suffer from both unnecessary causation and "treatments" that are torturous in their own right with the utilization of surgeries and chemotherapy. Women are getting fed up with this game, even going so far as to accuse doctors of blatant misogyny.

---

1.   *Lancet*, 2002, 360:187-195

The medical establishment dominated by male doctors pretends that the breast cancer epidemic will one day be reversed by some miracle cure, which we have now been promised for 50 years. Until that miracle arrives, we are told, there is nothing to be done except slice off women's breasts, pump their bodies full of toxic chemicals to kill cancer cells, burn them with radiation, and bury our dead. Meanwhile, the normal public health approach of primary prevention languishes without mention and without funding. We know what causes the vast majority of cancers: exposure to carcinogens. What would a normal public health approach entail? Reduce the burden of cancer by reducing our exposure to carcinogens. One key idea has defined public health for more than 100 years: PREVENTION. But with cancer, everything is different. In the case of cancer, prevention has been banished from polite discussion.[2]

It is no coincidence that the advertisers and owners of our media do all they can to keep the finger of blame pointed far away from them. MILLIONS of our fellow citizens are suffering to death from cancer and other diseases DIRECTLY CAUSED by these industries, with not one word uttered on our nightly news about this horrible reality. Liberal media? Think again.

## WHAT DOES THE MEDIA HAVE TO DO WITH ENVIRONMENTAL TOXICITY, CANCER & OTHER DISEASES?

What has happened to our media? Where did all of the muckrakers and investigative journalists go? They disappeared, because now that the major media is owned by a handful of corporations, the truth is taboo on the nightly news if the finger of guilt points to the owners and supporters of the media.

The sooner America sees that the media is the mouthpiece of corporate giants, the sooner we can be on our way to finding other sources of news. Dr. Peter Phillips, Department Chair and Professor of Sociology at Sonoma State University and director of Project Censored a media research organization, notes, "Governmental spin transmitted by a willing US media establishes simplistic mythologies of good vs. evil often leaving out historical context, special transnational corporate interests, and prior strategic relationships with the dreaded evil ones."[3]

2.  RACHEL'S ENVIRONMENT & HEALTH NEWS #723, April 26, 2001; revised May 24, 2001
3.  Phillips, Phd, Peter, "Corporate Media Ignores US Hypocrisy on War Crimes," December 9, 2003

Critics of today's media propose that, without a free and unbiased media, there can be no democracy, as democracy is dependent upon a free flow and exchange of ideas. If we cannot get the truth about pollution, polluters, government activities, political agendas, wars, chemical poisoning and corporate connections to government officials, then we cannot make important decisions affecting our lives. Of course, the evil geniuses understand this better than anyone, which is why they continue to buy up all the media. Dr. Phillips explains today's media dilemma:

> Since the passage of the Telecommunications Act of 1996, a gold rush of media mergers and takeovers has occurred in the United States. Over half of all radio stations have been sold in the past six years, and the repeatedly merged AOL–Time-Warner (CNN) is the largest media organization in the world. Less then ten major media corporations dominate U.S. news and information systems. Clear Channel owns over 1200 radio stations. Ninety-eight percent of all cities have only one daily newspaper and these are increasingly owned by huge chains like Gannett and Knight-Ridder. In medicine it is called Managed Care—in media it's Managed News. Corporate media today are in the entertainment business. Market share, advertising dollars and political self-interest drive the corporate media agenda. Lost to society is a diversity of political viewpoints and news story sources that are so important for democracy and freedom. We can see this quite clearly in the news coverage after the 9-11 attacks. Media's criticism of the government has become unpatriotic. The corporate media's line reads more like a government press release than a free society's analysis of important events of the day. We cannot have an active democracy with a news system that self-censors stories based on their political acceptability or marketability ratings rather than considering the importance of the news story for maintaining an informed electorate.[4]

Robert W. McChesney, associate professor of journalism at the University of Wisconsin-Madison, explains:

> A specter now haunts the world: a global commercial media system dominated by a small number of super-powerful, mostly U.S.-based transnational media corporations. It is a system that works to advance the cause of the global market and promote commercial values, while denigrating journalism and culture not conducive to the immediate bottom line or long-run corporate interests. It is a disaster for anything but the most superficial notion of democracy—a

---

4.   Phillips, PhD, Peter, "The Importance of Independent News Sources for Freedom and Democracy," 2003, http://www.projectcensored.org/resources/complete.html

democracy where, to paraphrase John Jay's maxim, those who own the world ought to govern it...

The global media system is now dominated by a first tier of nine giant firms. The five largest are Time Warner (1997 sales: $24 billion), Disney ($22 billion), Bertelsmann ($15 billion), Viacom ($13 billion), and Rupert Murdoch's News Corporation ($11 billion). Besides needing global scope to compete, the rules of thumb for global media giants are twofold: First, get bigger so you dominate markets and your competition can't buy you out. Firms like Disney and Time Warner have almost tripled in size this decade...

Behind these firms is a second tier of some three or four dozen media firms that do between $1 billion and $8 billion per year in media-related business. These firms tend to have national or regional strongholds or to specialize in global niche markets. About one-half of them come from North America, including the likes of Westinghouse (CBS), the New York Times Co., Hearst, Comcast and Gannett. Most of the rest come from Europe, with a handful based in East Asia and Latin America.[5]

In short, the overwhelming majority (in revenue terms) of the world's film production, TV show production, cable channel ownership, cable and satellite system ownership, book publishing, magazine publishing and music production is provided by these 50 or so firms, and the first nine firms thoroughly dominate many of these sectors. By any standard of democracy, such a concentration of media power is troubling, if not unacceptable.

## TODAY'S NEWS IS MOSTLY PR

We cannot expect the media to be objective watchdogs on environmental and health issues when they are influenced, supported and owned by disease-enablers. What's worse (if this could be any worse in a so-called "democracy") is that most news isn't really news at all. It's PR—public relations. That's right, tonight's news is not put together by busy reporters digging up facts and figures, but instead by public relations experts hired by corporations. Noam Chomsky, media watchdog, says, "The media present themselves as objective, balanced and free from any agenda. Reality suggests a different construct. Much of what passes as news is—sometimes subtle, sometimes crude—propaganda. The media are large conglomerates that serve to mobilize support for the special interests that dominate state and corporate power. In democratic societies populations are not controlled by force. Rather, they are subject to more refined forms of ideological manipulation. Necessary illusions are created. Consent is manufactured. The public is marginalized."[6]

---

5.    McChesney, Robert W., The Gllobal Media Giants, The nine firms that dominate the world," Extra!, November/December 1997

Public relations is a form of advertising. Instead of placing ads and creating commercials, public relations firms represent their clients by creating and writing so-called "news" articles, filming and videotaping "news" segments that highlight the activities of their clients, and working to get their clients publicity. If they are highly successful, PR firms fool the public into believing that we are watching news, not propaganda. When I was in journalism school in the 1970s, we learned of the difficulties public relations firms had in trying to get their clients' news in the media. This took a lot of networking, personal relationships, media connections and talent. No more. Now that the major media are actually owned by mega-corporations and cater to industry constituents, the balance of power has shifted. Instead of receiving mostly news and just a little PR, the American reader-viewer receives mostly PR and very little news. This is true, but not well-known. PR industry investigators John Stauber and Sheldon Rampton write:

> There is a precise and predictable inverse relationship between the work of journalists and the work of the public relations industry.
>
> Good investigative journalists work to inform the public about the activities of the rich and powerful. They uncover secrets known only to a few, and share those secrets with the rest of us.
>
> Public relations, on the other hand, works to control and limit the public's access to information about the rich and powerful. PR has its own techniques of investigation—techniques which range from opinion polling to covert surveillance of citizen activists. Rather than studying the *few* for the benefit of the *many*, these techniques study the *many* for the benefit of the *few*.[7]

What appears to be "news" about cancer studies, the wonders of new drugs, corporate news, introduction of new automobiles coming off the assembly line in Detroit, great innovations in science and industry, and outstanding leaders and scientists in our midst (never mind the fact that they wouldn't be caught dead living in your neighborhood) are really public relations features and mini-features. These pseudo-news stories are not limited to the mainstream media, but are also found in trade publications, specialty magazines and medical journals. "Even the *New England Journal of Medicine*—often described as the world's most prestigious medical journal—has been involved in controversies regarding hidden economic interests that shape its content and conclusions."[8] So prevalent and

---

6.  Chomsky, Noam, national broadcast, January 22, 1993, alternativeradio.org
7.  Stauber, John and Sheldon Rampton Flack Attack, prwatch.org 2002
8.  Stauber, John and Sheldon Ramptom, Trust Us, We're Experts!, Penguin Books, New York, p. 202

pervasive are PR-generated "news" stories that some experts say most news in the major media is really just propaganda in disguise.

## MIND OVER MATTER?
## THEY DON'T MIND BECAUSE WE DON'T MATTER

The most powerful stranglehold on freedom, health and happiness in our free world is the one industries have over the minds and emotions of the general public. The psychology of corporate warfare is far beyond the comprehension of most Americans. Most of us don't think like snakes and con men, so we don't expect to find this mentality in our leaders, corporate mucky-mucks or nightly news broadcasters. The degree to which our minds are manipulated is based on a calculated, specialized and powerful enterprise headed up by corporate psychologists, public relations specialists, advertising agencies, public speakers, media specialists, marketing professionals and political lobbyists. Even anthropologists have been called in as specialists, making monkeys out of us all.

## WHERE IS THE BUY BUTTON
## IN YOUR BRAIN?

Need more proof that corporate evil geniuses are working hard to get us to buy more, more, more? Consider what's going on at Emory University. Researchers at the school, as of this writing, are "undergoing intensive studies of the human brain looking for what has been coined the 'buy button.' This new pursuit of consumer control, known as neuromarketing, involves Magnetic Resonance Imaging (MRI) on live subjects to find the specific part of the brain that is activated when a consumer is successfully wooed by an advertisement into purchasing a product. Using the data from this research, marketers hope to be able to create ads that follow the exact neurological pathways that ultimately activate the "buy button" in consumers. According to a letter to the Emory University from a coalition of groups opposed to this research, 'If Emory University takes its own mission seriously, it should challenge this abuse of medical knowledge and technology to manipulate people for commercial purposes.'"[9]

> Neuromarketing is a controversial new field of marketing which uses functional Magnetic Resonance Imaging (fMRI)—a medical technology—not to

---

9.   The Latest in Consumer Brainwashing—Neuromarketing, Commercial Alert Asks Emory University to Halt Neuromarketing Experiments, December 2003, www.commondreams.org/news2003/1201-01.htm

heal, but to sell products. A BrightHouse Institute for Thought Sciences news release issued June 22, 2002 explains that it uses fMRI to identify patterns of brain activity that reveal how a consumer is actually evaluating a product, object or advertisement. Thought Sciences marketing analysts use this information to more accurately measure consumer preference, and then apply this knowledge to help marketers better create products and services and to design more effective marketing campaigns.[10]

The fact that the general public is unaware of how corporations control and influence our thinking patterns makes these enterprises even more successful. It makes the nightly national news believable and perceived as dependable, when it is mostly made up of public relations propaganda created to promote moneymaking. You cannot rely on MOST of the news in the major media to be factual and fair.

## WHERE'S THE OBJECTIVITY?

The cornerstone of journalism used to be OBJECTIVITY—the art of presenting all the sides involved in a news story. This would allow the viewer or reader to garner all of the facts and make a decision. No more. News is mostly one-sided these days.

Is the news lying to you? Lying is a harsh word, and it doesn't really hit the nail on the coffin. Rather than blatantly lying, news stories are actually the result of one-sided reporting, stories that make corporations and their employees look good in the public eye, and omission of important—and often life threatening—news. If we don't hear about a major chemical plant dumping tons of waste into our neighborhood creek where people fish and children swim, then such an omission is unspeakably without conscience. It is analogous to watching a mugger walk down the street with a loaded weapon and not calling the cops. This makes the media accomplices to murder, cancer, lung disease, childhood suffering, corporate cheating and stealing, and untold deaths. Not reporting the news is as unAmerican as fascism, and often worse. Wouldn't you want to know if the nuclear power plant ten miles away was melting down and about to spew radioactive materials all over your house and children? How about if a big chemical company was pouring toxins into your local stream or creek? What about if trucks carrying radioactive waste were driving along a highway less than a mile from your house? Or how about if Home Depot gave millions of dollars to the Bush campaign[11] despite the fact that, thanks to the Bush Administration, the EPA

---

10. ibid.

announced that it plans to suspend requirements for power plants to reduce their emissions of toxic mercury over the next four years?[12]

Here's a story that never made it onto the nightly news, yet appeared in the newspaper. Keep in mind that this news is far more common than you might think. In September 2002, just outside Denver, Colorado, the *Sunday Denver Post* reported that residents in Globeville were at risk of arsenic and lead poisoning in the air, water and soil. Globeville, the article notes, "became famous in the early 1990s for lead and arsenic contamination. Its residents sued ASARCO, Inc., a nearby metals extraction company, alleging that smokestack emissions had tainted the neighborhood soil. ASARCO later settled the lawsuit, agreeing to clean up the contamination in Globeville."[13] But guess what! Ten years went by and they never stopped poisoning the families living in the area. One mother in the neighborhood didn't know how to explain to her sick toddler "that her blood contains unhealthy levels of lead, which can hinder cognitive development, decrease a child's IQ, and cause mental retardation and possibly death…Arsenic can cause brain damage, nervous system disorders and cancer."[14] Soil tests conducted by the EPA (Environmental Protection Agency) four years previous, showed the affected neighborhoods were contaminated from emissions from defunct smelters operating in the area during the early 20th century. This statement tells any rational human being three main things: First, toxic waste in our environment lingers and continues to cause death and health problems long after industry has gone out of business or relocated. Secondly, that industry is irresponsible and that the federal, state and local governments are impotent at the expense of us citizens! Third, the news media isn't informing the public of environmental hazards affecting us all. In this particular case in the Denver neighborhood, ASARCO reported that it conducted its own study and "determined the contamination was not the result of smelting operations." Company spokespersons said the reported toxicity was from pesticides and lead-based paints instead. Whom do we believe? Or does it matter? The really important issue here is one that faces most families in the United States today: There are so many poisons in our environment, and it remains legal to continue to pollute the environment when it is a scientific fact that toxins kill and cause cancer and diseases of the brain, nervous system, skin, kidneys, liver, lungs and reproductive systems.

---

11.  Presidential Mystery Solved: Why Bush Is Stopping at Home Depot; *Public Citizen, Bush Rewards Generous GOP Donor with Visit to Maryland Store on Friday;* Energy Bill Includes $48 Million Tax Break that Benefits the Giant Retailer, December 3, 2003

## PERSISTENT POISONS

Poisons in the environment are all too often *persistent*, meaning that they hang around for years. Radioactive waste can keep polluting for 20,000 years or more! Many toxic substances such as mercury, lead and aluminum, are stored in our bodies' tissues for a lifetime, slowly killing us. Other toxins linger for weeks to many years in the environment, long after the polluter has packed his bags and moved his family and bank account to another community. Persistent Organic Pollutants (POPs) "persist for years in the environment, travel great distances on wind and water currents, and accumulate in food chains. Americans are exposed to POPs every day through foods like fish, meat, and dairy products. Scientific evidence has linked POPs to decreased birth weights, cancers, learning disorders, and reproductive disorders."[15]

## DO YOU LIVE NEAR A SUPERFUND SITE?

The word "Superfund" sounds like something you get after winning the Publishing Clearinghouse Sweepstakes. Not even close. A Superfund site is "any land in the United States that has been contaminated by hazardous waste and identified

---

12. "The latest payback to the utility industry from the Bush Administration: EPA's announcement that it plans to suspend requirements for power plants to reduce their emissions of toxic mercury over the next four years. Instead, the White House will give utilities *twenty-three years* to meet a standard that could have been met in four. Worse yet, the White House proposal would allow companies to buy and sell the right to emit mercury, a persistent reproductive and neurological toxin, as though it were an economic commodity like porkbelly futures. Research shows that we can achieve a 70% or more reduction in mercury from power plants with technologies that are available today AND save energy in the bargain.

   The Bush Administration's plan to let utilities off the hook on mercury is a threat to our children and our future. Toxic mercury is linked to cerebral palsy and other developmental and cognitive disorders in infants and children. The Centers for Disease Control have reported that more than one in twelve pregnant women has unsafe levels of mercury in their bloodstream, and forty-three states have issued fishing advisories urging people to limit their consumption of fish caught from local streams and rivers due to mercury contamination. Because people living closest to large, coal-burning power plants may be at the greatest risk from pollution fall-out, it is unconscionable to allow these sources to trade their way out of emission controls by buying the rig ht to pollute from cleaner plants that may be far away." Source: Environmental Integrity Project, Statement by Eric Schaeffer, Director of Environmental Integrity Project/Former EPA Chief of Civil Enforcement, December 5, 2003

by the Environmental Protection Agency (EPA) as a candidate for cleanup because it poses a risk to human health and/or the environment."[16] Most disturbing is the fact that one out of four people in America lives within four miles of a Superfund site. The EPA reports, "There are tens of thousands of abandoned hazardous waste sites in our nation, and accidental releases occur daily."[17] Eighty-five percent of all Superfund sites have contaminated groundwater, and half the people in this country—and virtually everyone in many rural areas—rely on groundwater for their drinking water.[18] Further, just because an area is not determined by the government to be a Superfund site does not mean that it is safe and free of deadly poisons!

Here are the 20 most prevalent toxins and their health effects at Superfund sites:[19]

### ARSENIC

Health Effects: Arsenic is a known to cause cancer of the lungs, bladder, and skin. Arsenic is also linked to cancer of the liver, kidney, colon and nasal passages, and to a variety of non-cancer health effects, including heart disease, diabetes, adverse impacts on the immune system, lungs, and gastrointestinal track, and thickening and discoloration of the skin. There is also evidence linking arsenic to adverse reproductive and developmental impacts.

### LEAD

Health Effects: Lead can damage almost every organ and system in the human body, especially the immune and reproductive systems, and can cause heart disease and kidney damage. Lead is exceptionally damaging to the central nervous system, particularly in children where it can cause brain damage. Lead has can also decrease IQ scores, slow growth, and cause hearing problems in infants or young children.

13.   Aguilera, Elizabeth, *The Sunday Denver Post*, September 15, 2002

14.   ibid

15.   SaveOurEnvironment.org Action Center Update: September 18, 2002

16.   United States Environmental Protection Agency: "Superfund Frequently Asked Questions," Superfund Hotline Training Module-January 1997-The Superfund Response Process), online: 2002

17.   ibid

18.   Public Interest Research Group, 2002, PIRG.org

19.   ibid

## MERCURY

Health Effects: Mercury can cause brain and kidney damage, and poses an especially high risk of adverse neurological development of fetuses.

## VINYL CHLORIDE

Health Effects: Vinyl chloride can cause cancer, and may damage the liver and immune and nervous systems.

## POLYCHLORINATED BIPHENYLS (PCBs)

Health Effects: PCBs can cause cancer and adverse developmental impacts. These impacts may include lowered IQ and behavioral problems such as Attention Deficit Disorder. PCBs are also linked to adverse reproductive impacts, including low birth weight, damage to the immune system.

## BENZENE

Health Effects: Benzene causes cancer, and adverse developmental and reproductive impacts. Benzene may also cause damage to the immune, respiratory, endocrine and cardiovascular system.

## CADMIUM

Health Effects: Cadmium causes cancer and adverse reproductive and developmental impacts. It may also damage the lungs, kidneys and digestive track, and has been linked to weakening of the immune system and human skeletal system.

## BENZO(A)PYRENE

Health Effects: Benzo(a)pyrene, a Polycyclic Aromatic Hydrocarbon (PAH), causes cancer and may damage to the developmental, immune and respiratory systems.

## POLYCYCLIC AROMATIC HYDROCARBONS (PAH)

Health Effects: Polycyclic Aromatic Hydrocarbons (PAHs) are a group of over 100 different chemicals formed during the incomplete burning of coal, oil and gas, garbage, or other organic substances. Some PAHs cause cancer, and may adversely affect the reproductive and immune systems.

## CHLOROFORM

Health Effects: Chloroform can cause cancer, and may damage the liver, kidneys, and endocrine and respiratory systems. Chloroform may also cause birth defects and miscarriages.

### DDT, P, P1

Health Effects: DDT can cause cancer and adverse developmental and reproductive impacts. DDT may also damage the liver and central nervous system, causing excitability, tremors, and seizures in people.

### AROCLOR 1254

Health Effects: Aroclor 1254 is a form of polychlorinated biphenyl (PCB). PCBs can cause cancer and adverse developmental impacts. These impacts may include lowered IQ and behavioral problems such as Attention Deficit Disorder. PCBs are also linked to adverse reproductive impacts, including low birth weight, damage to the immune system.

### AROCLOR 1260

Health Effects: Aroclor 1260 is a form of polychlorinated biphenyl (PCB). PCBs can cause cancer and adverse developmental impacts. These impacts may include lowered IQ and behavioral problems such as Attention Deficit Disorder. PCBs are also linked to adverse reproductive impacts, including low birth weight, damage to the immune system.

### TRICHLOROETHYLENE

Health Effects: Trichloroethylene can cause cancer and may damage the nervous system, liver, and lungs. It may also cause adverse reproductive and developmental impacts, and damage to the cardiovascular and immune system.

### DIBENZO(A,H)ANTHRACENE

Health Effects: Dibenzo(a,h)anthracene is a Polycyclic Aromatic Hydrocarbon (PAH) suspected of causing cancer. PAHs are a group of over 100 different chemicals formed during the incomplete burning of coal, oil and gas, garbage, or other organic substances. Some PAHs cause cancer, and may adversely affect the reproductive and immune systems.

### DIELDRIN

Health Effects: Dieldrin causes cancer and damage to the nervous system. Dieldrin may also damage the cardiovascular, immune, reproductive, and respiratory systems. Low exposure can cause headaches, dizziness, vomiting, irritability, and uncontrolled muscle movements.

### HEXAVALENT CHROMIUM

Health Effects: Hexavalent chromium (or chromium (VI)) causes cancer and may damage the kidney and liver. Large exposures of hexavalent chromium can cause death.

## CHLORDANE

Health Effects: Chlordane causes cancer and may damage the nervous, cardio-vascular, reproductive, and digestive system and the liver. Low doses of chlordane can also cause headaches, irritability, confusion, weakness, vision problems, vomiting, stomach cramps, diarrhea, and jaundice. Ingesting large amounts can cause convulsions and death.

## HEXACHLOROBUTADIENE

Health Effects: Hexachlorobutadiene may cause cancer and damage the cardiovascular system, and kidneys and liver. It may also cause adverse developmental, and reproductive impacts.

## *DO YOU POISON YOURSELF WITHOUT KNOWING THE DANGERS?*

There are several toxic substances that people are misled to believe are health-promoting and beneficial when they are actually the opposite. Chief among these are chlorine and fluoride. Chlorine is used, of course, for bleaching clothes and bathroom tiles, and "purifying" water, including water in swimming pools and the water coming out of your tap at home. Yet chlorine is a highly toxic chemical that causes illnesses from headaches to flu-like symptoms and much worse. Chlorine should not be ingested through your pores when you swim nor through your lungs via water vapor as you shower. On the dangers of chlorine, biochemist, clinical nutritionist, past president of the Canadian Holistic Medical Association and author of the Canadian bestseller *The Joy of Health,* Dr. Zoltan P. Rona writes:

> Most people never give it a thought. After all, our elected public officials keep assuring us that chlorinated city tap water is completely safe for human consumption. Numerous scientific studies report that chlorinated tap water is a skin irritant and can be associated with rashes like eczema. Chlorinated water can destroy polyunsaturated fatty acids and vitamin E in the body while generating toxins capable of free radical damage (oxidation). This might explain why supplementation of the diet with essential fatty acids like flax seed oil, evening primrose oil, borage oil and antioxidants like vitamin E, selenium and others helps so many cases of eczema and dry skin.
>
> Chlorinated water destroys much of the intestinal flora, the friendly bacteria that help in the digestion of food and which protects the body from harmful pathogens. These bacteria are also responsible for the manufacture of several important vitamins like vitamin B12 and vitamin K. It is not uncommon for chronic skin conditions like acne, psoriasis, seborrhea and eczema to clear up or to be significantly improved by switching to unchlorinated drink-

ing water and supplementing the diet with lactobacillus acidophilus and bifidus.

Chlorinated water contains chemical compounds called trihalomethanes which are carcinogens resulting from the combination of chlorine with compounds in water. These chemicals, also known as organochlorides, do not degrade very well and are generally stored in the fatty tissues of the body (breast, other fatty areas, mother's milk, blood and semen). Organochlorides can cause mutations by altering DNA, suppress immune system function and interfere with the natural controls of cell growth.

Chlorine has been documented to aggravate asthma, especially in those children who make use of chlorinated swimming pools. Several studies also link chlorine and chlorinated by-products to a greater incidence of bladder, breast and bowel cancer as well as malignant melanoma. One study even links the use of chlorinated tap water to congenital cardiac anomalies.[20]

Probably the most disturbing byproduct of chlorine is dioxin, a chemical family so deadly that a mere fistful is enough kill every human being on earth.[21] Dioxin is not only cancerous, but also disrupts the hormonal system of living beings, including humans. "Formed as an accidental by-product of many industrial processes, including the creation of plastic and the bleaching of paper, dioxin accumulates in the body's fatty tissue. It can cause chloracne, a disfiguring skin condition that produces skin eruptions, cysts and pustules. Long-term or prenatal exposure to dioxin can cause birth defects, cardiovascular and nervous system damage, endometriosis, and a variety of cancers, including leukemia and cancer of the breast and prostate."[22] There are also studies showing that chlorine ingestion is linked to bladder cancer.

For all the bad news about chlorine, log onto www.chlorinefreeproducts.org, the Chlorine Free Products Association. The best advice is not to use chlorine ever again. Purchase a shower filter and a whole house water filter, and don't swim in pools that are chlorinated. If you are staying at a hotel, bathe in a nearby lake (since this may not be practical, think about bringing a shower filter with you wherever you go).

---

20.   4optimallife.com/Dangers-Of-Chlorine-To-Your-Health, 2002, citing: Fackelman, K.A., *Hints of a chlorine-cancer connection. Science News*; Flaten, T.P., *Chlorination of drinking water and cancer incidence in Norway. International Journal of Epidermiology*; Messina V., *Chlorine and cancer. Good Medicine*

21.   Erickson, Kim, *Drop Dead Gorgeous*, Contemporary Books, NY, 2002, p. 19

22.   ibid, p. 19

If you are the kind of person who needs proof that chlorine is bad for human health, here are some references you can look up on your next day off from work:[23]

1. STATISTICAL ABSTRACT OF THE UNITED STATES 1997 [117th edition] (Washington, D.C.: U.S. Government Printing Office, October, 1997). See Table 88.

2. The STATISTICAL ABSTRACT for 1997, cited above, Table 123, says there were 7.4 fetal deaths per 1000 live births in 1992, so the total number of fetal deaths that year was 7.4 4,065 = 30,000.

3. STATISTICAL ABSTRACT for 1997, cited above, table 117.

4. S. Hamamah and others, "The effect of male factors in repeated spontaneous abortion: lessons from in-vitro fertilization and intracytoplasmic sperm injection," HUMAN REPRODUCTION UPDATE Vol. 3, No. 4 (July 1997), pgs. 393-400.

5. Kirsten Waller and others, "Trihalomethanes in Drinking Water and Spontaneous Abortion," EPIDEMIOLOGY Vol. 9, No. 2 (March 1998), pgs. 134-140.

6. Judith B. Klotz and Laurie A. Pyrch, A CASE-CONTROL STUDY OF NEURAL TUBE DEFECTS AND DRINKING WATER CONTAMINANTS (Atlanta, Ga.: Agency for Toxic Substances and Disease Registry, January, 1998).

7. Frank L. Bove and others, "Public Drinking Water Contamination and Birth Outcomes," AMERICAN JOURNAL OF EPIDEMIOLOGY Vol. 141, No. 9 (May 1, 1995), pgs. 850-862.

8. Andrew T. L. Chen and others, "RE: 'Public Drinking Water Contamination and Birth Outcomes,'" AMERICAN JOURNAL OF EPIDEMIOLOGY Vol. 143, No. 11 (June 1, 1996), pgs. 1179-1180.

9. Ann Aschengrau and others, "Quality of Community Drinking Water and the Occurrence of Late Adverse Pregnancy Outcomes," ARCHIVES OF ENVIRONMENTAL HEALTH Vol. 48, No. 2 (March/April 1993), pgs. 105-113.

---

23. RACHEL'S ENVIRONMENT & HEALTH WEEKLY #599, May 21, 1998, DANGERS OF CHLORINE IN WATER, Environmental Research Foundation, P.O. Box 5036, Annapolis, MD 21403

10.  David A. Savitz and others, "Drinking Water and Pregnancy Outcome in Central North Carolina: Source, Amount, and Trihalomethane Levels," ENVIRONMENTAL HEALTH PERSPECTIVES Vol. 103, No. 6 (June 1995), pgs. 592-596.

11.  Shanna H. Swan and others, "A Prospective Study of Spontaneous Abortion: Relation to Amount and Source of Drinking Water Consumed in Early Pregnancy," EPIDEMIOLOGY Vol. 9, No. 2 (March 1998), pgs. 126-133.

12.  Kellyn S. Betts, "Miscarriages associated with drinking water disinfection byproducts, study says," ENVIRONMENTAL SCIENCE & TECHNOLOGY [ES&T] April 1, 1998, pgs. 169A-170A.

## FLUORIDE IS BAD FOR YOUR HEALTH

Fluoride is another socially accepted toxin. Most people believe it is safe, beneficial and important, yet leading scientists are telling us that we have been scammed by big business and government. And the scam is continuing to this day as water "experts" and dentists continue to poison us with this toxic metal that has an affinity to bone and the potential to interfere with hormonal function. If you care about your health, look into the fluoride issue. Wouldn't you want to know whether fluoride causes thyroid and bone disease before giving your kids a fluoride treatment at the dentist?

What is fluoride anyway? You have never heard both sides of the fluoride story on the television news because the truth would damage the fertilizer and aluminum industries, as well as the prestigious dental profession. This would be good for you, but bad for them. Even your dentist is kept in the dark about this issue! If your dentist does know the truth, chances are he/she will not be candid with you, because to do so may be self-incrimination and get him/her in trouble with the dental association.

Fluoride is so dangerous, and the issue regarding its advocacy is so disputed, that I've devoted the next chapter to fluoride and its opposition by leading scientists, dental researchers and medical doctors.

## WHAT YOU CAN DO TO FIND OUT MORE ABOUT THE HEALTH OF YOUR OWN NEIGHBORHOOD & REDUCING TOXIC EXPOSURE

Do you know how polluted your neighborhood is? Do you know whether you and your family are being poisoned through your air or water?

- For starters, go online to the website scorecard.org and type in your zip code to find out how big of a risk you are in right where you live. You may be surprised at the discovery.

- Next, go to http://map3.epa.gov/enviromapper/index.html to find out where the nearest Superfund site is near you.

- Protest the use of fluoride in your area's drinking water. Many areas have stopped poisoning their water with fluoride thanks to citizens protests.

- Support only companies practicing safe, sustainable business. Do this with your buying power. Choose environmentally clean businesses and products.

- Buy a whole house water filter system to assure cleaner drinking water and bath water. Never use unfiltered tap water for drinking, bathing or cooking.

- Throw away all aluminum cookware, measuring cups, baking pans and cookie sheets. Replace these with iron or stainless steel.

- One way to convince corporations to change anti-environmental practices is through **ecopledge.com**. Consumers, investors and students are harnessing their power to leverage concrete changes in corporate environmental behavior. Sign the ecopledge online.

## BOYCOTTING IS ONE WAY TO MAKE A DIFFERENCE

Visiting ecopledge.com, there are several case studies showing how corporations can be persuaded to change their environmentally destructive policies. Here's one example of how students made a difference in influencing Ford Motor Company. An Ecopledge press release reports:

> Students across the country successfully pushed Ford Motor Company to resign their membership in the Global Climate Coalition (GCC). The GCC, an industry funded lobby group in Washington DC, is dedicated to undermining the science behind global warming and devoted to halting political measures to stop its increasing devastation. GCC members include General Motors, Chevron, Exxon, Mobil and Allegheny Energy.
>
> Ford's recent announcement resulted in both the company's removal from the ecopledge.com list of targets, and in the addition to the list of General Motors. "Now that we have forced Ford to take global warming seriously, we will force General Motors to do the same. And once we've done that, we'll keep moving on down the list until the Global Climate Coalition is a thing of the past," said Andy MacDonald, field director for ecopledge.com.

Ford was one of three targets of ecopledge.com, a nationwide effort by students for corporate environmental reform. Through ecopledge.com, students place pressure on target companies by pledging to not accept employment from them until they take simple, important steps to protect the environment. ecopledge.com was launched on October 15, 1999 at ECOnference 2000 at the University of Pennsylvania where thousands of college students from all over the country gathered to launch the environmental movement into the next millennium.

Students at over 40 other [universities] around the country have been running campaigns calling for Ford to pull out of the GCC. They have used a variety of strategies including the employment boycott, university divestment campaigns, and media campaigns to put pressure on Ford. "Our elected officials have failed to stop global warming because of industry opposition," said MacDonald, "We knew we needed to act to urge concerned companies like Ford reconsider their position on global warming."

Ford's announcement comes at a time when the scientific evidence that global warming is happening [and] is becoming increasingly overwhelming. In research released last week in the journal *Science*, top climate scientists stated that the amount of sea ice in the arctic waters "is shrinking, on average, by about 14,000 square miles a year." The scientists agree that all signs point to global warming as the cause.

Ford's departure from the coalition also comes on the heels of similar moves made by Shell and British Petroleum and is a further indication of the growing industry recognition of the threat of global warming. In anticipation of pressure from activists, Daimler Chrysler quickly followed Ford's lead by withdrawing from the GCC. "These companies' recent move shows how students can make powerful choices that have significant impacts on the environment," concluded MacDonald.[24]

Only time will tell whether these corporations are just playing PR games or are really making changes for the better. But some changes are better than none, right? And if public pressure works, why not keep at it?

## LEARN ABOUT IMPORTANT EVENTS
## NOT BROADCAST ON THE NIGHTLY NEWS

If you really want to know what's going on without hearing the corporate propaganda/public relations view of the news, here are some excellent sources. You can find them online or at many book stores.

---

24. "Boycott Campaign Successful in Changing Ford Motor Company's Global Warming Position, General Motors Named as Next Target," ecopledge.com, November 23, 1999.

- *The Nation* (thenation.com)

- 20/20 Vision (http://www.2020vision.org)

- *Mother Jones*

- *E Environmental Magazine*

- Environmental News Network (http://www.enn.com)

- *Earth Island Journal*

- *Z Magazine* (zmag.org)

- *Ad Busters* (adbusters.org)

- Project Censored books (projectcensored.org)

- Environmental Working Group (ewg.org)

- Greenpeace (greenpeace.org)

# Fluoride is Poisonous
# Even Though Your Dentist
# Recommends It

*"The plain fact that fluorine is an insidious poison harmful, toxic and cumulative in its effects, even when ingested in minimal amounts, will remain unchanged no matter how many times it will be repeated in print that fluoridation of the water supply is 'safe.'"*

*—Dr. Ludwig Grosse,*
*Chief of Cancer Research*
*U.S. Veterans Administration*

Perhaps one of the greatest ongoing battles between corporate science and the victimized public (you and I) is the one over the use of fluoride. Almost every dentist says fluoride is safe and helpful. To this I say that dentists, like medical doctors, rely on corporate-supplied research for their decision-making. Dentists listen to reports handed out through the dental association. They do not do their own, independent research. If they did, they would discover volumes of scientific research about the dangers of fluoride that their industry-influenced dental association would not dare tell them. Dentists who use fluoride are doing the public a disservice. This does not mean that dentists are evil or lying to you (at least not on purpose). It only means they are the pawns of their industry leaders when it comes to the use and recommendation of fluoride. They ignore the fact that fluoride is a toxic substance that greatly impairs the human physiology.

Charles Gordon Heyd, M.D., Past President, American Medical Association, said, "I am appalled at the prospect of using water as a vehicle for drugs. Fluoride is a corrosive poison that will produce serious effect on a long-range basis. Any attempt to use the water this way is deplorable."[1]

---

1.  http://www.fluoridedebate.com/conclusion.html

Fluoride's reported value as a deterrent of cavities is unproved. The voice of the fluoride industry has been louder and more persistent than the voice of those brave scientists who know better than to use this toxic substance on human beings due to its harmful effects. Fluoride has been linked to cancer, bone disease, thyroid dysfunction, attention deficit disorder and other health problems. Rarely are the truths about fluoride published in the mainstream media because the political and economic power behind the fluoride industry is formidable. Perhaps the most sobering statement ever made about the use of fluoride was by world renowned microbiologist, Nobel Prize winner and discoverer of streptomycin, Professor Albert Schatz, Ph.D., who said, "Fluoridation is the greatest fraud that has ever been perpetrated, and it has been perpetrated on more people than any other fraud."[2]

## FLUORIDE, TECHNICALLY SPEAKING

Fluorine is a highly reactive element with an affinity to bond with other elements. These combinations are often salts, and the fluorine part is called *fluoride*. Hence, fluorine added to water has commonly become known as fluoride. Chemically speaking, fluoride as it is naturally found in water is calcium fluoride ($CaF2$). This means that it is calcium bound to fluorine. When water is artificially fluoridated, sodium fluoride ($NaF$), sodium silicofluoride or hydrofluosilic acid is added. These are all human-made chemical concoctions. Natural (found in nature) fluoride is safer because calcium binds relatively strongly with the fluoride ion, which is much less available (free-floating and looking for something to bond with) than in artificially produced (human-made) fluoride. "The artificial [human-made] compounds are more toxic because they are more soluble in water and the fluoride dissociates from the compound. In the [human] body this fluoride becomes the 'most exclusive bone seeking element, owing to its affinity for calcium phosphate.' Studies have shown that the lethal dose of $NaF$ is approximately 50 times smaller than that of $CaF2$ (naturally-occurring fluoride)."[3] In essence, fluoride found in drinking water, toothpaste and other media is looking for places to bond—and most commonly it bonds to your bone tissue.

---

2.   Oregon Citizens for Safe Drinking Water, 2003; http://homepages.ihug.co.nz/~dcandmkw/fluoride/flqest12.htm

3.   "Fluoride Fact Sheet," EarthLife, earthlife.org.za/factsheets, 2002

## WHAT'S WRONG WITH FLUORIDE?

It's true that we've all grown up being told that fluoride prevents cavities. We've heard this so many times that we've become brainwashed, forgetting that there is always another side to every claim. We've been listening to the voice of the fluoride industry without recognizing the voice of sane scientists who know that the public has long been the victim of a sickening deception. We've been so fooled by the industrial rhetoric that we've allowed fluoride into our mouthwashes, tooth-pastes and drinking water for generations.

As we have discussed, today's evil geniuses are fighting like crazy to keep news of their destructive practices out of the major news media, according to their profits-first, public-health-second philosophy. Yet the toll on human health, live-stock and the environment is scientifically undeniable, with fluoride being often more than 100 times more toxic than the known poison sulfur dioxide:

> In 1969, a massive fish kill that turned Placentia Bay, Newfoundland, into "a biological desert" was traced to fluoride effluent from a plant that produced elemental phosphorus for metal finishing and consumer goods. Some 22,800 pounds of fluoride effluent poured into [was dumped into] the bay each day, primarily in the form of hydrofluosilicic acid—the same substance used to fluoridate city water supplies.
>
> According to US Department of Agriculture Handbook No. 380: "Airborne fluorides have caused more worldwide damage to domestic animals than any other air pollutant." The handbook's list of fluorosis symptoms included: "dental mottling, respiratory distress, stiffness in knees or elbows or both" and concluded with the observation that "Man is much more sensitive than domestic animals to F [fluoride] intoxication."
>
> In a 1970 report on "The Effects of Fluorides on Man," Harold C. Hodge (See *Earth Island Journal*, Winter, Spring '98) listed some of the symptoms of fluoride poisoning found in industrial workers: osteosclerosis, ossifications of ligamentous attachments, sinus trouble, perforation of the nasal septum, chest pains, coughs, thyroid disorders, anemia, dizziness, weakness and nausea.[4]

Most commonly, fluoride is a waste byproduct of the aluminum and fertilizer industries. It is **industrial waste**. Now, let's do a little multiple choice quiz. If you were Dr. Evil and you were making millions of dollars a day processing aluminum and synthetic fertilizers that were unfortunately producing millions of tons of industrial waste (pollution) that can kill people, what would you do:

---

4.    Smith, Gar, "Why Fluoride is an Environmental Issue," *Earth Island Journal* archives online, 2002

a.   stop production at once, cancel your vacation to Rome, sell your fleet of Rolls Royces, pull your kid out of Yale, return your blue blazer with the emblem to the millionaire's club and apologize to the citizens of your country for accidentally ruining their health and their environment; or

b.   bury your waste under your house in the cover of night; or

c.   hire some scientists and dentists to claim on your behalf that fluoride is a beneficial compound then find a way to get everyone to believe it to the point where it will be incorporated into toothpaste, dental treatments and national water supplies.

The answer is "c."

The truth is that fluoride is highly toxic, quite aside from any possible tendency to cause or promote cancer. A few grams can kill you. Poisoning from fluoride may range from discoloration and pitting of the teeth (dental fluorosis) to skeletal abnormalities, vomiting and diarrhea, kidney failure and spasms. Depending on your particular tolerance level (which is a variable for any degree of toxicity), fluoride's effects vary from person to person. "Sensitive individuals suffer from fluoride even at extremely low levels. And people with kidney problems are especially at risk because they cannot flush fluoride efficiently from their system. These effects may be compounded by the largely unnoticed increase in average fluoride consumption. Foods and beverages processed with fluoridated water didn't exist when health authorities set recommended fluoride levels in the water."[5]

## BUT DOESN'T FLUORIDE PREVENT CAVITIES?

We've been told that fluoride prevents cavities. We've been hoodwinked, fooled, lied to, deceived and conned. Studies showing that fluoride is beneficial have been proffered by fluoride producers whose research has been proven to be flawed, focusing on small groups of people and showing inconsistencies in information gathering. Conversely, there are many more reliable studies showing that fluoride **does not** prevent decay, and is in fact harmful. Some of these are included below (note that the word "caries" means cavities; and ppm means parts per million):

- A study has been done of the dental records of 39,207 schoolchildren aged 5 to 17 in 84 areas of the USA. These areas were divided according to not fluoridated, partially fluoridated (less than 17 years or some of the time)

---

5.   *The Oakland Tribune,* "The Fluoride Bombshell," Feb. 16, 1990

and fluoridated. No statistical difference was found in decay rates of permanent teeth or percentages of decay free children between the areas. The only group of children which showed a difference were 5-year-olds who had less decay in deciduous teeth in fluoridated areas. However, by age 6 this advantage disappears leading to the conclusion that fluoridation causes a delay in tooth eruption.

- R Ziegelbecker has made two studies by taking a random sample of all available data on caries (decay) prevalence. He selected 48,000 12- to 14-year-old children from 136 communities in seven countries. No correlation was found between caries or dental health and fluoride concentration.

- Further studies have shown that not only does fluoride not improve dental health but it may cause decay.

- A study of 400,000 Indian school children from 1973–1993 showed that the higher the fluoride concentration in the water, the more caries occurred.

- A similar study of 22,000 Japanese school children showed that above 0.4 ppm the decay increased significantly. When the concentration was below 0.2 ppm it also increased. This was thought to be caused by a lack of calcium in the water when fluoride was below 0.2 ppm.

- A study of 26,000 Tucson elementary school children was performed by Cornelius Steelink, Professor Emeritus, Dept. of Chemistry, University of Arizona. He compared tooth decay with the fluoride in the water. He found that the more fluoride a child drank, the more cavities occurred. On further investigation it was also found that decay related to low family income, bad diet and oral hygiene and lack of access to dental facilities.

- The decline in DMFT (decayed, missing, filled teeth) of 12-year-old children in the USA declined by 25% from 1974 to 1988. The USA is partially fluoridated. Unfluoridated countries such as the Netherlands, Sweden and Finland had a decline.[6]

Fluoride poses not just a personal health risk, but is an environmental poison as well, affecting both the plant and animal kingdoms without bias. *Earth Island Journal* reports:

> Fluoride is hazardous to human health. But this is not where the hazard begins or ends, because the toll it is taking on the environment is just as serious. "Fluorides are pollutants with considerable potential for producing ecological

---

6.    "Fluoride Fact Sheet," EarthLife, earthlife.org.za/factsheets, 2002

damage," Edward Groth III warned in an article in the April/May 1975 issue of *Environment*. By the end of the 1960s, the EPA estimated that 155,000 tons of fluoride (calculated as hydrogen fluoride) was pouring into the atmosphere each year from aluminum smelters, phosphate processing, coal combustion and the manufacturing of steel, bricks and glass products.

Several types of coniferous forests are vulnerable to fluoride damage at one part per billion (ppb) or less. Because fluoride does not breakdown, it slowly accumulates in the environment. As early as 1971, the National Research Council warned that fluoride pollution from US industry (in concentrations as low as 1 ppb) had caused serious damage to plants and posed a threat to livestock as far as 20 miles downwind of the emission points. Some grasses consumed by livestock have been found to contain 200,000 times more fluoride than in the ambient air.

A 1971 National Park Service study of the area downwind of an Anaconda aluminum company smelter and a phosphate plant found excessive elevations of fluoride in pines, firs, grasses, shrubs, herbs and hay. Honey bees had the highest fluoride levels among insects. Wildlife, from birds and ground squirrels to larger mammal predators, had fluoride levels that reached as high as 13,333 parts per million (ppm).

Foraging on grasses containing 30 to 40 ppm of fluoride can be toxic to cattle. Mussels, oysters, crabs, shrimp and prawns have been killed by aquatic fluoride pollution.[7]

## DOCTORS, RESEARCHERS SPEAK OUT AGAINST FLUORIDATION

Here is what a few doctors, scientists, association spokespeople and researchers are saying about fluoride (special thanks to Citizens for Safe Drinking Water, Mountainview, California, www.nofluoride.com, for granting permission to reprint the following research):

- "The American Medical Association is NOT prepared to state that no harm will be done to any person by water fluoridation. The AMA has not carried out any research work, either long-term or short-term, regarding the possibility of any side effects."—Dr. Flanagan, Assistant Director of Environmental Health, American Medical Association. [actual letter]

- "Based on data from the National Academy of Sciences, current levels of fluoride exposure in drinking water may cause arthritis in a substantial por-

---

7.    Smith, Gar, "Why Fluoride is an Environmental Issue," *Earth Island Journal*, archives online, 2002

tion of the population long before they reach old age"—Dr. Robert Carton, former EPA [Environmental Protection Agency] scientist.

- "Fluorides are general protoplasmic poisons, probably because of their capacity to modify the metabolism of cells by changing the permeability of the cell membrane and by inhibiting certain enzyme systems." *Journal of the American Medical Association*, Sept 18, 1943

- Segments of the population are unusually susceptible to the toxic effects of fluoride. They include "post menopausal women and elderly men, pregnant woman and their fetuses, people with deficiencies of calcium, magnesium and/or vitamin C, and people with cardiovascular and kidney problems." United States Public Health Service Report (ATSDR TP-91/17, pg. 112, Sec.2.7, April 1993)

- "Fluoride exposure, at levels that are experienced by a significant proportion of the population whose drinking water is fluoridated, may have adverse impacts on the developing brain." Greater Boston Physicians for Social Responsibility, May 2000

- "It is now clear that fluoride is a potentially harmful substance when present in the drinking water in any amount." Dr. Simon Beisler, Chief of Urology, Roosevelt Hospital and Past President of the American Urological Association.

- "The plain fact that fluorine is an insidious poison, harmful, toxic and cumulative in its effects, even when ingested in minimal amounts, will remain unchanged no matter how many times it will be repeated in print that fluoridation of the water supply is 'safe.'" Dr. Ludwig Grosse, Chief of Cancer Research, U.S. Veterans Administration.

- In Harlem, NY, which has been fluoridated for 32 years, "There's more dental decay among these kids; we see the beginning of inflamed gingivitis in their mouths." American Dental Association, May 2000

- "Fluoride has been shown to adversely effect the central nervous system, causing behavioral changes, increased hip fractures and reproduction problems." Natick Report Research Team [Research Microbiologist, U.S. Army, Dr. B. J. Gallo, Environmental Chemist, J. Kupperschmidt Apollo Program Project Scientist, Dr. N.R. Mancuso, U.S. Army Natick Research Labs, A. Murray, Molecular Biologist, Dr. Strauss]

- "I am appalled at the prospect of using water as a vehicle for drugs. Fluoride is a corrosive poison that will produce serious effects on a long range basis. Any attempt to use water this way is deplorable."—Dr. Charles Gordon Heyd, Past President of the American Medical Association.

- Fluoride may be destroying our bones, our teeth and overall health. It doesn't need to be added to our water and we may be taking unnecessary risks by doing so.—Dr. Hardy Limeback, a leading Canadian fluoride authority, former fluoride advocate and long-standing consultant to Canadian Dental Association.

- "The evidence against the safety of this public health policy keeps mounting; it is too compelling to ignore."—Dr. Phyllis Mullenix, Children's Hospital, Boston

- "By 1983 I was thoroughly convinced that fluoridation caused more harm than good. I expressed the opinion that some of these children with dental fluorosis could, just possibly, have also suffered harm to their bones"—Dr. Colquhoun, former Principal Dental Officer for Auckland New Zealand.

- "…the evidence is quite convincing that the addition of sodium fluoride to the public water supply at one part per million is extremely deleterious to the human body".—Chief Justice John Flaherty, of the Supreme Court of Pennsylvania (presided over litigation involving fluoridation)

- "This record is barren of any credible and reputable scientific epidemiological studies and/or analysis of statistical data which would support the Illinois Legislatures determination that fluoridation of the water supplies is both a safe and effective means of promoting public health."—Illinois Judge Ronald Niemann (presided over litigation involving fluoridation)

- "The artificial fluoridation of public water supplies, such as contemplated by (Houston) City ordinance No. 80—2530 may cause or may contribute to the cause of cancer, genetic damage, intolerant reactions, and chronic toxicity, including dental mottling, in man; that the said artificial fluoridation may aggravate malnutrition and existing illnesses in man; and that the value of said artificial fluoridation is in doubt as to the reduction of tooth decay in man."—Texas Judge Anthony Farris (presided over litigation involving fluoridation)

- "E.P.A. should act immediately to protect the public, not just on the cancer data, but on the evidence of bone fractures, arthritis, mutagenicity and other effects."—Dr. William Marcus, Senior Toxicologist at E.P.A.

- "…fluoride damages bone even at levels added to public drinking water" *American Journal of Epidemiology*, October 1999

- "Since 1990, five major epidemiological studies from three countries—the United States, United Kingdom and France—showing a higher rate of hip fractures in fluoridated regions." Australian & New Zealand *Journal of Public Health*, 1997 vol. 21 no. 24

- "...significant increase in the risk of hip fracture in both men and women exposed to artificial fluoridation at 1 ppm." *Journal of the American Medical Association*, August 1992

- In 1996, there were approximately 340,000 hospital admissions for hip fractures in the United States. Women sustain 75 percent to 80 percent of all hip fractures. Medicare costs for hip fractures were estimated at $2.9 billion in 1991. Centers for Disease Control

- "About one-half of the people with hip fractures end up in nursing homes, and in the year following the fracture, 20 per cent of them die." Harold Slavkin, Director of National Institute of Dental Research (JADA 1999)

- "Water contains a number of substances that are undesirable, and fluorides are just one of them" stated Dr. F. A. Bull, State Dental Director of Wisconsin, speaking at the Fourth Annual Conference of State Dental Directors.

- Hundreds of millions of dollars may be wasted annually on children's fluoride treatments by dentists. Typically given once or twice a year at routine checkups, the treatments do nothing to reduce cavities in kids, says a study of insurance records. Journal of Public Health Dentistry

- In June of 1999, the Majority Chairman of the Environmental Resources Committee, Pennsylvania House of Representatives stated "...there is no solid scientific or medical evidence to show that fluoridation is of any beneficial help to public health, safety or welfare."

- The Washington Bureau editor of *AD Impact*, the monthly publication of the Academy of General Dentistry, wrote last year that supporters of fluoridation have had an "unwillingness to release any information that would cast fluorides in a negative light, "and that organized dentistry has lost "its objectivity—the ability to consider varying viewpoints together with scientific data to reach a sensible conclusion."

- "All of the organizations promoting water fluoridation agree that dental fluorosis, which is the first visible sign of systemic poisoning, increases with water fluoride levels." Dr. Kennedy, Past President of International Academy of Oral Medicine and Toxicology and a practicing Dentist for 20 years.[8]

---

8.   "Respected Medical Professionals and Scientists are warning that water fluoridation has dangerous long-term consequences to health," Citizens for Safe Drinking Water, Mountain View, California website: www.nofluoride.com/index.html, 2002

During your next visit to the dentist, you can take this chapter with you and have a nice argument. But I have to warn you that you probably won't even make a dent in your dentist's brain, because brainwashing is more powerful than a bunch of quotes from scientific experts who dare to challenge corporate industrialists who have controlled the media for the past 50 years. Good luck anyway.

# State of the
# Union Address

The president traditionally prepares a speech with his professional writers, goes on television and delivers to the American public his "State of the Union" address. He gets all pretentious, feigns a smile, dresses in a dark blue suit and red tie as he sits at his desk in front of the American flag, then tells us to tighten our belts because the economy is, will be, or has gone through, a trying time. He tells us that we must band together because we are the greatest nation on earth and we are the leaders of the free world. He tells us that we must take responsibility for our actions and have family values and share the American dream and work hard. Yes, we've heard it over and over and over again—the same exact way.

Just once, I would like to see the president—Ms. President, perhaps—sit down by her swimming pool wearing gardening clothes and sipping on an organically grown lemonade beneath a big umbrella and deliver this State of the Union Address:

> Good morning, fellow Americans. I have just taken office and, unlike anyone ever before me, I have made a real plan that is going to take some hard work, dedication and sacrifice. But this time it is the huge industrial giants that are going to bear the responsibility. We're starting by making them pay taxes they've been avoiding for all these years.
>
> We are sick and tired of being abused by shameless corporate activities that support the few while the rest of Americans have to eat their toxic dust.
>
> That's right, I am calling on Monsanto, Union Carbide, Ford Motor Company, Kellogg, General Mills, General Motors, Kodak, Halliburton, all the electric companies, Exxon, Shell Oil, Westinghouse, the Disney characters, and all the others to tighten their belts, fasten their seat belts and take a shot of organic carrot juice, because I'm going to drive their asses screaming and kicking if necessary into a cleaner, more responsible, environmentally friendlier and peaceful coexistence with the American people who are now paying with their lives and health for innumerable misdeeds stemming from their shameless greed and lack of conscience. No product shall be manufactured, sold or made legal if it destroys life, gives our families cancer and other

diseases, ruins the planet, robs our children of their future, or contains sub-stances that are not natural. Period.

Further, if our industries want to plunder and abuse our citizens while lying to them through crafty public relations and slick television ads, then out you go! Out! You cannot do business in this great nation. And you can't rake in billions of dollars and do your banking offshore so that this nation cannot benefit from supporting you.

We shall not tolerate another moment as you wipe out our forests, turn our air black, change the weather patterns of the world with global warming, murder other peoples in other nations for their natural resources, poison our foods with synthetic pesticides and fertilizers or produce waste products that we have no way of getting rid of.

This is tough love, baby! And don't talk back to your mother, because I'm driving the car now, and I'm really pissed!

I hope she gets elected soon, makes this State of the Union address and forces the big bad boys to behave like human beings, because we are all running out of time (and resources) FAST.

## WHAT IS THE STATE OF OUR UNION?

We are in no condition to say what condition we are in. While during every State of the Union address the president talks about our military might, defending our homeland, fighting drug abuse, making America more prosperous (not Ameri-cans, but America), extolling the importance of education and promoting a bud-get to benefit the few, he continues to ignore a problem historically swept under the rug. Now the rug can't hold any more dirt. The truth, Mr. President? The truth is that our nation is suffering from chemical poisoning and you aren't doing a damn thing about it, because you really don't care. In fact, you're actually part of the problem. You (whether Democrat or Republican—it doesn't matter which) are rich and greedy and so are the other politicians in your circle who are drinking cocktails up on the Hill [Washington, D.C., where important decisions about our families' futures are discussed by powerful millionaires with private corporations involved in public affairs]. Poisonous chemicals from America's industries are killing children, disfiguring women and breaking men. How can this be kept secret any longer? It can't.

Just a thought.

# Most People
# Eat Poisoned Foods

Most of today's modern foods contain toxic substances—the kinds of food you buy in most grocery stores across the nation—and the government allows companies to put them in your food supply. This statement is true as well for cosmetic products and other substances people put on their bodies, use to clean their homes and spray on themselves, their lawns and their toe nails, but this comes as a shock to most people. Instead of just trusting me on this poison issue, it would be a better idea if you took a trip to the local grocery store—or even your food pantry for that matter—and start reading labels with great curiosity and verve.

Just like the rest of America, I never used to read labels either. I used to buy the foods that tasted best to me then go home and eat them. Topping my list were pasta sauce, spaghetti, frozen vegetables, ice cream, chocolate chip cookies featuring funny little cartoon people on the package, cheese, crackers, soft drinks, soups and bread. Plus more. Then, many years ago, my wife was driving home from work and was stopped in traffic. She looked to her right and noticed a small health food store on the corner. Neither one of us ever set foot in a health food store up until that point, because, like most of the rest of America at that time, we thought it would be too weird and the food would be strange and disgusting. I guess I was afraid that I would be force-fed seaweed and purple beans by a band of bead-clad hippies chanting a monosyllabic sound designed to launch people into the astral plane. This day was different because, alone and courageous, my wife contemplated on the store while stuck in traffic. The clouds parted and a shaft of light beamed down onto the roof and set the whole place aglow. She didn't actually tell me this, but maybe there was even some heavenly, angelic music ringing out of some white light. In any event, my wife's car was mysteriously guided to the parking lot. She got out of her car and boldly entered the store. The clerk behind the counter asked her if he could be of service, and she said, "I want to know if there's a book I can read about how to feed my family healthier food." Why it occurred to her to seek a healthier diet for her family is still a mystery, but this was the beginning of a long, fun and healthy journey for our family, friends, acquaintances, and anyone reading this book.

The book my wife was given was written by Dr. Bernard Jensen, one of the pioneers of healthful eating and natural health care. It was called *Better Health Through Your Kitchen*, and talked all about how most people are not eating real foods anymore in today's modern world, and this was making everyone sick. Quite a premise, and quite a shock to us. This is what set us on the path to reading food labels every time we went shopping. Instead of just buying foods for their taste, we began to look at foods for their health value. We found that not many foods in the grocery store qualified as health-builders, but instead were health-destroyers. Before long, we realized that we could not eat most of the food that lined the shelves of our longtime grocery store because the foods were filled with chemical ingredients never meant to be ingested by human beings—chemicals our whole family had been consuming for years. Some of these chemicals contained within packaged foods include dyes, colorings, emulsifiers, separators, artificial flavors, stabilizers, MSG, artificial sweeteners, thickeners and preservatives. Then we found out that all of the produce—from the lettuce to the tomatoes, from the potatoes to the squash, and from the green beans to the apples—contain pesticides and synthetic fertilizer residues. Finally we discovered that meats—from chicken to beef—contain hormones, steroids, sulfites, antibiotics, mineral salts and drug residues. Even our drinking water, we learned, was contaminated with poisons and heavy metals. All of these chemicals are bad for your health, and most can cause cancer, so we decided to stop eating foods that contain them. We had to start shopping at the health food store. We started buying only organically grown foods. And we got healthier and healthier over the years. Now as a matter of course I read every label on every food package as if I've been doing it all my life. The moral of this story is that the foods most people eat make them sick without them knowing it, and there are better, healthier alternatives that not only taste much better, but actually promote good health.

## *POISONS IN YOUR FOODS*

We may be a little far along in this book to ask this question, but now is as good a time as any: What is a poison? One dictionary describes a poison as "any agent which, when introduced into the animal organism, is capable of producing a morbid, noxious, or deadly effect upon it."[1] This covers a lot of ground. By this a definition, a poison can be emitted through your car's exhaust pipe, sprayed from

---

1.   dictionary.com

a can of bug repellent, found on your food as pesticide residues, or mixed in with your drinking water in the form of fluoride. The word "toxin" is used interchangeably. In either case, toxic and poisonous substances make us sick and may cause death. This having been said, you may ask, "What would poisons be doing on or in my food?" I wondered the same thing before realizing that it is not illegal for companies to put poisons in their foods. The reason for this is rather complex, including that the packaged, processed food industry pulls a lot of political weight and exerts a lot of political pressure and influence to perpetuate their poisonous practices. The monetary benefit of putting chemicals in their foods outweighs any concern for public health. Chemicals in processed foods serve a number of benefits for the food manufacturer, as the following Australian/New Zealand report shows.

> Some food additives have more than one use. Food additives are listed according to their functional or class names. Examples of the most common functions are:
>
> - **Colourings** add or restore colour to foods
>
> - **Colour retentions agents** retain or intensify the colour of food
>
> - **Preservatives** help protect against deterioration caused by microorganisms
>
> - **Artificial sweetening substances** are substances which impart a sweet taste for fewer kilojoules or calories than sugar
>
> - **Flavour enhancers** improve the flavour and/or aroma of food
>
> - **Flavourings** restore taste losses due to processing, maintain uniformity and make food more palatable
>
> - **Anti-caking agents** keep powdered products such as salt, flowing freely when poured
>
> - **Emulsifiers** help to prevent oil and water mixtures from separating into layers
>
> - **Food acids** help maintain a constant level of sourness in food
>
> - **Humectants** prevent foods such as dried fruit from drying out
>
> - **Mineral salts** improve the texture of foods, such as processed meats

- **Thickeners and vegetable gums** improve texture and maintain uniform consistency

- **Stabilisers** maintain the uniform dispersion of substances in a food

- **Flour treatment agents** are substances added to flour to improve baking quality and appearance

- **Glazing agents** impart a shiny appearance or provide a protective coating to a food

- **Propellants** are gases which help propel food from a container[2]

There are several scientists, universities, associations, trade groups and doctors who are now saying that artificial chemicals in foods are safe and do not cause cancer. Here is one typical example of their absurd hogwash:

Stories in newspapers and on television have focused public attention on synthetic chemicals in food—things like pesticides, or chemicals that form during processing. But current scientific research indicates that the small amounts of individual chemicals in the foods we eat are not a major cause of human cancers. In fact, the cancer risk posed by any individual chemical in food is probably negligible.

It's a good thing, too, because people cannot avoid eating the wide variety of chemicals in foods, including some toxic chemicals [I guess this "expert" never heard of organic foods]. Many plants contain naturally occurring toxins. In other cases, naturally occurring contaminants—like the mycotoxins generated by fungi that contaminate grains and nuts—have been shown to cause cancer.

These naturally occurring chemicals are just as potent as the synthetic chemicals more often identified as carcinogens. And we probably are exposed to many more of the naturally occurring kind—partly because regulations protect us by preventing many synthetic carcinogens from entering foods.

Foods do contribute to cancer. It is estimated that as many as one third of the half million deaths caused by cancer in this country each year may be linked to what people eat or do not eat. But the primary culprit in these deaths seems to be the total amount of calories eaten—and perhaps too many fats as a proportion of those calories.[3]

---

2.    "Food Additives Shoppers' Guide," Food Standards, Australia/New Zealand, April 2001

3.    Estabrook, Ronald W., "Answering Questions About Diet and Cancer," National Academy of Sciences, Washington, DC, March 15, 1996

Is this the best they can come up with? It's pretty pathetic. The Evil Genius who wrote this stupid stuff is saying that natural, real foods are the cause of cancer. Curious, because the cancer rate has been correlated with the rise in industry, yet human beings have been eating natural foods since they appeared in the misty recesses of time.

The above PR crappola is wrong on a number of counts. In fact, it's an insult to the intelligence! The first thing is that the writer is choosing to ignore the most fundamental of all facts, which is that the human body is not equipped to be fed human-made chemicals, flecks of Teflon, aluminum powder, golf balls, socket wrenches, bug spray, herbicides or hockey pucks. The body is designed to consume NATURAL foods because the body is not a robot, but rather a living, dynamic, complex entity that gets sick when you feed it artificial ingredients. This is undeniable to anyone who has eaten a chemical-free-only diet for more than several years. Once you have weaned yourself off chemicals, you realize how they were sapping the life out of you, not to mention causing so many health problems that you couldn't keep track of them all. Also, we have to remind the industry-paid "experts" they have no way to determine the infinite varieties and combinations of chemicals that people are ingesting through their foods. Chemicals are combining with other chemicals, creating chemical concoctions unforeseen in the laboratory. They cannot determine whether chemicals are safe for everyone, because we are all so different in our body types, dispositions, genetic strengths and weaknesses, and so on.

Corporate scientists and other food industry mouth-pieces are fond of telling us that it's not the chemicals in foods that are hazardous to your health, but rather the calories, fats, microbes (germs) and even naturally occurring phytochemicals that we should be concerned about. This is just a foul smokescreen to take the pressure off of them, and keep the public from giving anything more than a cursory thought about ARTIFICIAL chemicals and their ever-present, real dangers. As the health food industry continues to gain strength and popularity, this is the best they can come up with—trying to tell mothers that it's okay if their children eat artificial ingredients. If you listen to them, they will also tell you that breast milk, which has sustained human life on this planet since the beginning—is not as good as chemicalized baby foods.

On this topic, journalist Peter Montague has shown that "Heavy marketing by the baby food industry has contributed to a drop in breastfeeding rates in both the United States and Third World nations. Advertisers intend to convince women that breastfeeding their babies isn't modern, and that bottle-feeding is healthier. The premise of such advertising is medically unfounded. Breastfeeding provides infants with significant immunity to disease, as well as creating an emotional bond between mother and child."[4] Further, babies are designed, biologically, to nurse from their mothers breasts, whereas baby formulas are unnatural concoctions of modern scientists hired by the processed food industry. Baby formula, Montague writes, "leads to 1.5 million infant deaths each year in Third World countries, as mothers often unwittingly prepare the formula with contaminated water, causing fatal diarrhea. According to the United Nations Children's Fund (UNCF) only 44 percent of women in Third World countries currently breastfeed."[5]

There are a number of questionable ingredients in today's baby formulas and baby foods, chief of which are meat, milk, pesticides, soy protein isolates and other chemicals that alter, accelerate and disrupt normal hormonal activity. Of course, the baby food and chemical industries disagree, but the evidence of premature sexual development is mounting worldwide. Time magazine reported that there is a "disturbing increase in early puberty among girls in the US. According to a recent study reported in the journal *Pediatrics*, one percent of all American girls now show signs of puberty, such as breast development or pubic hair, before the age of three; by age eight, 14.7 percent of white girls and almost 50 percent of African-American girls had one or both of these characteristics."[6] In response, writes researcher Sally Fallon, a 1998 issue of *Nutrition Reviews...*

> published an article by K. O. Klein of DuPont Hospital for Children as proof that soy infant formulas do no harm. Yet in the article Klein notes that effects of isoflavones on various animal species include hormonal changes, increased uterine weight and infertility. "It is clear from the literature," says Klein, "that different species and different tissues are affected by isoflavones in markedly different ways. It is difficult to know which tissues, if any, are affected in infants, and the variation among species makes extrapolation to infants inappropriate." This is scientific double talk. Scientists may be reluctant to extrapolate but parents would certainly err on the side of caution if they knew that "isoflavones affect different tissues in markedly different ways."
>
> Klein says that medical literature provides "no evidence of endocrine effects...and no changes in timing of puberty." But she makes no mention of the Puerto Rican study which strongly implicated soy formula. Why would Dr. Klein leave out any reference to the Puerto Rican study in her review? Is it

---

4.  Phillips, PhD, Peter, *Censored* 2001, p. 77
5.  ibid
6.  Fallon, Sally and Mary G. Enig, PhD, "Teens Before Their Time," Weston Price Foundation

because DuPont, owner of Protein Technologies International, is the leading manufacturer of soy protein isolate?

Or is it because her review was sponsored by the Infant Formula Council? Or because *Nutrition Reviews*, which published her whitewash, is funded by industry giants, including Pillsbury, Hershey Foods, Kellogg, Roche, General Mills, Kraft, Campbell Soup, Monsanto, Coca-Cola, Cargill, Heinz, Nabisco, Proctor and Gamble and Pepsi-Cola?[7]

The alternative to processed baby foods? Breastfeeding is, of course, the most natural way to go. When your baby is old enough to eat solid foods, instead of getting jarred food, feed him/her real, organic foods mushed and mashed in the blender. Remember that many so-called food allergies among children may be due to artificial ingredients and pesticide residues rather than the food itself. Your pediatrician should be supportive of your desire to feed your baby a well-rounded, raw vegetable and fruit medley. Also, avoid feeding your baby cow's milk for two main reasons: First, the milk you buy at the store is pasteurized, which means it's dead, contains altered fats and proteins and is not, for the most part, nutritious. Second, your baby is not a calf.

## LET'S PICK ON ASPARTAME
### Artificial sweeteners are not foods and are certainly not natural.

There are so many health-harming chemicals in foods that it is safe to say that any spokesperson, researcher, scientist or university professor claiming that there is no danger has to be a liar. They are feeding us lies in hopes that we won't look any further into the issue. Consider the effects of aspartame, the artificial sweetener found in soft drinks and fake-sugar packets in every restaurant and grocery store from New Jersey to Oregon, for example:

> In February of 1994, the U.S. Department of Health and Human Services released the listing of adverse reactions reported to the FDA (DHHS 1994). Aspartame accounted for more than 75% of all adverse reactions reported to the FDA's Adverse Reaction Monitoring System (ARMS). Many reactions to aspartame were very serious, including seizures and death. Other reactions reported included:
>
> Headaches/Migraines Dizziness
>
> Joint Pain Nausea

---

7.   ibid

Numbness Muscle spasms

Weight gain Rashes

Depression Fatigue

Irritability Tachycardia

Insomnia Vision Loss

Hearing Loss Heart palpitations

Breathing difficulties Anxiety attacks

Slurred Speech Loss of taste

Tinnitus Vertigo

Memory loss

Both the U.S. Air Force's magazine "Flying Safety" and the U.S. Navy's magazine, "Navy Physiology" published articles warning about the many dangers of aspartame including the cumulative deleterious effects of methanol and the greater likelihood of birth defects. The articles note that the ingestion of aspartame may make pilots more susceptible to seizures and vertigo (US Air Force 1992).

Recently, a hotline was set up for pilots suffering from acute reactions to aspartame ingestion. Nearly 1,000 pilots have reported symptoms including some who have reported suffering grand mal seizures in the cockpit due to aspartame (Stoddard 1995b). The danger to pilots of tunnel vision, blurred vision, seizures, vertigo and other serious adverse reactions, who may ingest large amounts of aspartame products during flight, are so great that articles and letters warning about aspartame have appeared in many aviation-related journals including *The Aviation Consumer* (1988), *Aviation Medical Bulletin* (1988), *Pacific Flyer* (1988), *CAA General Aviation* (1989), *Aviation Safety Digest* (1989), *General Aviation News* (1989), *Plane & Pilot* (1990), *Canadian General Aviation News* (1990), *National Business Aircraft Association Digest* (*NBAA Digest* 1993), International Council of Air Shows (ICAS 1995), *Pacific Flyer* (1995) and a paper warning about aspartame was presented at the 57th Annual Meeting of the Aerospace Medical Association (Gaffney 1986).

Well over 7,000 citizens have submitted adverse reaction reports to the FDA since 1982 (DHHS 1993b, DHHS 1995). These reports detail well over 10,000 complaints of 92 different symptoms, many of them very serious. Many more people may have called the FDA to report adverse reactions only to get turned away.[8]

---

8.    Galloway, Paul, http://allergies.about.com/cs/additives/index_2.htm, Sept. 1996

Aspartame remains an uncontrolled substance packaged and sold without warning while an herbal sweetener called stevia is considered illegal due to the political influence of chemical food manufacturers. As discussed, the food manufacturing industry employs scientists, doctors and other "experts" who even work for universities receiving **huge financial donations**, to prove that chemicals are safe, wonderful and life-enhancing. Studies on aspartame, to name one of thousands of artificial ingredients that follow the same hazardous trail, are questionable at best, and downright fraudulent at worst. Regarding aspartame, the following shows how industry-funded studies report industry propaganda in the guise of scientific findings:

An analysis of peer reviewed medical literature using MEDLINE and other databases was conducted by Ralph G. Walton, MD, Chairman, The Center for Behavioral Medicine, Professor of Clinical Psychiatry, Northeastern Ohio Universities College of Medicine. Dr. Walton analyzed 164 studies which were felt to have relevance to human safety questions. Of those studies, 74 studies had aspartame industry-related sponsorship and 90 were funded without any industry money.

> Of the 90 non-industry-sponsored studies, 83 (92%) identified one or more problems with aspartame. Of the 7 studies which did not find a problems, 6 of those studies were conducted by the FDA. Given that a number of FDA officials went to work for the aspartame industry immediately following approval (including the former FDA Commissioner), many consider these studies to be equivalent to industry-sponsored research.
>
> Of the 74 aspartame industry-sponsored studies, all 74 (100%) claimed that no problems were found with aspartame. This is reminiscent of tobacco industry research where it is primarily the tobacco research which never finds problems with the product, but nearly all of the independent studies do find problems.
>
> The 74 aspartame industry-sponsored studies are those which one invariably sees cited in PR/news reports and reported by organizations funded by Monsanto/Benevia/NutraSweet (e.g., IFIC, ADA). These studies have severe design deficiencies which help to guarantee the "desired" outcomes. These design deficiencies may not be apparent to the inexperienced scientist.[9]

Nor are these design differences made apparent to endangered consumers—i.e., you and I.

---

9.    "Analysis Shows Nearly 100% of Independent Research Finds Problems With Aspartame," http://www.holisticmed.com/aspartame/100.html, October 17, 1996

## WHAT ARE THE 'INDEPENDENT' ASSOCIATIONS SAYING? WHO CARES? THEY'RE INDUSTRY-FUNDED

This brings us to the subject of research, researchers and research-funding organizations. Can we believe what associations report through our media? We have to closely scrutinize any association to find out if it is an industry front posing as a detached, objective entity.

Since some evil genius figured out that research could be created, massaged, bought-off, bought up and influenced, chemicals have ubiquitously been delivered to our dinner plates posing as food. Industry's evil geniuses invented "Independent associations" to back up their corporation's claims that people are healthier—or not affected by—(depending on the propaganda slant) chemical consumption. Now we can see (read *Trust Us, We're Experts* and *Global Spin* for in-depth exposés on industry-directed research and reporting) that "independent research" may not be so independent, making their "findings" and reports nothing short of public deception. One such example of an association with an impressive name is the American Council on Science and Health. Why believe what we hear out of this group (or others that we really know very little about)? Now let's look a little closer and see what the American Council on Science and Health (ACSH) is made of:

> Corporate funders for the American Council on Science and Health have included American Cyanamid, American Meat Institute, Amoco, Anheuser-Busch, Archer Daniels Midland, Ashland Oil Foundation, Boise Cascade, Bristol-Myers Squibb, Burger King, Chevron, Ciba-Geigy, Coca-Cola, Consolidated Edison, Coors, Dow Chemical, DuPont, Exxon, Ford Motor Co., Frito-Lay, General Electric, General Mills, General Motors, Hershey Foods, Johnson & Johnson, Joseph E. Seagrams & Sons, Kraft Foundation, Kraft General Foods, Merck Pharmaceuticals, Mobil, Monsanto, National Agricultural Chemicals Association, National Dairy Council, National Soft Drink Association, National Starch and Chemical Foundation, Nestlé, NutraSweet Co. (owned by Monsanto), Oscar Mayer Foods, Pepsi-Cola, Pfizer, Procter & Gamble, Shell Oil, Sugar Association, Union Carbide Corp., Uniroyal Chemical Co., USX Corp., and Wine Growers of California.[10]

---

10. PR Watch Archives, http://www.prwatch.org/prissues/1998Q4/kellogs.html, "Integrity Ain't Cheap," Volume 5, No. 4, 2002

At least a couple of these companies seem like they'd be a bit biased in trying to achieve objective reporting. Can you trust the Sugar Association, for instance, to tell you that sugar is bad for your health? What about The Dairy Council? Do you think they would give you an honest answer about the health effects of hormone residues in their milk? Companies supporting the American Council on Science and Health and similar groups have a boatload to lose should the public start questioning why their foods are loaded with chemicals scientifically proven to cause allergies, headaches, cancer, heart disease, clogged arteries, infertility or diabetes.

The degree to which America's associations are tainted by industry money is phenomenal. We have come to think of the American Heart Association and others as above the rhetoric and commercialism associated with corporate ways of doing business; but we have been duped, because the long tentacles of the corporate octopus have reached the shores of the most prestigious and high-profile of our nonprofit institutions. The Center for Media & Democracy explains:

> Corporate sponsors have formed "partnerships" with a number of leading nonprofit organizations in which they pay for the right to use the organizations' names and logos in advertisements. Bristol-Myers Squibb, for example, paid $600,000 to the American Heart Association for the right to display the AHA's name and logo in ads for its cholesterol-lowering drug Pravachol. The American Cancer Society reeled in $1 million from SmithKline Beecham for the right to use its logo in ads for Beecham's NicoDerm CQ and Nicorette antismoking aids. A Johnson & Johnson subsidiary countered by shelling out $2.5 million for similar rights from the American Lung Association in its ads for Nicotrol, a rival nicotine patch. In 1999 manufacturers spent $630 million on these and similar kinds of sponsorship deals, some unseemly, such as a deal between the Eskimo Pie Corporation and the American Diabetes Association, which was designed to create the impression that Eskimo's "Sugar Freedom" line of frozen desserts was endorsed by the American Diabetes Association, when in fact the desserts contain high levels of both total and saturated fat—a risky dietary choice for diabetics, who have a propensity for obesity and heart disease. Although the nonprofit organizations involved in these deals deny that the use of their names and logos constitutes an endorsement, the corporate sponsors have no such illusions. "PR pros view those third-party endorsements as invaluable ways to build goodwill among consumers for a client's product line," noted O'*Dwyer's PR Services Report.*[11]

---

11.   Center for Media & Democracy, "What is Impropaganda?", prwatch.org, 2002

## *ARTIFICIAL CHEMICALS DON'T BELONG IN OUR BODIES*

For non-profit associations to be free of the temptation to espouse industry-corporate scientific findings, they'd have to forego millions of dollars in payoffs—I mean, donations. Not gonna happen. The fact that industry funds these associations makes them, by default, untrustworthy and unable to fully devote themselves to the public good.

When it comes to artificial chemicals in your food, use your logic and think. Artificial chemicals are not indigenous to the human organism. The body revolts and tries to get rid of them, and they cause pimples, indigestion, headaches, hormonal interference, tooth decay, aching joints, weight gain, rashes, hair fallout, and yes, even cancer. To blame health problems on calories and naturally occurring food ingredients is ridiculous rhetoric from an industry trying to justify the reasoning for poisoning your family. Where is it written that human beings need to have human-made chemicals in their foods for health and survival? Maybe it's in the Bible in the story of Exodus:

> Go forth, Moses, God commanded. Go forth and tell thy people to eat not of My Food nor off My Lands, but rather artificial chemicals because scientists are smarter than I. Now take thine staff and get the flock out of here!

Or maybe we missed this concept during the Last Supper where Jesus was surrounded by the apostles at the Passover dinner. On the table was a rack of lamb, wine, soup, matzoh and a box of chocolate chip cookies filled with food dyes, artificial colorings, preservatives and chemical flavorings. Playing with little pink packets of NutraSweet, Jesus joshed with his disciples, saying, "To Satan with all this wonderful food at this blessed supper, Thou shalt partake only in the Twinkies and Cheese-Ohs, for they are filled with chemicals made by scientists who know better than thy Father."

## *WHAT ARE SOME ARTIFICIAL INGREDIENTS TO PURGE FROM YOUR DIET?*

There is a plethora of artificial chemicals contained in today's grocery store foods. My personal opinion is that you should avoid all of them, in an ideal situation. The fewer you have in your body, the healthier you will be. Here are ten chemicals to avoid right off the bat:

**ASPARTAME**: This chemical sweetener has the longest list of complaints the FDA has ever received. Aspartame also goes under such brands as NutraSweet and Equal. Symptoms associated with aspartame sensitivity can range from rashes, mild depression, headaches, nausea, ringing ears, vertigo and insomnia to loss of motor control, loss or change of taste, slurred speech, memory loss, blurred vision, blindness, suicidal depression and seizures.

**BROMINATED VEGETABLE OIL (BVO)**: A potentially dangerous additive for some people, BVO is used as an emulsifier in some foods and as a clouding agent in many popular soft drinks, Bromate, the main ingredient of BVO, is a poison. Just two to four ounces of a 2 percent solution of BVO can severely poison a child.

**BUTYLATED HYDROXYANISOLE (BHA) AND BUTYLATED HYDROXYTOLUENE (BHT)**: Used to prevent fats, oils and fat-containing foods from becoming rancid, BHA or BHT is often added to food packaging materials. Researchers report that BHA in the diet of the pregnant mice results in brain enzyme changes in their offspring including a 50% decreased activity in brain cholinesterase, which is responsible for the transmission of nerve impulses. BHA and BHT also affect the animals' sleep, levels of aggression, and weight. The authors of the study speculate that BHA and BHT can affect the normal sequence of neurological development in young animals too. Many consumers eat nearly 20 milligrams or more of BHA or BHT daily. Babies who are beginning to eat solid foods are estimated to ingest as much as eight milligrams per day.

**CITRUS RED DYE NO. 2**: Used to color orange skins, Citrus Red Dye No.2 is a probable carcinogen and may cause chromosomal damage. Some experts contend that this compound does not migrate from the orange skin onto the pulp but the FDA has recommended a ban. Its continued use should be one more reason to seek organically grown foods.

**MONOSODIUM GLUTAMATE**: Also known as MSG, monosodium glutamate is a "flavor enhancer" often found in fast food, and packaged food. Sensitivity symptoms include headaches, flushing of the skin, tightness of the chest, heart palpitations, and nausea.

**NITRATES**: Nitrates are used as preservatives in cured meats such as bacon, ham and smoked fish to prevent spoilage. Nitrates form cancer causing compounds, known as nitrosamines in the gastrointestinal tract. They have been associated with human cancer and birth defects.

**SACCHARIN**: Still widely used as an artificial sweetener in soft drinks, this additive is a possible human carcinogen. Every packet of Sweet'n'Low has forty milligrams of saccharin.

**SULFUR DIOXIDE, SODIUM BISULFITE AND SULFITES**: These are used to preserve foods such as dried fruits to prevent them from drying and stiffening, and are also used on shrimp and frozen potatoes. The FDA has received hundreds of letters reporting adverse reactions in asthma sufferers who have consumed food with sulfating agents. At least four deaths caused by acute reactions to sulfites have been reported to the FDA.

**TERTIARY BUTYHYDROQUINONE (TBHQ)**: This chemical is often used along with BHA or BHT to spray the insides of cereal and cheeses packages. TBHQ, which is toxic at extremely low doses, has been implicated in childhood behavioral problems. It is mainly found in candy bars, baking sprays, and fast foods.

**YELLOW DYE NO. 6**: Used in candy and carbonated beverages, Yellow Dye No. 6 increases the number of kidney and adrenal gland tumors in rats. It may also cause chromosomal damage as well as allergic reactions. It has been banned in Norway and Sweden.[12]

Unfortunately, there are thousands more. And more are being created every day. If you want a complete list, you will be involved for a long time in a lot of research, because the different types and numbers of chemicals used in today's foods are staggering. Here are a few of sources to begin your own research:

- http://www.truthinlabeling.org/

- http://www.fedupwithfoodadditives.info/THE%20BIG%2050.html (includes a list of 50 food additives to avoid)

- http://www.allergysupport.org/index.php?contents=articles.php&topic=30

- http://www.parentsofallergicchildren.org/food_additives_to_avoid.htm

- http://allergies.about.com/cs/additives/index_2.htm

## WHAT ARE THE HEALTHIEST FOODS TO EAT?

The healthiest foods to eat are organically grown and do not have to list any ingredients because none are added. Examples include **organically grown** apples, pears, peaches, bananas, nuts, seeds, squash, spinach, red leaf lettuce, kale, green beans, eggs, raw cheese, pineapple, carrots, zucchini and more.

---

12.  "TOP TEN FOOD ADDITIVES TO AVOID,"
     http://www.parentsofallergicchildren.org/food_additives_to_avoid.htm,
     Excerpts for "Alternative Medicine", The Definitive Guide. Future Medicine Publishing, Allan Lieberman, M.D., 2002

## WHY DOES THE GOVERNMENT ALLOW
## POISONS TO BE IN OUR FOODS?

If you are asking why the government allows poisonous chemicals to exist in manufactured foods, then you may be the product of mass deception. Join the growing club.

A sucker is created every day. This very truth is what keeps chemical creators in the dough (figuratively and literally). Not only does our government allow harmful chemicals to exist and be included in commercial foods, but they are a huge part of the problem. Instead of watching out for the public's interest, the government is in bed with industry. If we break this down into more personal terms, you can see how this would happen. Have you ever been in school, a club or at work and noticed there are certain groups of individuals who want to take over and control everything? They are selfish, snobby and power-hungry. Well, we have to stop seeing the government as some giant machine that exists to serve us faithfully and protect us from ill health. We have to see it as an institution made up of imperfect individuals with personal agendas who are willing to trade our health for some benefit meaningful for themselves. Is this corruption? It sure is! And it's here to stay, because history shows that government corruption goes back to Ancient Egypt and beyond. Bible Stories and ancient mythologies depict corruption and back-stabbing. Societies are forever battling government corruption and individual greed that injures the public in more ways than one. Every year we see some government official being carted off to jail because of some self-serving activity that ended when he or she got a hand caught in the cookie jar. Admission of wrong-doing is becoming as scarce as truth these days, and hiding nefarious activities, by way of media compliance, is now an art form.

Our most powerful government department overseeing foods is the Food and Drug Administration (FDA), which has come under attack over the years for being a better friend and confidant of industry than of the taxpayer. The FDA consistently gives its stamp of official approval on questionable, toxic, poisonous and health-destroying chemicals at the expense of our public health. Take the MSG issue, for example. It seems that everybody admits that MSG is bad for your health except our own government officials. MSG (monosodium glutamate) is used as a preservative and flavor-enhancer, but it has been known to hospitalize many people who have consumed it. The lightest side effect may be a mild headache, but severe reactions, which are not uncommon, are far more devastating. Nowadays, MSG is found not only in Chinese restaurant food, but in thousands of other products, from soups to seasonings. Even baby food is tainted. Here's one writer's plea regarding the FDA's approval of MSG in baby formula:

> One would think that even an agency as financially and morally corrupt as the FDA would have a finite limit to its [bias], but that imaginary "envelope" gets pushed harder with each passing year. Even those of you who have grown jaded with the accumulating data suggesting FDA corruption will be appalled to know that MSG and Aspartic acid have been found, in alarming quantities, in baby food and infant formula. If you are the parent of an infant, or know someone who is, please take note of the following information, posted on http://www.truthinlabeling.org on January 8, 2000.
>
> Why are no members of the national news core conducting ANY investigation into this outrage? Has their objectivity been compromised by the millions of dollars in advertising revenue they receive from the guilty parties in this case? Why are so few elected officials voicing suspicion about the conduct of the FDA? Why are so many members of government regulatory agencies also former employees of Monsanto? How many problems of depression, sickness, crime, and insanity are at least partly attributable to the American diet? How much farther must our collective health sink before a SINGLE "respected" journalist will dare to ask these questions? It's truly sad that in 2000 America, people must be ferociously diligent when making nutritional choices for themselves and their families. Eating what you "feel like" or what is convenient is no longer an option, and infants are obviously unable to make health choices for themselves. Since we can't rely on our elected, un-elected, and universally unaccountable officials to do the right thing, we must empower ourselves to protect our children and ourselves.[13]

Another example of how the FDA favors industry (in this case the seafood industry) and ignores public health may be found in a recent failure to inform mothers about known mercury toxicity. The Environmental Working Group (EWG) reported:

> Washington—Internal Food and Drug Administration (FDA) documents obtained by the Environmental Working Group (EWG) reveal that the agency is failing in its public health obligation to protect pregnant women and the developing fetus from the toxic effects of mercury. The FDA cites focus group research as a justification for its severely limited consumer advisory on fish that should be avoided by pregnant women. However, transcripts of the focus groups reveal that the agency knows its standards don't protect the fetus, knows that adequate protection would mean adding tuna to the list of

---

13.   Goodspeed, Michael MSG In Baby Food—It Doesn't Get Any Worse Than This, http://jassekhmet.tripod.com/msg_BF.htm

restricted fish, and knows that women want as much information as possible, preferably from their doctors.

"The FDA is ignoring the science on mercury and ignoring health information women want and need, while using focus groups as an excuse," said Jane Houlihan, EWG's Vice President for Research. "The problem is not FDA using focus groups to determine **how** it should communicate concerns about mercury in fish to women. The problem is the FDA using focus groups to determine **if** it should communicate concerns about mercury in fish to women."

Both the U.S. Environmental Protection Agency (EPA) and the National Academy of Sciences (NAS) have recognized that mercury is a substantial public health problem, and recommend much stricter standards for allowable levels of mercury in fish than the FDA. The NAS estimates that every year approximately 60,000 children are born at a significantly increased risk of neurological effects from mercury because of the contaminated fish their mothers ate. The NAS is also concerned that, aside from the extremely high exposure cases, there is a broad, low-level mercury exposure potential that could push a greater percentage of the population into the group of children who struggle to keep up in school or who require remedial education. Furthermore, a 2001 Centers for Disease Control study found that 10% of reproductive-age American women already carry so much mercury in their blood that if they got pregnant it could pose a threat of neurological damage to the fetus.[14]

## A LITTLE MORE ABOUT ORGANICALLY GROWN FOODS

Foods that are organically grown are healthier, richer in nutrients and kinder to the environment that we all depend on for life on this planet. However, organic farming gets a bad reputation and a persistently heavy dose of defamation from corporate farming concerns and the chemical industry. Why? Because the latter makes fortunes selling chemicals (despite the fact that they are killing our family members). So the chemical companies make up lies such as "Organic farming just isn't economically viable. Sure, it may look prettier and tread lighter on the land. Heck, it may even produce healthier food. But there's just no way we can produce enough food to feed a hungry world without the help of pesticides and other unhealthy strategies."[15] Despite this kind of brain-bursting rhetoric, here's a sensible viewpoint:

---

14.  Agency Ignores Womens' Opinions in Focus Group Research, Gets Chummy with Seafood Industry, *Environmental Working Group,* February 28, 2002, Focus Pocus: EWG Study Finds FDA Out to Lunch on Protecting Women from Mercury in Fish; http://www.ewg.org/reports/focuspocus/

According to the longest running study in the history of organic agriculture, organic farming is an economically viable alternative to conventional farms that rely on synthetic inputs and toxic chemicals to ensure a successful harvest.

The mammoth 21-year Swiss study compared organic test plots growing barley, potatoes, beets, and wheat to conventionally farmed plots growing the same foods. A total of 96 plots divided into 2 types each of organic and conventional growing methods were extensively studied for over two decades. In that time, researchers found that the organic plots, on average, used 50% less energy, 97% less pesticides and about half as much fertilizer as so-called "traditional" fields.

Furthermore, at the end of the project, the soil in the organic plots remained nutrient rich and water absorbent (i.e. healthy). The amount of microorganisms and root-assisting fungi in the organic soils was far larger and consisted of more total species than was found in the conventional plots. Insects were two times as common, showed similar diversity, and beneficial species like pest-eating spiders and beetles abounded. Also present in the organic fields was a more diverse community of non-crop plant species including some endangered species. These results suggested that in addition to food, organic farms also make a significant contribution to biodiversity.[16]

There is a tremendous cost, impacting the environment, human health and finance, that comes from non-organic farming resulting from soil loss, ground water pollution, air pollution, loss of biodiversity, medical bills, medications, suffering and pain, loss of work and degeneration. When other side effects of conventional (non-organic) farming are factored into the equation, organic methods emerge as more than merely competitive; organic foods are less expensive. It is important for we citizens of the world to realize that conventional farmers do not account on their balance sheets for any of the environmental effects of their operations. Such hidden costs are born by the public. "If better accounting standards were to prevail and force factory farms to report and pay for such obvious expenses, the superiority of organic methods would be crystal clear."[17]

---

15. "Organic Food To Factory Farms: Eat Me…I Passed The Test," The Non—Toxic Times, Seventh Generation electronic report, August 2002
16. ibid
17. ibid

## WHAT YOU CAN DO IF YOU WANT TO STOP POISONING YOUR FAMILY THROUGH THE FOODS THEY EAT:

Beware of the fact that chemical companies, drug companies and giant food manufacturers periodically buy out natural health companies. You have to keep abreast of the fact that today's healthy food choice can be tomorrow's chemical concoction. The playing field is constantly changing. Today's healthy soft drink owned by Mother Nature's Bubbly Soda brand can be tomorrow's same drink owned and operated by the Coca Cola corporation. Of this new wave of corporate buyout, one report states:

> Once, of course, natural foods were an obscure niche product. They were good for maybe a chuckle or two at traditional food company board meetings, but little else as far as the major players were concerned. Now, however, Corporate America couldn't be more interested in gobbling up the companies that are seen by many as the last bastion of healthy independence in an increasingly unsustainable food system. After all, as more and more Americans discover the sordid truth about just what's in their dinner and just how that dinner was made, natural foods are experiencing the kind of growth rates most analysts drool over.

Can we trust Coca-Cola to provide consumers with a healthy drink—even if so-called "organic"—when it's traditional line of soda is packaged in toxic aluminum cans, filled with ridiculous quantities of refined sugars and has no redeeming health value? It may be argued that bigger companies buying out health food manufacturers intend to continue producing health foods under their newly acquired divisions, but suspicion and skepticism are not out of place here. Only time can tell whether huge food manufacturers will stab the consumer in the back by ruining, altering or replacing once-healthy products under trusted brand names. Many such companies have a long history of deceiving and poisoning the public. Why should we believe they are not going to continue such practices under the guise of producing so-called health foods just because they've taken over the production of healthier brands? Or what if their ultimate goal is to buy out their health food competitors to once and for all eradicate health food from the world marketplace? This is not such an unbelievable idea, especially in light of the genetic engineering campaign aimed at replacing all natural seed and food crops with scientifically altered varieties bearing a patent.

Healthy, untrusting paranoids remember that giant corporations on the whole became rich, famous and widespread due to their callous disregard for human health and suffering and their aggressive, cut-throat business practices that have long included hostile and deceptive marketing practices, lies, paid-off scientists, and cost-cutting buying practices. What makes us think that just because they now own a "health food product" that they will not practice business as usual?

Here are some helpful healthy tips:

- Buy organically grown foods ONLY

- Eat mostly raw, organic foods.

- Avoid foods that are genetically engineered/genetically modified (GMO)

- Do not eat refined OR artificial sugars. Stick to raw, unfiltered honey, stevia, and raw maple syrup for your sweeteners.

- Read all labels carefully, but beware that MSG and other chemicals may be present in foods even when not listed on the label

- Be very selective of the types of restaurants you visit. Insist on having the restaurant tell you if MSG, hydrogenated oils, sulfites, sulfates or other chemicals are in their foods

- Stop eating fast foods—they are not healthy and their owners are destroying the environment and indigenous cultures by the minute

- Get involved by pressuring legislators and the FDA to do their jobs and protect you from artificial chemicals in foods

- Go online and lookup the food additives that you find on labels

- If it isn't food, don't eat it. Foods are not named by chemicals

- Support local, organic farmers

- Never assume that any restaurant food is organically grown or devoid of dangerous chemicals

- Eat only organically raised meat and poultry and eggs rather than the commercial alternatives. Commercial beef, pork and poultry farmers have historically abused their animals and inject them with drugs that you ultimately ingest.

# How Toxic Is
# Your Environment?

*"The most alarming of all man's assaults upon the environment is the contamination
of air, earth, rivers and sea with dangerous and even lethal materials."*

—Rachel Carson
author, *Silent Spring*

Have you ever walked along a busy street and noticed that the air is filled with
exhaust? Have you ever washed paint, chlorine or some other chemical down the
drain? Did you notice the air in the airport stinks? Did you ever drive by your
town's dump site and notice how bad it smells? Have you ever eaten out at a restaurant only to return home and vomit your guts out all night long? Welcome to
our saturated world of toxic substances!

The U.S. Environmental Protection Agency estimates that 60,000 people a
year die in the United States alone from particulate air pollution—the kind
caused when small particles of smoke pervade the air.[1] The World Health Organization reports that three million people now die each year from the effects of air
pollution—three times the one million who die each year in automobile accidents. While governments spend millions of dollars in warnings, medical care
and technologies in response to deaths caused by accidents, they are doing almost
nothing in response to even a bigger death machine on American's highways…

> In the United States, traffic fatalities total just over 40,000 per year, while air
> pollution claims 70,000 lives annually. U.S. air pollution deaths are equal to
> deaths from breast cancer and prostate cancer combined. This scourge of cities
> in industrial and developing countries alike threatens the health of billions of
> people. Governments go to great lengths to reduce traffic accidents by fining
> those who drive at dangerous speeds, arresting those who drive under the
> influence of alcohol, and even sometimes revoking drivers' licenses. But they

---

1.　Fox, Maggie, "Pollution, heart disease linked," Reuters news service, 2001

pay much less attention to the deaths people cause by simply driving the cars. While deaths from heart disease and respiratory illness from breathing polluted air may lack the drama of deaths from an automobile crash, with flashing lights and sirens, they are no less real.[2]

The next time Ford Motor and General Motors tell you to "buckle up," remember that the biggest threat to your life may be coming out of the exhaust pipe, and that the automobile industry really doesn't care if you live or die, evidenced by their choice to ignore their generous and ceaseless contribution to air pollution. When is the last time you heard a report on television's major networks about the ravages of air pollution caused by vehicle emissions? Investigative reporters NEVER take Ford, GM or Exxon Oil to the mat and force them to explain to America's moms and dads why they knowingly produce cars that kill more Americans than wars. Because automobile manufacturers are one of the biggest advertisers on television and in print, you won't find any such investigative muckraking in the major media. Too bad for us. Good for them.

## TAKING THE PIPE

A Greenpeace report warns that much of the world's food is contaminated with human made, highly toxic chemicals called persistent organic pollutants (POPs), some of the most problematic chemicals to which humans can be exposed. The report, "Recipe for Disaster," reviews existing data on food worldwide and reveals that some foodstuffs, particularly fish," meat and dairy products, contain levels of POPs that "even exceed internationally agreed limits."[3] Pennsylvania's industries and sewage treatment plants, for example, dump more toxic chemicals into state waters than those in all but one other state, and the amount is increasing, according to a study released yesterday by a coalition of environmental groups. The study found that more than 40 million pounds of toxic pollutants were released into Pennsylvania waterways in 1997, the latest year for which federal statistics are available. While most of the discharges were within limits set by state and federal permits, 18 percent of the state's largest industrial facilities violated the Clean Water Act.[4]

---

2.   Fischlowitz-Roberts, Bernie, "Air Pollution Fatalities Now Exceed Traffic Fatalities by 3 to 1," http://www.earth policy.org/Updates/Update17.htm, 2002

3.   Greenpeace report: "World Food Supplies Contaminated with Toxic Chemicals," March 2000

4.   Hopey, Don, "Pennsylvania ranks 2nd worst in toxic dumping," postgazette.com, February 18, 2000

## GETTING PERSONAL

What's so toxic about your personal environment? Let's remember that the word "environment" does not just apply to the forests and rivers and streams. It applies to the place where you live, your city, your neighborhood, and especially your home—even the mattress you lie upon to count sheep. Here are some of the main offenders (and their adverse health effects) most Americans face personally on a daily basis (courtesy of Rick Dennam, Denham Enterprises, 30ways.com):

> **Alcohols—Acid and Alkali:** rashes, muscle weakness, headaches, dizziness, nerve damage, vision problems, sleeping problems, stomach cramps, disorientation, coughing, depression, respiratory problems, anemia, organ damage, fatigue, heart damage, cancer, death.
> **Chlorines:** headaches, mental function difficulties, pulmonary edemas and heart disease, diabetes, gastrointestinal and urinary tract cancer, organ and gland cancer, severe eye problems, immune system breakdown, child development problems, anemia, and more.
> **Detergents/Emulsifiers:** strip skin of protective oils, interference with nutrient absorption, skin irritation, scalp eruptions, hair loss, allergic reaction, cataract formation, organ damage, reproductive damage, blindness, cancer.
> **Synthetic Fragrance & Dyes:** allergic reaction, skin rashes, ADD, stomach upsets, muscular aches and pains, violent coughing and sneezing, irritability, vertigo, hyperactivity, convulsions, emotional and behavioral problems, Leukemia, Hodgkin's, multiple tumors, reproductive damage, headaches, dizziness, organ damage, depression, cancer.
> **Heavy Metals:** abdominal cramps, nausea, joint and bone pain, muscle weakness, mouth sores, muscle, joint, and bone pain; cancer, reduced intelligence, motor difficulties, brain disorders, short attention span, aging, hyperactivity, emotional disorders, immune disorders, genetic damage, aging.
> **Pesticides & Fungicides:** flu-like symptoms, (fatigue, muscle and joint pain), stomach cramps, nervous system disorders, insomnia, memory loss, swelling of body parts, dizziness, genetic mutations, birth defects, gland tumors, organ damage, cancer, death.
> **Petrochemicals:** inhibit skin functions, pimples, rashes, splitting nails, sensitivity to sun, headaches, premature aging, allergic reactions, fatigue, depression, intestinal gas, asthma, respiratory failure, immune disorders.
> **Preservatives (synthetic):** headaches, skin rashes, eye damage, asthma, respiratory problems, tumors, cancer, digestive problems, mental confusion, organ damage, muscle weakness & cramps, loss of motor control, joint pain, reproductive damage, etc.[5]

---

5.    Denham, Rick, Denham Enterprises, 30ways.com, www.denhamenterprises.com, 2002

## STATISTICS ON OUR
## CHEMICALIZED ENVIRONMENT

I know what you're thinking right now: Hey, you promised a boatload of juicy statistics that I can use for my next speech at the United Nations—where are they already? To this query, I offer the following hair-raising, mind-razing, number-crunching, spoiled-lunching stats on how toxic our world has grown:

- A new report issued today by Environmental Defense appraises for the first time the carbon dioxide ($CO_2$) produced by the new vehicles sold each year by major auto manufacturers. General Motors' fleet imposes the largest "carbon burden," producing 6.7 million metric tons per year. GM is followed closely by Ford, whose fleet produces 5.6 million tons. The carbon burden is the total $CO_2$ emitted by a group of vehicles each year and represents their lifetime average global warming impact. A copy of the report is available at www.environmentaldefense.org[6]

- More than one-fourth of the nation's lakes have advisories warning consumers that fresh-caught fish may be contaminated with mercury, dioxins, or other chemicals, according to the Environmental Protection Agency (EPA).

  The EPA said state regulators issued 2,618 fishing advisories or bans in 2001 because of contaminants. Eating fish that contain high concentrations of mercury, dioxins, PCBs, and other industrial chemicals can be especially harmful to pregnant women and children, according to the EPA.

  In 2001, the state advisories covered 28 percent of the nation's total lake acreage, up from 26 percent in 2000, the EPA said. Some 14 percent of U.S. rivers were covered by advisories in 2001, up from 10.5 percent in the previous year.[7]

- A federal survey that found trace levels of medications in rivers and streams throughout the U.S. could prompt the Food and Drug Administration to revitalize its environmental investigations into drug safety. The first-of-its-kind survey of more than 100 waterways found low levels of dozens of antibiotics, hormones, painkillers, cough suppressants, disinfectants, and other products excreted by humans and animals. Many of these substances fall

---

6.   "Environmental Defense", "New Report Measures U.S. Automakers' Corporate Culpabilities For Global Warming Pollution," http://www.cleancarcampaign.org/releases/20020731carbon.shtml, July 2002

7.   "EPA Warns that Fish in 28% of US Lakes Are Toxic," Organic Consumers Association: Reuters, June 28, 2002

through regulatory cracks, because they are not defined as pollution under clean water laws, and the FDA has not examined the environmental impact of most drugs since 1997.[8]

- 50% of all illness is due to poor indoor air quality. (Source: 1989 State of Massachusetts Study)

- Each weekend, about 54 million Americans mow their lawns, using 800 million gallons of gas per year and producing tons of air pollutants. Garden equipment engines, which have had unregulated emissions until very recently, emit high levels of carbon monoxide, volatile organic compounds and nitrogen oxides, producing up to 5% of the nation's air pollution and a good deal more in metropolitan areas.

- 70 million computers already have been sent to landfills. In another five years, five hundred million more computers may be joining them.

- A conventional lawn mower pollutes as much in an hour as 40 late model cars (or as much air pollution as driving a car for 100 miles).[9]

- Liquid Dish Soap is the leading cause of poisonings in the home for children under the age of 6 (over 2.1 million accidental poisonings per year) (contains formaldehyde and ammonia in most brands)

Of the chemicals found in personal care products:

884 are toxic
146 cause tumors
218 cause reproductive complications
314 cause biological mutation
376 cause skin and eye irritations
(Source: United States House of Representatives report, 1989)

- Over the last 20—30 years, as more toxic chemicals have been introduced in greater amounts, the level of toxins stored in adipose tissues (fat cells) of our bodies has risen. Bio-accumulation studies have shown that some toxins store in our bodies for life. Greater and greater amounts are being stored at younger ages. Diseases that used to occur later in life are now appearing at younger ages. Diseases that used to be rare are more frequent.

For Example: There has been a 28% increase in childhood cancer since the addition of pesticides into household products. (Source: National Cancer Institute)

---

8.  "Drug Residues in US Water Supply," www.gristmagazine.com, March, 2002
9.  "Cleaner Air: Gas Mower Facts," www.peoplepoweredmachines.com

- In one decade, there has been a 42% increase in asthma (29% for men; 82% for women—the higher rate for women is believed to be due to women's longer exposure times to household chemicals). (Source: Center for Disease Control)[10]

In many cases, whole neighborhoods, towns and cities have been devastated by pollution, toxic emissions, manufacturing and dumping, with death, cancer, lung disease and other illness rates to prove the disastrous impact. At the outset of this book we mentioned "Cancer Alley" in Louisiana. Here is an instance wherein industry has destroyed lives as a course of doing business. Investigative journalist Barbara Koeppel writes:

> Something is rotten in the state of Louisiana. It is the stretch along the Mississippi River between Baton Rouge and just south of New Orleans. Locals call it Cancer Alley. The corridor is home to seven oil refineries and somewhere between 175 and 350 heavy industrial plants, depending on how you count. Together, they produce staggering amounts of waste, much of which they treat onsite or spew into the air, land and water. Waste-processing companies also set up shop here to handle the industrial overflow. Because the laws are laxer in Louisiana than elsewhere, they cart in [import] even more waste from outside the state to bolster business—a whopping 330 million pounds in 1993, which dropped to about 52 million pounds in 1995, partly because the federal government closed down Marine Shale, one of the state's three waste-processing companies.
>
> People living nearest the factories and waste dumps are sick and dying. Clusters of asthma, stillbirths, miscarriages, neurological diseases and cancers have mushroomed. And residents have long claimed that the waste has poisoned domestic animals, wildlife and fish.[11]

The natural question is: Why isn't something done about this problem that is causing an alarming rate of cancer in children, destroying the water system, air and land? Always lurking in the wings is the troubling link between big money and lack of government intervention. Koeppel writes:

> Perhaps the biggest obstacle to proving the pollution-cancer link is the industries' immense wealth and influence. In 1998 oil, petrochemical products and gas extraction accounted for $28 billion of the state's $110 billion gross state product. Some of the worst polluters donate lavishly to all sorts of institutions and are particularly generous to "environmental" causes.

---

10. http://www.enviroalternatives.com/nontoxichome.html
11. Koeppel, Barbara, "Cancer Alley, Louisiana," The Nation, November 1999

...Most troubling, however, are the massive gifts these industries make to the universities and medical centers, which, together with the State Health Department, run the cancer studies. According to press accounts, oilman C.B. Pennington gave LSU $125 million in the eighties to build a Bio-Medical Research Center, whose main task is to study nutrition; and Lod Cook, chairman of Arco, footed most of the bill for LSU's three-story alumni center, which opened in the mid-nineties. In August of 1997, when Pennington died, he left about $250 million to be shared among the LSU center, the Pennington Foundation and his grandchildren.

Tulane [university] has also thrived, according to Earl Bihlmeyer, senior associate vice president of the university. Texaco donated a twenty-year free lease for a building that houses its Public Health School facility. And because the lease will soon expire, Tidewater Industries, which services oil rigs, has given it a twenty-four-story building that will also be used by Tulane's medical and hospital departments. In 1996 Freeport donated $1 million to the university's Bio-Environmental Research Center and, along with Shell and Exxon, pumped another $2 million into its Environmental and Waste Management Program. In fact, dollars flow for countless projects, such as endowed chairs, which cost donors $600,000 each, matched by $400,000 from the Oil and Gas Trust Fund (financed by gas and oil royalties). Since the early nineties, Ethyl, Texaco and Claiborne Gasoline have each endowed an LSU chair, Freeport has endowed one Tulane chair and two LSU chairs, and Pennington has given two chairs to Tulane.

The problem, say critics, is that contributions profoundly affect the kinds of studies designed: Until the mid-nineties, for example, scientists investigating lung cancer limited research to the link with smoking, says Ben Fontaine, executive director of Louisiana's American Lung Association. Efforts by journalists and others to get the universities to reveal their funding sources (apart from data about endowed chairs) have been stonewalled: Tulane's status as a private institution allows it to remain silent, and although LSU is a public university, it created a private foundation through which it funnels its grants.

The industries and firms servicing them also contribute heavily to politicians on both sides of the aisle. For example, oil and gas companies contributed just under $342,000 to the 1990 campaign of Democratic Senator J. Bennett Johnston, chairman of the Energy and Natural Resources Committee. In the early nineties, the committee again exempted oil field waste—which contains carcinogens, heavy metals and radioactive materials—from federal hazardous waste laws (the first time it was classified as non hazardous was in 1970). Thus, oil companies can inject it underground or just dump it into pits, with far fewer controls. Similarly, Louisiana state legislators got $294,000 in 1993—94 from the industries. Soon after, the lawmakers killed a bill that would have sharply hiked industry taxes.

Sometimes, the links between industry and government are even closer: Republican Mike Foster, the current governor, who owns prime oil and gas land, earns $200,000 in annual royalties from Exxon, along with smaller sums from Quintaine Petroleum, Meridian Oil and others, according to his campaign disclosure form. Moreover, according to press reports, firms such as Chevron, Occidental, Ciba-Geigy, Freeport and Cryptopolymers were among a long list of industry contributors to Foster's 1996 gubernatorial campaign. Edwin Edwards, who held the governor's chair in 1972—80, 1984—88 and 1992—96, earned, in the years he was out of office, at least $100,000 a year in oil and gas royalties from Exxon, Superior Oil and others, and large legal retainers from several oil corporations, including Texaco and Texas International.[12]

As long as we have these kinds of problems, it cannot be said too many times that the biggest stumbling block to citizens' rights and public welfare is the conflict that is created when private corporations—the same ones who are involved in toxic dumping and the production of toxic industrial waste—financially support (and undermine) politicians, universities and researchers. With so many billions of corporate dollars in circulation, nearly everybody sides with industry, from the media to the city commission to the governor to the president, and even physicians who promise to stand behind you (so long as they have a syringe in their hand ready to give you the business). When people start dropping like flies from disease, the cover-up continues, and the victims of industrial pollution are defamed, belittled, paid-off, lied to and ignored. Parents cannot help their children, mothers and fathers lose their way of supporting their families and women suffer from breast cancer while the corporations launch a powerful propaganda campaign to squelch the voices of the suffering. Maybe you've seen this in your town. Maybe you've seen the movies Erin Brockovich, Civil Action or Silkwood dealing with industry's ugly role in manifesting, perpetrating and ignoring human suffering. This horror is real, but it's nearly impossible to get anyone to listen and make a change; and even when a change is made, it's always after innocent children have suffered. In her article, "Multiple Sensitivities Under Siege," Anne McCampbell, M.D., Chair, Multiple Chemical Sensitivities Task Force of New Mexico, elaborates:

> Movies like Erin Brockovich and A Civil Action depict the true stories of communities whose members became ill from drinking water contaminated with industrial waste. Their struggles clearly show how difficult it is for people to hold corporations responsible for the harm they have caused. Whether individuals are injured by exposures to contaminated air or water, silicone breast implants, cigarettes, or other chemicals, their quest for justice is usually a

---

12.  ibid

David versus Goliath battle that pits average citizens against giant corporations.

When confronted with the harm they have caused, corporations typically blame the victims, deny the problem, and try to avoid responsibility for the harm caused. The corporate response to people with multiple chemical sensitivities (MCS) has been no different. People with MCS are made sick from exposures to many common products, such as pesticides, paints, solvents, perfumes, carpets, building materials, and many cleaning and other products. But the manufacturers of these products would rather silence the messenger than acknowledge the message that their products are not safe. To that end, the chemical manufacturing industry has launched an anti-MCS campaign designed to create the illusion of controversy about MCS and cast doubt on its existence. What has been said about the tobacco industry could easily apply to the chemical industry regarding MCS, that is, "the only diversity of opinion comes from the authors with…industry affiliations."

It is a credit to the chemical industry's public relations efforts that we frequently hear that multiple chemical sensitivities (MCS) is "controversial" or find journalists who feel obligated to report "both sides" of the MCS story, or attempt to give equal weight to those who say MCS exists and those who say it does not. But this is very misleading, since there are not two legitimate views of MCS. Rather, there is a serious, chronic, and often disabling illness that is under attack by the chemical industry.

The manufacturers of pesticides, carpets, perfumes, and other products associated with the cause or exacerbation of chemical sensitivities adamantly want MCS to go away. Even though a significant and growing portion of the population report being chemically sensitive, chemical manufacturers appear to think that if they can just beat on the illness long enough, it will disappear. To that end, they have launched a multipronged attack on MCS that consists of labeling sufferers as "neurotic" and "lazy," doctors who help them as "quacks," scientific studies which support MCS as "flawed," calls for more research as "unnecessary," laboratory tests that document physiologic damage in people with MCS as "unreliable," government assistance programs helping those with MCS as "abused," and anyone sympathetic to people with MCS as "cruel" for reinforcing patients' "beliefs" that they are sick. They also have been influential in blocking the admission of MCS testimony in lawsuits through their apparent influence on judges.[13]

While on the subject of Erin Brokovich, her battle against toxic polluters continues, as reported in the online new magazine, The Grist (April 30, 2003)…

BEVERLY HILLS FLOP

---

13. McCampbell, MD, Ann, "Multiple Chemical Sensitivities Under Siege," Santa Fe, NM, 2002

Erin Brockovich, the tenacious eco-crusader made famous by Hollywood, is back in the news: She says that many former Beverly Hills High School students have been stricken with cancer because of exposure to toxic fumes from an active oil field on school property. Brockovich and her boss, attorney Ed Masry, yesterday filed 25 personal injury claims for damages against the city of Beverly Hills and its school district—and they say that hundreds more claims could be forthcoming. They also plan to go after three oil companies and two government entities. The duo argues that contamination on the campus has led to 280 cases of thyroid cancer, Hodgkin's disease, and non-Hodgkin's lymphoma since the 1970s, giving the school a cancer rate 20 to 30 times higher than the national average. The school district and the South Coast Air Quality Management District, which monitors air pollution in the region, dispute Brockovich and Masry's findings.[14]

Journalist Bill Moyers, one of the few mainstream professional journalists who dares to investigate the wrongdoings of industry and its role in causing cancer, produced a PBS (Public Broadcasting System) television show called "Chemical Papers," rousing a national coalition of activists to combat the lies of the chemical industry. Instead of being welcomed for exposing how citizens are being lied to, cheated of their health and futures, the mainstream media chose either to ignore Moyers' exposé or to defame him and his work. In accord with industry's history of truth-twisting, critics of Moyers claimed that somehow he was standing in the way of "progress" and acting in a most undemocratic way by interfering with industry's right to make a profit. After all, it has been stated by pro-industry voices that the unfortunate tradeoff for great inventions, "progress" and "beneficial" chemicals is the possible loss of health here and there. However,

> no one on [Bill Moyers'] program argued against tradeoffs or democracy. The issue Moyers presented was quite simple: Do companies have the right to lie and mislead their workers and the public about the potentially harmful effects of their products? If tradeoffs or democracy were the issue, then the victims of these companies would at least have been given the relevant information about the likelihood that they might contract cancer or other life-threatening diseases as a result of their exposure to toxic chemicals. Yet, as Moyers reported, that information was deliberately withheld or covered up by the companies.
>
> People died or were permanently disfigured as a result of the coverups Bill Moyers exposed. Yet the [New York] *Times* likened acceptance of (slow) murder by corporations for profits to growing up. It's hard to know which is more offensive: the actions of the corporations or the willingness of journalists to act as apologists for them.[15]

---

14.  San Diego Union-Tribune, Associated Press, 28; Apr 2003

We have to ponder whether we want industry and greedy politicians to decide whether they should be the final arbiters over whether it is worth sacrificing our children for their profits. Is it okay with you if your son or daughter is the "tradeoff" for progress? No? It's not okay with me either. In fact, it's insulting to the intelligence of the American people who suffer as industry pours billions of gallons of toxic sludge into the ground, pays off scientists to say that there's no proof any of it is harmful, then tells us it's okay for our children to play in it. They must think we're stupid, or at least too weak and poor to speak out against the injustices.

## WHAT'S THE DEAL WITH GENETICALLY ENGINEERED FOODS?

The latest battle between human decency and the evil geniuses centers around Genetically Engineered Foods, which are foods that have been so genetically tampered with by scientists that critics are calling them Frankenfoods. Industrial proponents of genetically engineered foods tell us that their invention is a blessing and they will uplift life on earth by saving the planet from starvation. Is this true, or just another industry excuse for selling the public the proverbial bag of magic beans? Who profits from controlling most of the world's food supply?

The most basic way to explain genetic engineering of foods is that the genetic codes of plants are artificially altered (tampered with) so that they no longer reproduce a natural end-product. The end result of genetic engineered is unstable and unpredictable in the widest sense.

Genetic engineering changes the DNA of living organisms. DNA is the complex, intricate molecular structure found in cells that determines the characteristics of each living organism. As explained on the Mothers For Natural Law website,

> The organism relies upon the information stored in its DNA for the management of every biochemical process. The life, growth and unique features of the organism depend on its DNA. The segments of DNA which have been associated with specific features or functions of an organism are called **genes**. Molecular biologists have discovered many enzymes which change the structure of DNA in living organisms. Some of these enzymes can cut and join strands of DNA. Using such enzymes, scientists learned to cut specific genes from DNA and to build customized DNA using these genes. They also

15.  *The Nation*, Editorial, April 2002

learned about **vectors**, strands of DNA such as viruses, which can infect a cell and insert themselves into its DNA.

With this knowledge, scientists started to build vectors which incorporated genes of their choosing and used the new vectors to insert these genes into the DNA of living organisms. Genetic engineers believe they can improve the foods we eat by doing this. For example, tomatoes are sensitive to frost. This shortens their growing season. Fish, on the other hand, survive in very cold water. Scientists identified a particular gene which enables a flounder to resist cold and used the technology of genetic engineering to insert this 'antifreeze' gene into a tomato. This makes it possible to extend the growing season of the tomato.

At first glance, this might look exciting to some people. Deeper consideration reveals <u>serious dangers</u>.[16]

Among other things, by melding genetic coding of unlike species, such as pigs and corn, genetic engineering involves creating a new plant that is a mixture of plant and animal genetic material—something that is literally impossible to ever occur naturally. Einstein was appalled when he found out how horrific his atomic energy could be manifested when he witnessed the bombing of Hiroshima and Nagasaki to end World War II. He never imagined that his scientific knowledge would be put to such a devastating use. If he could see the goings-on with genetic engineering today, he would rise up out of his grave and die of a heart attack. We (you or I or any scientist on earth) cannot begin to guess the degree to which genetic scientists will affect the world, species on earth, seasons, food chains, microorganisms, the ecology and human health. This is why genetically engineered food is referred to as **Frankenfood**. It's as insane as Dr. Frankenstein, the popular classical character invented by author Mary Shelley. Dr. Frankenstein created a monster out of nonliving parts only to find out that his creation got out of hand and began to forge an uncontrollable path of mass destruction. It's almost impossible to believe that corporate scientists would be so shortsighted, arrogant, corrupted by money and willing to tempt the hands of fate and the course of life on earth for profit. Scientists do not yet understand living systems completely enough to perform DNA surgery without creating mutations which could be harmful to the environment and our health. They are experimenting with very delicate, yet powerful forces of nature, without full knowledge of the repercussions (*Washington Times* 1997, *The Village Voice* 1998). There are literally infinite combinations of problems (disasters) that may result from genetic engineering:

---

16. Mothers for Natural Law, 2002, www.safe—food.org/—issue/ge.html

- **Widespread Crop Failure**—Genetic engineers intend to profit by patenting genetically engineered seeds. This means that, when a farmer plants genetically engineered seeds, all the seeds have identical genetic structure. As a result, if a fungus, a virus, or a pest develops which can attack this particular crop, there could be widespread crop failure. (Robinson 1996)

- **Threatens Our Entire Food Supply**—Insects, birds, and wind can carry genetically altered seeds into neighboring fields and beyond. Pollen from transgenic plants can cross-pollinate with genetically natural crops and wild relatives. All crops, organic and non-organic, are vulnerable to contamination from cross-pollination. (Emberlin et al 1999)

### Health Hazards

- **No Long—Term Safety Testing**—Genetic engineering uses material from organisms that have never been part of the human food supply to change the fundamental nature of the food we eat. Without long-term testing no one knows if these foods are safe.

- **Toxins**—Genetic engineering can cause unexpected mutations in an organism, which can create new and higher levels of toxins in foods. (Inose 1995, Mayeno 1994)

- **Allergic Reactions**—Genetic engineering can also produce unforeseen and unknown allergens in foods. (Nordlee 1996)

- **Decreased Nutritional Value**—Transgenic foods may mislead consumers with counterfeit freshness. A luscious-looking, bright red genetically engineered tomato could be several weeks old and of little nutritional worth.

- **Antibiotic Resistant Bacteria**—Genetic engineers use antibiotic-resistance genes to mark genetically engineered cells. This means that genetically engineered crops contain genes which confer resistance to antibiotics. These genes may be picked up by bacteria which may infect us. (New Scientist 1999)

- **Problems Cannot Be Traced**—Without labels, our public health agencies are powerless to trace problems of any kind back to their source. The potential for tragedy is staggering.

- **Side Effects can Kill**—37 people died, 1500 were partially paralyzed, and 5000 more were temporarily disabled by a syndrome that was finally linked to tryptophan made by genetically-engineered bacteria. (Mayeno 1994)[17]

---

17. Mothers for Natural Law, Safe Food Campaign, 2001, www.safe—food.org/ —issue/dangers.html

You may ask, as do the rest of us who are clutching onto the sinking U.S.S. Sanity: Why is genetic engineering being pushed upon us with such force for acceptance? If you guessed the fact that huge profits and power are at stake, then you would get the prize. Like so many other stories, the genetically engineered food concept is a tragedy in progress all because of corporate greed. Industry is transfixed on today's profits at the expense of life on earth. Dr. Barry Commoner, author of the article "Unraveling the DNA Myth: The Spurious Foundation of Genetic Engineering," writes, "The genetically engineered crops now being grown represent a massive uncontrolled experiment whose outcome is inherently unpredictable. The results could be catastrophic."[18] Yet the major media remains all but silent on the issue for reasons already stated. The Organic Consumers Association reports, "...Reading the mainstream press, it's hard to find anything critical of genetic engineering. The public interest think tank, Food First, released a report April 29 demonstrating that 13 of the U.S.'s major newspapers and magazines "have all but shut out criticism of genetically modified (GM) food and crops from their opinion pages."[19]

Makers of genetically engineered foods have put their heads together to come up with some reasons why their Frankenfoods are so needed in our world, including to wipe out world hunger due to crop destruction by pests, to produce bigger and more weather-resistant foods, to create more nutritious foods and so forth. However, the real reason is to control all of the world's food supply, making it necessary for everyone on earth to purchase their foods from Monsanto and others who create genetically engineered foods while choking out their competitors. Word domination of the food supply is evil genius. It's hard to believe, but it's happening. Dr. Frankenstein has arisen from the dead and is now wearing a business suit as he smiles to your face while poisoning you and your family at the supper table. Most of Europe has disallowed genetic engineering, or at least forced food manufacturers to state on their labels that their products contain genetically engineered ingredients; because they can see the dangers. We should only be so wise.

But hold your horses! Even as I write these words, political pressure is being brought to bear on European nations to continually relax their standards against genetically engineered ingredients. Time will tell whether these countries collapse under the weight of blackmail and bribery.

---

18. BioDemocracy News #40 of the Organic Consumers Association: Dr. Barry Commoner, "Unraveling the DNA Myth: The Spurious Foundation of Genetic Engineering," Harpers magazine, February 2002

19. ibid

### Genetic Monkey Business
### During the World Summit

During the World Summit 2002 (a meeting of the world's nations in South Africa), during a drought and famine in southern Africa, the United States sent Monsanto corporation's genetically engineered grain for "relief." The Africans told the U.S. to take it back, knowing that genetically engineered grain would contaminate the African landscape. South Africans were appalled at the U.S.'s "take it or leave it" lack of compassion for sending foul food. George W. Bush's Secretary of Defense, Colin Powell, addressed world leaders and ambassadors at the Summit and called the relief-*refusal* "crazy." He was booed off the stage. Greenpeace reported:

> On the Summit's closing day, Secretary of State Colin Powell addressed the packed plenary session. "There were probably groups from more than a hundred countries in there," explained Greenpeace delegate Matt Gianni. "There were no organised plans to have a demonstration…But when Colin Powell chastised countries for saying "no" to US genetically modified food, the room simply erupted in boos and catcalls. And when he tried to claim that the US was defending biodiversity and promoting renewables, there was this incredible roar of disbelief—nobody was silent."
>
> Powell was unable to continue for several minutes as the gallery of the conference room voiced its protest. Several representatives were escorted out by security, still voicing their disbelief. Chairperson Nkosazana Dlamini-Zuma called for order, saying "This is totally unacceptable," but the spontaneous outpouring of protest simply would not be silenced.[20]

## HERE'S WHAT YOU CAN DO TO
## REVERSE THE TOXIC TIDE:

If this doesn't make you want to march on the nation's Capitol, you can just do what everyone else does and ignore the facts on your way to the local cheeseburger factory. Or you can make a change for the better, even if it means taking one or two little measures that require very little effort to save yourself and your family. The first step is to stop personally contributing to the problem.

Next, start recycling, using earth-friendly, non-toxic products at home, school and at work. Here are some earth-friendly companies and their websites:

---

20.   Greenpeace Australia-Pacific, "Action against inaction," 2002

- Do not buy genetically engineered or GMO foods. Do not buy any product from a company producing or selling genetically engineered foods.

- Eco Wise: ecowise.com, 512-326-4474

- Green Home: www.greenhome.com: 415-282-6400

- Florida Naturally: floridanaturally.com/shopping_non_toxic.htm

- Environmental Health Center Catalog, (214) 368-4132, www.aehf.com

- Nirvana Safe Heaven: nontoxic.com

- Earth Friendly Products: available in many stores

- Seventh Generation: www.seventhgeneration.com

- Nutrition Research Center: nutritionresearchcenter.org

- Go to the website www.broward.org/aqi01900.htm and look at all of the helpful tips on becoming toxic-free

- Use environmentally friendly dry cleaners

- Switch all of your dish detergent and soaps to nontoxic brands such as those made by Seventh Generation

- Buy a low emission, maximum-miles-per-gallon, or electric/hybrid automobile. Look into the Honda Civic hybrid, the Toyota RAV4 electric vehicle, Toyota Prius hybrid, Chrysler-Daimon's neighborhood electric vehicles, and the ZENN electric vehicle; or find out about the new vehicle powered by compressed air, offered by MDI—www.zeropollution.com. **Imagine driving a car that uses no gasoline!** This car is a lighter load on your pocketbook and the environment at the same time. All of downtown New York City should be running on air-cars only, disallowing other vehicles from entering Manhattan. Think of the pollution and noise savings, not to mention the elimination of oil dependence!

- Recycle

- Stop ingesting fluoride and chlorine. Get a whole-house water filter system and a reverse osmosis filter for all of your ice cubes and drinking water

- Make your city commission become involved with pollution issues

- Switch to a non-motorized, electric or solar lawn mower and trimmer; and ban the cursed leaf blower. Leaf blowers are stupid inventions that blow dirt onto everyone else's property while polluting the air and causing enough noise to make Helen Keller scream, "Cut it out!!" Lawn mowers pollute the air far more than you might realize:

A typical 3.5 horsepower gas mower can emit the same amount of VOCs—key precursors to smog—in an hour as a new car driven 340 miles. The replacement of every 500 gas mowers with non-motorized mowers would spare the air:

- 212 pounds of hydrocarbons (smog ingredient)

- 1.7 pounds of nitrogen oxides (smog ingredient)

- 5.6 pounds of irritating particles 1,724 pounds of carbon dioxide

And speaking of gas, the EPA claims that 17 million gallons of fuel, mostly gasoline, are spilled each year while refueling lawn equipment. That's more than all the oil spilled by the Exxon Valdez, in the Gulf of Alaska.[21]

- If you are concerned about genetically engineered foods, go online to http://www.safe—food.org/—consumer/brands.html#natp and do as much research as you can about the foods you eat by searching the internet and environmental magazines for the truth. Don't buy any foods unless they are guaranteed on their labels to be non-GMO.

- Remember that there are toxins everywhere in the modern world, so switch to earth-friendly, human-friendly personal care products, clothing, carpeting, shampoos, soaps, dishwashing liquid, washing machine detergent, toothpaste, cologne and perfume, pet supplies, bug sprays, paints, drinking water and foods.

- Switch all your shopping to health-food stores and eat at natural-food restaurants. Boycott your local grocery store and restaurants to get them to stop selling and serving genetically engineered foods. Such boycotting has proven successful nationwide

This book is meant to open your eyes to the breadth of the toxic problem we all face every day, everywhere we turn. Once you are aware, you can do something to make things better, starting with your purchasing power.

---

21.  "Cleaner Air: Gas Mower Facts," www.peoplepoweredmachines.com

# What You Put ON Your Body Ends Up IN Your Body

*"Whether the issue is hair spray, or shampoo, or lipstick, or baby powder, suntan lotion, soap and toothpaste, Americans assume that the products they use are safe...But this confidence is too often unjustified—because Federal oversight of this $20 billion industry today is extremely limited. The basic Federal law regulating cosmetics has not been updated since 1938. The FDA has less than 30 employees overseeing this huge industry—and only two employees dealing with the critical issues of packaging, labeling, and consumer warnings. The FDA has no authority to require manufacturers to register their plants and products. It cannot require manufacturers to file data on the ingredients in their products. It cannot compel manufacturers to file reports on cosmetic-related injuries. It cannot require that products be tested for safety or that the results of safety testing be made available to the agency. It does not have the right of access to manufacturers' records. It cannot require recall of a product."*

*—Senator Ted Kennedy, 1997*

Some people's bathrooms look like the final scene from Casablanca where Bogart says to Bergman, "Here's looking at you, kid," in a fog so dense that you need a flashing light just to find your nose. Aerosol cans of hair spray, talcum powder, perfume, makeup powder, foot sprays and underarm deodorant produce a cloud so thick you can almost cut the air with a knife, if you could actually find a knife in the chemical mist.

When I was a child I once walked into a beauty salon where my mother was getting her hair coiffed. The air could have choked a horse. In fact, there were two horses right outside the door refusing to go in to have their manes braided. The smell inside gave me an instant headache which I didn't know at the time was caused by toxins from nail polish, polish removers, hair sprays, powder, hair dyes, curling agents, straightening agents, bleaching agents, hair dyes and even cigarette smoke from the employees who ran out back to take a puff but left the door open. (I guess the inside air wasn't killing them quite fast enough). Beauty parlors, hair salons and nail salons are death traps that are killing owners, employees and patrons. But you don't even have to go out of your house to experience the toxic cloud, because in the average American's bathroom is an arsenal of poisonous personal care products that warn you on the label that they are bad for your health and may cause cancer. Except for the fact that people don't read labels, it defies logic why anyone would put them on their skin, in their hair or into their body cavities, let alone be in the same room where they are being thoughtlessly, liberally and ubiquitously applied.

## SENATOR TED KENNEDY
## HAD SOMETHING TO SAY

A few years ago, Sen. Ted Kennedy delivered a paper and address in an effort to reform the cosmetics industry. There are far too many dangers from the use of personal care products to be ignored. Do you use one or many of these products on a daily basis without thinking twice about cancers, skin irritations, persistent rashes, bone disease or allergic reactions? Vanity is a big business largely because people will generally be more interested in their outward appearance than whether the products they use cause long-term illnesses. **What you put on your skin ends up inside your body**, yet the cosmetics industry does little, if anything, to warn consumers of potential health hazards. The industry remains free of oversight and regulation, with only a handful of companies taking measures to ensure the safety of their products. Sen. Kennedy wrote:

> A study by the respected, nonpartisan General Accounting Office reported that more than 125 ingredients available for use in cosmetics are suspected of causing cancer. Twenty cosmetic ingredients may cause adverse effects on the nervous system, including headaches, drowsiness, and convulsions. Twenty cosmetic ingredients are suspected of causing birth defects. The GAO concluded that "cosmetics are being marketed in the United States which may pose a serious hazard to the public."
>
> The cosmetics industry wants the public to believe that no effective regulation is necessary at either the state or federal level. They are masters of the slick ad and expensive public relations campaign. But all the glamorous pictures in the world cannot obscure the basic facts: this is an industry that is under-regulated and too often hazardous. A mother of a beautiful six-year-old girl in Oakland, California found this out when she used a hair product on her child that resulted in second degree burns on her ears and neck. A 59-year-old California woman almost died from an allergic reaction to hair dye. A 47-year-old woman had her cornea destroyed by a mascara wand. In another tragic case, a

woman's hair caught fire as the result of an inflammable hair treatment gel. She lost her hair and was severely scarred.

In fact, for every one million cosmetic products purchased, there are more than 200 visits to the doctor to treat cosmetic-caused illnesses. A 1987 study for the Consumer Product Safety Commission found that in one year alone, cosmetic products resulted in 47,000 emergency room visits. Another study found that between 1985 and 1987, more than 151,000 cosmetic-related injuries occurred.[1]

Think of how many more cases of injury go unreported. Most people do not seek medical treatment for minor side effects, rashes or irritations—and many wouldn't even make the immediate connection between the cosmetics and their symptoms.

## TOXIC TAMPONS

You can't get more personal than talking about feminine hygiene products. But despite the risk of cancer and other diseases, the major news media has failed once again to adequately inform the public of some horrendous side effects affecting female health. Did you know that countless women are being poisoned from tampons?

An American woman uses as many as 11,000 tampons in her lifetime. Most tampons sold by companies such as Tampax, OB, Playtex and Kotex are made of rayon or rayon-cotton blends. Rayon, a wood pulp derivative commonly bleached with chlorine, contains dioxin, an organochlorine formed during the bleaching process.

Mounting evidence suggests that low levels of dioxin may be linked to cancer (especially breast cancer), immune system suppression and low sperm counts. A February 7 *Village Voice* article estimated that 73 million US women regularly risk dioxin exposure when they put bleached sanitary products in contact with highly absorbent mucous membranes.

In 1992, a congressional subcommittee discovered a March 1989 memo stating that Food and Drug Administration (FDA) scientists had detected trace levels of dioxin in tampons.

The memo warned that "the risk of dioxin in tampons can be quite high," and that "the most effective risk-management strategy would be to assure that tampons contain no dioxin." Subcommittee chair Ted Weiss accused the FDA of purposely ignoring the dioxin danger in tampons. A New York University School of Medicine study, published in the July 1994 issue of *Infectious*

---

1.   Kennedy, Senator Edward M., www.senate.gov/~kennedy/statements/970908fdafloor.html

*Diseases in Obstetrics and Gynecology*, suggested that rayon also produces *Staphylococcus aureus* bacteria, which cause toxic shock syndrome (TSS). When researchers tested 20 varieties of tampons for their ability to induce TSS toxins, the bacteria were detected in all US brands.

Despite the deaths of 38 women in 1980 from tampon-related TSS, the tampon industry continues to deny that there is a connection between TSS and rayon.[2]

Maybe the industry-influenced media consensus is that feminine health is too sensitive a subject for the nightly news, but the fact is that violence, murder, rape and terror make up the majority of their prime time programming.

## WHAT ARE YOU PUTTING ON YOUR SKIN?

When we think of ingesting poisons into our bodies, especially concerning our children, we first think of what goes in through the mouth—food, drink, air and drugs. We can't afford to forget that the skin drinks in (ingests) poisons as well, and those poisons enter our bloodstream as well, as assuredly as if we swallowed them. Chemicals on our skin don't necessarily have to manifest as skin diseases, rashes, pimples, blotches and boils. They may manifest as headaches, liver disease, infertility, birth defects, cancer and hormonal interruption, to name but a few consequences.

Compared to other body parts, our skin is uniquely and perpetually exposed to the environment. The rate of chemical absorption through the skin has to do with a combination of what type of chemicals we are exposed to, plus the amount of surface area that is affected and the thickness of the skin, as well as frequency and duration of exposure. Thicker skin may provide a greater barrier to chemical invasion, yet skin thickness varies depending on the part of the body in question. For instance, scientists have shown that hydrocortisone (a chemical used to treat inflammatory problems) is absorbed more than 50 times greater through the skin of the genitalia than the skin of the palms. In addition, the wider the contact area and the more concentrated the substance, the greater the absorption.[3] "Damage to skin, both through disease or direct environmental influence, can also alter the barrier properties of skin and enhance absorption of substances. Even something

---

2.    Chamberlain, Sarah, "Toxic Tampons Pose Health Risk," Earth Island Journal, 1995

3.    "Dermal Absorption as an Exposure Route," Canadian Association of Physicians for the Environment, 2000

as innocuous as the removal of outer layers of skin with cellophane tape can apparently dramatically increase dermal absorption."[4]

The most common clinical signs of chemical exposure affecting the skin itself include rashes, intense to mild itching, swelling, redness, sores, changes in skin coloring, sensitivity to the sun, heat or cold, tingling, burning, skin cancer and growths. However, as stated, absorption of toxins through the skin may also manifest in illnesses and symptoms seemingly unrelated to the site of invasion. (Conversely, skin eruptions, rashes and other abnormalities may be related to internal toxicity that manifests on the skin's surface. Therefore, not all skin problems are topical. Some examples include acne, warts, skin cancer and liver spots.)

## CHLORINE: THINK TWICE BEFORE
## YOU POUR BLEACH IN YOUR WASHLOAD

Chlorine, chlorine bleach, bleaching detergents, tile spray, and a host of cleaners contain chlorine and chlorine compounds that are absorbed through the skin and cause illness. Many children also become sick from swimming pools, as they are exposed to prolonged and concentrated amounts of chlorine. Doctors may say your child has come down with a cold, while the truth is that the illness is more likely due to chemical toxicity—chlorine poisoning.

The American Chemical Society meeting in Anaheim, CA released this statement in 1986: "People are exposed to more potentially harmful indoor pollutants in home, office or car than outdoors." A five-year study by the Environmental Protection Agency concurred. Studies by Dr. Julian Andelman, Professor of Water Chemistry, University of Pittsburgh Graduate School of Public Health, found less chemical exposure from *drinking* chlorine contaminated water than using it to wash the clothes or take a shower.[5]

> The researchers concluded that skin absorption of contaminants in municipal water has been underestimated and that ingestion may not constitute the sole or even primary route of exposure. In addition to penetration of contaminants through the skin to the body as a whole, the contaminants can adversely affect the skin itself.
>
> Chlorine chemically bonds with proteins in the hair, skin and scalp. Hair can become rough and brittle and lose color. Skin can dry out with itchy, flaky

---

4.   ibid
5.   "Hazards in the bath & shower—State health departments insist on use of chlorine!," www.nontoxic.com/nontoxic/chlorine.html, 2002

scalp occurring. Chlorine can aggravate sensitive areas in the eyes, nose, throat and lungs.

Buy a water filtration system for your entire house. In the least, install a shower filter, because, in addition to absorbing several cups of chlorinated water through your skin each shower or bath, you're also breathing in chlorine vapors from the steam.

## DR. NEEDLEMAN, AN AMERICAN HERO, TEACHES US TO GET THE LEAD OUT

And now we return to the Adventures of Dr. Needleman, superhero by day and scientist by night…Through the persistent effort and scientific findings of Herbert Needleman, MD, for the past 40 years, most of us now know that lead is a deadly poison that destroys brain function. Before Needleman came along, industry kept this fact hidden from the public as children lost their sanity and lives from lead poisoning. Since his public condemnation of lead toxicity, lead-producing industries have tried to defame Dr. Needleman, dragging him into court to defend his research, calling him a quack and a hack scientist, and challenging his professional and personal credibility. But his detractors lost out in the long run, as Dr. Needleman consistently proved that industries were carelessly causing brain damage in children. Dr. Needleman's more recent work has linked lead exposure to anti-social and potentially criminal behavior.

> Children who are exposed to lead while growing up are at greater risk of developing delinquent-behavior patterns, according to a new study.
> Using a special X-ray technique, Needleman measured bone lead levels in the tibias of 216 youths convicted in the Juvenile Court of Allegheny County, Pennsylvania, and of 201 Pittsburgh high school students who did not tend toward delinquent behavior.
> The results showed that the delinquent youths had significantly higher mean concentrations of lead in their bones—13.7 parts per million—than the control group. This held true whether the individual was white, black, male or female.
> "This study provides further evidence that delinquent behavior can be caused, in part, by childhood exposure to lead," said Needleman. "Of all the causes of juvenile delinquency, lead exposure is perhaps the most preventable. These results should be a call to action for legislators to protect our children by requiring landlords to not simply disclose known instances of lead paint in their properties, but to remove it."

Needleman's work on the impact of lead on child behavior and development has been instrumental in bringing about nationwide bans of the metal in paint, gasoline and food and beverage cans.

Research conducted by Needleman in 1979 showed that children with high lead levels in their teeth, but no outward signs of lead poisoning, had low IQ scores, short attention spans and poor language skills.

Another Needleman study published in 1996 found that boys with relatively high levels of lead in their bones were more likely to engage in antisocial activities like bullying, vandalism, truancy and shoplifting.[6]

While most of Dr. Needleman's work involved lead from factories and industrial output that were poisoning children as they ate paint chips or placed toys and contaminated soil in their mouths, we must still be aware of lead's affect as it is absorbed through the skin. "The ability of the skin to absorb certain organic lead compounds, such as tetraethyl lead found in petrol [gasoline] has been recognized since the 1940s. Recent laboratory research suggests inorganic lead compounds (e.g., lead nitrate, lead acetate and lead oxide) can be absorbed through the skin but in very small quantities. Skin absorption may also pose a threat to workers in the construction trades and paint industry that are less likely to wear protective clothing to prevent lead dust from adhering to their skin."[7]

Lead exposure may come from lead industries, mining and smelting, petrol/gasoline, paint, piping, fixtures and solder, consumer products, hobbies and recreational activities using lead. Fumes, dust or pieces of lead can contaminate the work area, home and immediate environment. Children can be at considerable risk if they play in or near hobby work areas. Experts say hobbyists using lead should establish a separate work area with limited access for children and pets to prevent lead exposures. A number of hobbies that can expose the user or others to lead include antique furniture refinishing, stripping old lead paint, art conservation or restoration, automotive body or radiator repair and maintenance, soldering, welding fumes, using leaded gasoline, boat building, repair and maintenance, casting lead fishing sinkers, lead shot or lead or pewter toys, fumes from melting lead ready to cast, handling lead, ceramics or pottery, using lead paint and glazes, electronics, enameling, glass blowing, home renovation, disturbing old lead paint and lead contaminated dust, handling lead building materials, jewelry making,

---

6. Chubb, Lucy, "Lead exposure linked to delinquency," May 16, 2000, Environmental News Network

7. Environmental Protection Agency (EPA) paper, "How Lead Gets Into People," 2002

lead lighting, model making, print making, shooting at indoor firing ranges, combustion of firing, dust created by impact of bullets, and welding.

Personal care products—especially hair dyes—are another, lesser known, source of lead. "A study by Xavier University of Louisiana found a number of brands of hair dyes that contain up to ten times the amounts of lead allowed in household paint…The toxicity of lead is cumulative, building up in the body over the course of many years, and its effects can be severe…Because exposure to lead poses such an extreme threat to human health, the Center for Environmental Health recently filed a lawsuit against Combe, Inc., the manufacturer of the Grecial Formula line, under California's Proposition 65,"[8] which requires manufacturers to print warnings on their labels when their contents exceed safety standards.

## A PERSONAL STORY OF ITCHING, WELTS AND MISERY

There's nothing like a personal experience with misery and suffering to teach one a lesson. I am speaking of yours truly, and more than a year-and-a-half of constant itching and a skin rash that at times spread over my entire body. Imagine a mosquito bite that itches so bad you want to use a garden rake and a stick of dynamite for relief! Well, multiply this times a hundred and you begin to get the idea. Here is my tale of woe. One morning—New Year's Day to be exact—I woke up on the floor next to our fireplace where I had fallen asleep the night before listening to Pavarotti (not his fault). Two nights previous my daughter hosted a sleep-over whereupon she and three friends slept in the same cozy spot. I had fallen asleep there in the past, but not since we bought a beautiful new area rug that made the location even more cushy and attractive. Anyway, in the morning I woke up, stretched and noticed that my sides, the skin over my ribs—were a little itchy. I didn't think much about this until later in the day when the itching didn't go away. So I did what anybody else would do in the same circumstance—I scratched. Later that night I put some aloe on the light rash then went to bed, slightly annoyed at the persistent itch. During my sleep I itched and scratched a lot. I scratched so much that the itching and rash spread across my chest and up onto my arms. Within a week the rash was everywhere and I was cursing my dogs, my woolen sweaters, some hot sauce I had eaten a few days ear-

---

8.    Erickson, Kim, *Drop Dead Gorgeous? Protecting Yourself From The Hidden Dangers of Cosmetics,* Contemporary Books, 2002, p. 27

lier, carpet mites, and even my daughter's friends whom I suspected could have brought some unseen insect into my house.

To boil down my long experience into a shorter story, I had to figure out if there was any hope for me to live a normal, itch-free life ever again, and I began to examine my lifestyle and diet. Since my diet is very clean, consisting of about 95% organically grown foods, and I do not have any artificial chemicals in my house, I figured it must be some sort of dust mite that had invaded our house. I went online and found nontoxic mite killing powders, sprays and soaps. These were all excellent products, but none of them made me well. I still itched like a poison ivy victim. I went on a raw diet and this did not work. I visited a traditional Chinese medical doctor from Beijing, but his herbs only helped me just a little bit. I cleaned my clothes after every wearing, and showered before going to bed. My bed became my only haven—like a clean raft floating on a sea of scary unknown itchy creatures. Every piece of furniture in my house made me itch intensely. Even our dogs made me itch. The carpets and our new decorator rugs made me itch. Unless one of my family members was fresh out of the shower, they made me itch too. Soon my itching body developed oozing sores from all of the itching and scratching. I consulted experts on itching, but none of them had a good answer that applied to my condition.

Unlike most other people, I wouldn't consider going to a medical doctor, knowing he would just look at me, tell me he didn't know what it was, order $1000 worth of tests, then give me some cancer-causing steroids and tissue-destroying anti-inflammatory drugs—none of which would address the *source* of my itching.

I was going crazy. Nothing was working against the itch except my clean bed which didn't make my itching stop, but also did not contribute to the itching like every other piece furniture in my house. I had to wear long sleeve shirts and long pants because I was covered with sores, which is not good advertising for a doctor of natural health care. You may be wondering whether this story ever ends. I was wondering the same thing as I was going through the misery. I knew that every hardship has a finality to it, which, if I didn't find relief soon, may have come to fruition as I jumped off the top of a mountain.

Then it came to me as I was writing my second book, called *Illness Isn't Caused by a Drug Deficiency!* I was typing up a testimonial told to me the year before by a man who suffered from a terrible, itchy rash. The man said he only had the rash in the winter. He would put on his new suit, go to work and begin to itch intensely within an hour or so. By the end of the day the itching was severe, and welts were all over his legs and arms. In the late spring his itch and rash mysteriously subsided. Eventually he figured out that he only itched when wearing his suit—he merely discovered he had an allergy to wool. I contemplated the man's experience and began to wonder if my rash, too, could be from wool or some sort of fabric or fiber rather than from an insect. I thought back to a year prior and remembered that my rash and itch began while sleeping on the floor near our new area rug. Maybe, I thought, that rug and similar ones in the dining room and family room were causing my condition. I decided to remove all of the area rugs from my house by rolling them up and putting them in the basement away from humankind. Then I shampooed all of the wall-to-wall carpeting three times and then every piece of upholstered furniture in the house. My family pitched in and washed every single piece of clothing and bed linens stored in drawers, linen closets and hampers. We gave the dogs a bath, steam-cleaned the upholstery and carpets in our car, then waited to see what happened. I figured that if something in the rugs was making me itch and inflamed, then the fibers from the rug could literally be everywhere in the house; and the dogs could be carriers.

Did you ever notice how many dust and fiber particles are visible in a shaft of light streaming in across your living room? There are far more particles in our air than we realize. I suspected that I itched everywhere because rug fibers were everywhere, carried through the air. I did not feel better right away, but I gave this new idea a six-month trial. It would take a lot of time, I considered, for the fibers to filter out of the house and/or settle down to the floor to be vacuumed or mopped away. Within a few weeks I was itching less; within two months I was 95% better. That was it! The rugs, which were not made of natural fibers, contained some sort of toxic substance that made me sick. (By the way, others in my household were also itchy, but just not to the same severity as me. Their itching cleared up as well.)

Subsequent to this terrible experience, I began to research chemicals on rugs and carpets and found out that they can contain (especially if imported, as were mine) any one or more of the following:

- formaldehyde

- pesticides

- color fasteners

- plastics (most rugs and carpets are made of plastics)

- stain protectants

- chemical bonding agents

- PBBs (polybrominated biphenyls)

- 1,3-butadiene

- herbicides

- dyes

- wool (whereas wool is not a toxic substance and NOT a chemical, some people are allergic to it. Wool is a preferable fabric to make carpets out of, and there are many sources for woolen carpets and rugs on the Internet).

My rugs were made of synthetic naturals. By the way, without mentioning the name of the home improvement, national, orange-logoed chain store, when I explained my miserable experience to the store manager and to their representatives online, I was not even given an apology nor a refund for more than a quarter of their selling price!

We don't generally think of our houses as harbingers of toxins, but they are, as we shall see in the next chapter.

## WHAT TO LOOK OUT FOR:
## SUBSTANCES ABSORBED THROUGH YOUR SKIN

Here are some of the typical chemicals that cause health problems when absorbed through the skin:

- Chlorine in most water supplies, swimming pools, showers, and cleaning agents.

- Jewelry (toxic metals)

- Gasoline and engine oil; brake fluid and radiator fluid

- Paints, paint removers, nail polish and alcohol

- Makeup/cosmetics

- Over-the-counter and prescription skin medications such as cortisone creams

- Insect repellant

- Cologne and perfume

- Dishwashing liquid soap

- Bathing oil compounds, soaps, lotions and skin softeners

- Fluoride in toothpaste, drinking water and dental treatments

- Ammonia in cleaning agents

- Suntan lotion and sun block lotion

- Lead, copper, mercury and other heavy metals

- Aluminum in various compounds in deodorants, baking powder, baking pans, pots, pitchers, kettles, aluminum foil and aluminum cans (containing soda, beer, soft drinks, fruit juices, etc.)

- Skin lotions

## MAKEUP YOUR MIND

Is your face the entry port for toxins? Put another way, do you rub toxic chemicals into your face, legs, arms, chest and neck as part of your look-good, feel-good regime? I know of one woman who actually applied too much moisturizer, jumped into bed then slid out the window. When paramedics tried to lift her onto a stretcher she squirted out of their hands and became lodged in a nearby tree. (Some of this event is exaggerated.)

Most makeup products on the market today are hazardous to your health. Foundation, for instance, has been known to create inflammation, redness, small pimples, rashes and other blemishes. If you have skin problems on your face, try changing your brand of makeup, because foundation tops the list of causative factors in dermatitis among cosmetics users. You have to consider the fact that makeup is worn all day, almost every day, so not only is there a cumulative toxic effect, but also a perpetual irritation. Due to the cumulative effect, you may not see your condition improve right away after switching to non-toxic makeup; the improvement is usually gradual.

Consumer advocate and author of *Safe Shoppers Bible*, David Steinman has researched thousands of product ingredients for their potential health hazards. In personal care products he found:

> Brands containing 2-bromo-2-nitroproane-1, 3-diol or quaternium 15 could expose you to formaldehyde, a sensitizing and allergenic ingredient for a lot of people, or otherwise irritate your skin. Furthermore, people with sensitive skin

may have problems with fragrances and propylene glycol; both can sting. For some people, triethanolamine (TEA) can be irritating.

Foundations often cause a condition known medically as cosmetic acne, characterized by very small pimples that occur intermittently. Cosmetic acne affects about one-third of all women in their twenties through their fifties at one time or another. If you are suffering from small blemishes, especially pimples, and you are not sure why, try switching to our nontoxic formulas.

### Carcinogens

Stay away from products containing 2-bromo-2-nitroproane-1,3-diol, which can break down into formaldehyde or, under certain conditions, cause formation of carcinogenic nitrosamines. TEA should also be avoided, as it too can cause nitrosamine formation.

The extra-careful shopper may want to avoid ingredients ending in *eth* as in ceteareth—20. These may be contaminated with the carcinogen 1,4-dioxane. Polyethylene glycol or "PEG" compounds may also be contaminated with 1,4-dioxane or breakdown into formaldehyde. Shoppers may want to avoid these, too.[9]

Some other makeup ingredients (read labels carefully) to avoid include:

- Imidazolidinyl Urea and Diazolidinyl Urea

- Methyl and Propyl and Butyl and Ethyl Paraben

- Petrolatum

- Propylene Glycol

- PVP/VA Copolymer

- Sodium Lauryl Sulfate

- Stearalkonium Chloride

- Synthetic Colors

- Synthetic Fragrances

- Triethanolamine[10]

9.   Steinman, David, "Save Your Complexion with Nontoxic Makeup," *Healthy Living, 2001*

10.  Hampton, Aubrey, Aubrey Organics, "10 Synthetic Cosmetic Ingredients to Avoid," 2002

## PHTHALATES

Does your perfume contain phthalates (pronounced tha-lates)? The Centers for Disease Control (CDC) tested a group of 20- to 40-year-old females and discovered they are overdosing on phthalates. "While the CDC found evidence of phthalates in virtually every one of the cross-section of Americans tested, evidence of the highest levels of exposure to the phthalate DBP (dibutyl phthalate) were found in women of childbearing age.[11] This is significant, because phthalates have been linked to birth defects, among other health problems.

### What are phthalates?

Phthalates are a family of industrial chemicals that are used as plastic softeners or solvents in many different consumer products. They can be absorbed through the skin, inhaled as fumes, ingested when they contaminate food or when children bite or suck on toys, and are inadvertently but directly administered to patients from some PVC (polyvinyl chloride or vinyl) medical devices.

### Phthalates are dangerous.

Hundreds of animal studies have demonstrated that phthalates can damage the liver, the kidneys, the lungs and the reproductive system, especially the developing testes. Some patients who receive treatment using PVC medical devices softened with phthalates have developed the same health problems that animal studies show come from exposure to these chemicals. Other health problems seen in animal studies have never been looked for in people. But scientists in the Food and Drug Administration (FDA), Health Canada and the National Institutes of Health's Toxicology Program agree that animal studies predict that phthalates can be dangerous to humans.

In her highly recommended book, *Drop Dead Gorgeous? Protecting Yourself From The Hidden Dangers of Cosmetics*, author Kim Erickson takes a hard, close-up look at personal care ingredients, including ones that contain known disease-causing ingredients plus those that are non-toxic. This book is worth reading for anyone using anything on her skin other than plain aloe or filtered water. The cosmetics industry, like our food industry and others, is producing toxic substances within the confines of our lax laws. As consumers we are not protected by government oversight, inspection or regulation enough to ensure our safety. The

---

11. "Not Too Pretty: Phthalates, Beauty Products and the FDA," www. nottoopretty.org/more., 2002

reason for this, of course, is the power of big business whose rights to make a profit exceed our rights to safety. Erickson writes:

> During the past fifty years, science and big business have teamed up to bring a steady stream of new and "better" products to consumers, many of them aimed at our desire for instant beauty. With systems working at break-neck speed, and with billions of dollars at stake, the primary aim of this alliance was to protect the cosmetics trade. This method of ensuring continued industry profits and consumer demand was a strategy that worked well for many years. But during the 1970s, consumers began to question the safety of mainstream cosmetics. To counteract the growing skepticism on the part of consumers, manufacturers set out to prove how safe their products were by sponsoring research into several of the synthetic chemicals commonly found in cosmetics. While the results sounded reassuring, the politics and science behind the studies were anything but. Since the studies were paid for by the cosmetics companies, it was no surprise that the findings ultimately supported the industry's profit margin by using misleading research to soothe consumers' fears…The few independent studies that have been conducted have resulted in some alarming findings.[12]

Erickson boldly identifies by name specific brands and products that contain lead and other neurotoxins, carcinogens, irritants and hormone disrupters in hair dye, shampoo, perfumes, deodorizers, eye shadow and more. If you use any of these products, Erickson's book is worth reading, even if it scares the stuffing out of you. If you are a beautician, hair dresser, salon stylist or nail salon specialist, you may want to change your career to nautical engineering or something like that. Or wear gloves, or a mask or just cut hair, or switch to all natural products in your shop. Do something!

## WHAT CAN YOU DO?
### Start with non-toxic brands…

There are several companies offering non-toxic makeup, and a trip to the health food store, plus a little experimentation will eventually determine what's best for you. Some of the better/more popular brands of non-toxic makeup are:

- Aubrey Organics: www.aubrey—organics.com. The people at Aubrey offer this sound advice: "Look for natural ingredients in the products you buy. Do not use cosmetics that are artificially colored. Is the shampoo bright

---

12.  Erickson, Kim, *Drop Dead Gorgeous? Protecting Yourself From The Hidden Dangers of Cosmetics,* Contemporary Books, 2002, pages 3-4

green or blue? Very likely it contains a coal tar color. Does the product contain synthetic fragrances? Don't buy it. You may find that some of your allergy problems will suddenly disappear when you no longer use cosmetics formulated with petrochemicals and other synthetics."[13]

- Abundant Earth: www.abundantearth.com.

- Beauty Without Cruelty: www.avalonnaturalproducts.com; Products are 100% vegetarian, making optimum use of safe, natural and organic ingredients, without the use of animal testing for ingredients or finished formulas.

- Rachel Perry: www.rachelperry.net

- Ecco Bella: www.eccobella.com; Sally Malanga, founder of Ecco Bella, writes: "When I started Ecco Bella in 1992, I took a long, hard look at the ingredients women were using in their commercial body care products. I found many of the ingredients were potentially toxic, including talc, mercury, synthetic colors, fragrance, formaldehyde releasing preservatives, and a wide range of ingredients derived from petroleum.

  As bad as this was, I was also horrified by the cruelty of animal testing, which all the major cosmetic companies participated in. Many still do. The FDA does not require that ingredients be tested on animals. Yet, thousands of innocent animals are maimed and killed every year in the name of beauty.
  If a product is intended for human use, it makes sense to test it on people. If a product is going to be beneficial to human skin, it makes sense to use gentle natural ingredients that have been shown to be safe over time."[14]

A bit of good advice is to periodically check up on natural products companies to make sure they haven't been bought out by big corporate entities that have decided to corrupt the once-healthy products.

## WHAT ARE YOU PUTTING UNDER YOUR ARMS?

Underarm deodorants, like cosmetics, create a cumulative, perpetual toxic effect. Most popular brands are loaded with toxic chemicals and heavy metals that are bad for your health. Chief among these is aluminum compounds. Aluminum is a toxic metal that concentrates in your bones and brain, and in underarm deodorants the aluminum is fine enough to enter your bloodstream via your skin. The aluminum industry is one of the most powerful around, so most news on the

---

13.  http://www.aubrey—organics.com/about/treat_10synth.cfm
14.  eccobella.com

dangers of this heavy metal is squelched and kept from the public. Dr. Laura Thompson, author of *Smart Food, Smart Families, Our Children Are…What Our Children Eat* writes:

> The most common metal that I find in the people I consult with is aluminum. Today, aluminum is everywhere…under your arms, in your teeth, and on your baby's skin. Antiperspirants, toothpaste, dental amalgams, baby powder, cosmetics, and cigarette filters contain aluminum. We ingest it in some drinking waters, some commercial teas, cheeses, white flour, baking powder, aspirin, and table salt. We cook with it too; some pots and pans contain aluminum. Unfortunately, many over-the-counter and prescription antacids for digestive difficulties, contain aluminum.

In a nutshell, avoid all aluminum products, aluminum compounds and aluminum containers.

## *MORE ON HAIR DYES…*
## *GET THE GRAY OUT?*

Hair dyes are generally toxic. A recent British report on the BBC stated that scientists are particularly worried about two chemical ingredients, para-phenylenediamine and tetrahydro-6-nitroquinoxaline. Both substances, common in hair dyes, have been shown to damage the body's genetic material, and to cause cancer in animals. "It is not the first time that fears have been raised about the safety of permanent hair dyes, which have previously been linked to arthritis and damage to unborn children," say British scientists. "Last year a study by the University of Southern California [USC] found women who used permanent hair dyes at least once a month were up to three times more likely to develop bladder cancer. Researchers also found long-serving hairdressers were also at increased risk.[15]

> According to a study published in last February's issue of the *International Journal of Cancer*, the USC research team found that women who use permanent dyes at least once a month for a year or longer have twice the risk of bladder cancer as nonusers even after adjusting for smoking. Those who used dyes more often and for longer periods, as well as hairdressers (who use dyes on their clients), face an even higher risk…The findings were part of a continuing study on bladder cancer incidence.
>
> The hair dye study results raised concerns in Europe, where, as in the United States, about one-third of women over age 18 dye their hair.[16]

---

15. "Hair dye cancer alert," British Broadcasting Company, April 2002

Although the studies mentioned reflect risks of bladder cancer, it would be prudent to realize that other cancers, diseases and symptoms may result as well from both short-term and long-term hair dye usage.

## TRICLOSAN KILLS GERMS AND PEOPLE

The funny thing (only in an ironic sense) is that many products that are found in today's personal care products and foods kill not only insects and germs (as they are designed to do), but people as well. As much as chemical-makers deny the fact, cancer is a common side effect of toxic chemicals that enter our bodies. There are many such chemicals, but one of note is triclosan, a common ingredient in germ-killing soaps, cleaners, toothpastes, deodorants and other products found in your drawers—which includes your dresser drawers and your bicycle shorts. Triclosan, when not wreaking havoc inside your body, finds its way down your drain and breaks down into dioxins. Dioxins are a group of chemicals known to increase the likelihood of cancer:

> An unwanted byproduct, they [dioxins] are formed when heating processes create certain chemicals—chlorine is the best known. Environmental campaign groups describe them as among the most dangerous toxins known. Scientists are working to establish their exact toxicity, but a draft report from the US Environmental Protection Agency [EPA] indicates dioxins are considered a serious threat to public health.
>
> In 1997, a World Health Organisation group declared the most toxic dioxin—2,3,7,8-tetrachlorodibenzo-p-dioxin, or TCDD—a class 1 carcinogen, meaning it causes cancer in humans.[17]

Triclosan, which contains dioxins, are a member of the carcinogenic family of chlorophenols, and is now considered a specific biocide—a killing agent that targets specific cellular functions. "This kind of germ-killer is troubling because it can create 'super-bugs,' bacteria that have managed to survive their encounter with it and evolved into a resistant type."[18] Scientists at the University of Minne-

16. DiRado, Alicia, "Study linking hair dyes and cancer trigger policy changes in Europe," University of Southern California, 2002; "Coloring Your Hair Could Affect Your Bladder; Study Finds Link Between Permanent Dyes and Cancer," by Peggy Peck WebMD Medical News, 2002

17. "Dioxins: What are they," BBC News report, April, 2001

18. "The Devil's In The Details. (And The Dioxin's In The Tricolsan)," The Non—Toxic Times, Seventh Generation electronic news report, August 2002

sota have discovered that triclosan dissolved in water breaks down into dioxin in the presence of sun light, raising the alarming possibility that triclosan escaping into the general environment may be turning into one of the most toxic materials known.

> What's disturbing here is the fact that our collective appetite for antibacterial products may be turning our country's wastewater stream into a new source for a highly dangerous chemical we simply don't need any more of.
>
> ...Fanning the flames of this emerging triclosan controversy is a new study from the U.S. Geological Survey which tested the water from 139 streams in 30 states for 95 wastewater contaminants. Focusing on waterways that were located near wastewater treatment plants and large agricultural operations in an attempt to quantify what pollutants these sources might be releasing into the environment, researchers found that triclosan contaminated a hefty 57% of all surveyed sites. The findings were further proof that triclosan readily survives conventional wastewater treatment methods and is entering the environment in many locales.
>
> In addition to rivers and streams, scientists have also now found triclosan in human breast milk. Researchers at Stockholm University in Sweden found that three out of five tested samples contained this antibacterial chemical, sometimes in appreciable amounts. It's now clear that that triclosan can and does enter into and remain in the human body as a result of either direct contact with products containing it or exposure to triclosan-contaminated environments.
>
> It all adds up to a clear message that didn't really need to be any clearer: Triclosan is both a household hazard and a threat to the environment. **Though ironically marketed as an ingredient that increases personal health, it appears to do the precise opposite.** Its suspected contribution to bacterial resistance and the fact that it's likely contributing to dioxin pollution make it an ingredient to watch out for and avoid.[19]

## *WHAT YOU CAN DO TO GET THE TOXINS OUT OF YOUR PERSONAL LIFE*

Start to wean yourself and your family off of toxic personal care products. If the idea is overwhelming, just start with three items that you use the most and switch to non-toxic brands. Then do the same with three more items a couple of months later until you eventually purge your house and body of all of them. This should make a huge difference to your health.

---

19. ibid

- For safe tampon replacements, go online to www.organicessentials.com. Organic Essentials products are available through natural food stores, finer drug stores and some Internet and catalog companies.

- Use safer, non-toxic makeup. Read the book *Drop Dead Gorgeous* by Kim Erickson to study safer, cleaner brands

- Realize that everything you put on your skin ends up on the inside of your body—from gasoline to nail polish, and from soap to ink

- If you go to a state fair, nightclub or other event, don't let them stamp your hand with ink as a proof that you paid admission if you don't plan to leave and come back

- If you must work with chemicals, always wear gloves, a mask and other protective gear

- Discontinue using aerosol cans, both the ingredients and the propellant are almost always bad for your health

- Use only deodorants and toothpaste without fluorides, aluminum and other heavy metals

- Avoid products with artificial dyes. The price to pay for looking good can be your good health.

- Don't put any substance in your mouth or on your skin without understanding each ingredient on the label. As with any food you eat, read all labels carefully for anything you are going to inhale, put on your hair or skin, or ingest in any other way. Avoid all chemical names. If you are not sure of what something is on a can, bottle or tube, find a book wherein you can look up the substance, because your health depends upon it.

- If you are the activist type, or just want to get the toxins out of your hair (figuratively and literally), you may look at a website called chemicalbodyburden.org for whole long list of website links on the topic. This will not only give you a lot to look at, but it will also give you an idea of the immensity of the toxic burden we all face and the great numbers of people joining hands across the world to clean up the problem. The Chemical Body Burden website advises: "In the long term,...the best way to reduce the load of chemicals we all carry is to stop using them. This means creating public policies that encourage the production of safer products produced without dangerous chemicals. It means relying less and less on chemical pesticides to grow our food. We need policies that are truly protective of human health, so that future generations are not born with a chemical body burden that grows throughout their lifetime.

"Moving toward a cleaner economy and reducing our chemical body burden means changing policies, challenging chemical companies, changing consumer behavior and supporting cleaner industrial and agricultural production.
This can only happen with widespread involvement of concerned individuals
in communities across the country and around the world."[20]

There are many other products falling under the personal health care category
that we can critique for their toxicity levels. However, in this book we cannot
cover all of the products and all of the chemicals without putting you to sleep and
producing a volume bigger than the New York City phone directory. Consider
this chapter your starter kit—a mere taste for the immensity of this subject matter and a warning to avoid toxic chemicals as a means of preserving, fostering and
protecting your health and the health of your family members.

---

20.  chemicalbodyburden.org, 2002

# The War on Cancer Is A Joke,
# But Nobody's Laughing!

*Physicians give drugs of which they know little,*
*into bodies, of which they know less,*
*for diseases of which they know nothing at all.*

—Voltaire

The war on cancer is deplorable. It's being fought with feathers and paper swords instead of bazookas. The generals are all high and the soldiers are ill-equipped from the very start. When people get cancer, the doctor's face waxes over with a dazed expression. In all seriousness he/she tells you that "doctors just don't know enough yet as to why people get cancer, but they suspect it is genetics." Then he/she tells you there really is no cure. So the treatment consists of surgery and/or giving the sufferer powerful chemicals—chemicals that target cells and kill them all, good and bad alike. Chemotherapy is such a common word that you would think it would be good for something. Another approach, often in conjunction with chemotherapy, is surgery—cutting away diseased tissue. They don't know what causes it or how to treat it, but they poison you and hack you up.

One day, if humankind survives the next fifty years altogether, people will look back on this as the dark ages of health care—darker than the previous Dark Ages wherein leeches and incantations were used to drive evil spirits out of your blood. Today's scalpel is the replacement for yesterday's leeches; and chemotherapy replaces gizzards and newts' tongues. I don't know which approach is better, and neither do doctors, which is proof enough that we have not advanced one inch in cancer cure or therapy. What's worse is the whole joke that we refer to as "cancer research," which is comprised of paying scientists and their universities to look in all the wrong places so they will never discover and publicly report the fact that several of the corporations funding the research are the same characters producing the pollutants and chemicals causing cancer.

## MAJOR PLAYERS

Monsanto owns the drug company G.D. Searle and produces NutraSweet, rBGH (Bovine Growth Hormone) and a host of other chemicals and toxic chemical pollutants. And Dupont produces dimethyl sulfate (DMS) used to make surfactants, fabric softeners, water treating chemicals, pesticides, drugs, dyes and photographic chemicals. Dupont also produces abrasives, additives, adhesives, building and construction materials, carpet and flooring products, cleaning products, films, fluoropolymers, food ingredients, fungicides, herbicides, insecticides, paint and coatings, plastics, seed and specialty grains, to name a few of this company's offerings. Wait, it gets worse. Investigator Ashley Simmons (*Poison for Profit*) claims:

> The same chemical companies that produce toxic chemicals also produce prescription drugs, veterinary medicines, a wide array of medical products and imaging technologies, hold cancer treatment and medical device patents, and a produce a staggering assortment of over-the-counter palliatives.
>
> Families with toxin induced illnesses often spend large sums for drugs and medical treatment.
>
> This circle of profit is not conspiracy theory, but an easily provable fact.
>
> Below are chem/pharm web sites for the largest companies in the world. There you can see quickly and clearly that these companies profit from all sides of the picture.
>
> **Aventis** was launched in December 1999 through the merger of Hoechst AG of Germany and Rhône-Poulenc SA of France. www.aventis.com
> Aventis brought us Star Link genetically modified corn. Aventis "crop sciences" include herbicides, fungicides, pesticides and genetically engineered food. www.cropscience.aventis.com/products/products.htm
>
> **Aventis Pharma is the pharmaceutical division:** - www.aventis.com
>
> **Monsanto** is owned by **Pharmacia**. The Pharmacia Corporation was created through the merger of Pharmacia Upjohn with Monsanto Company and its G.D. Searle unit. Pharmacia employs 59,000 people worldwide and has research, manufacturing and administrative sales operations in more than 60 countries.
>
> **Merck** is known widely as a pharmaceutical company: www.merck.com
> Merck Research Company; Applications to Register Pesticide: -
> www.epa.gov/fedrgstr/EPA-PEST/1996/July/Day-10/pr-796.html
> Merck produces chemicals and precursors for pesticides and other neurotoxins.

**Dow Chemical** produces both toxic chemicals and pharmaceuticals. Dow's pesticide products include the organophosphate pesticide Dursban (a/k/a Chlorpyrifos/a/k/a RAID a/k/a Lorsban and is found in about 800 other pesticide products). Dursban was to be phased out and banned from indoor, yard and garden use last year because of what it does to the developing brain.

**Bayer.** Did you know that Bayer also makes other drugs, pesticides, chemicals? www.bayer.com

**Bayer pharmaceuticals:** www.pharma.bayer.com
It is interesting to note that the Bayer corporation was originally the I.G. Farben Company with deep ties to the Nazis during the 1920s and 30s. I.G. Farben produced Zyklon-B gas which was used in the Nazi death camps. Other big chem/pharm manufacturers became owners of pieces of I.G. Farben during the lengthy process of dissolving its assets after decades of lawsuits and pressures from international organizations for alleged I.G.Farben Nazi crimes. Here is a quote from the BBC:
"Most of the company's assets were confiscated after World War II and were transferred to four big German corporations: Bayer, Hoechst, Agfa and BASF."
http://news.bbc.co.uk/hi/english/business/newsid_1549000/1549092.stm
Many of these huge transnationals have merged with each other. For example, CibaGeigy, Sandoz and other multinational chemical/pharmaceutical companies merged to become Novartis. Then Novartis Agribusiness merged with Zeneca (Astra-Zeneca) Agrochemicals to form Syngenta: www.syngenta.com/en/syngenta/facts.asp

**Novartis** www.novartis.com **Novartis** owns **Syngenta**—produces pesticides, herbicides, etc: - www.syngenta-us.com

**AMVAC** makes the insecticide NALED a/k/a DIBROM, and nineteen other products. AMVAC Chemical Company is owned by American Vanguard Corporation, which makes herbicides, pesticides. A major portion of its revenues comes from selling its specialty chemicals to the pharmaceutical industry. It is also in the business of "environmental remediation" and "toxic waste management." (Like other chem/pharm companies, American Vanguard profits from pollution that they help make, and then get paid to clean up). www.thestandard.com/companies/dossier/0,1922,271462,00.html

**American Home Products** pharmaceuticals and veterinary medicines has subsidiaries galore, including American Cyanimid among others. American Cyanimid produced many chemical products including pesticides and pharmaceutical chemicals.
www.amvac-chemical.com/investor_page/Subsidiaries/subsidiaries.htm

AHP later changed its name to WYETH, a major holding company: www.wyeth.com[1]

This is evil genius, pure and simple, profiting at both ends of the spectrum—"The huge transnational companies that produce toxic chemicals found in pesticides, herbicides and industrial and household products profit not only from the sale of these products, but also from the symptoms and chronic illnesses that they can trigger."[2]

It's amazing, but it's really no secret if you just do a little background checking. The companies making chemicals that cause cancer also make the chemicals that make the drugs to treat the cancer. Is this a coincidence? You decide if this is a wonderfully evil genius enterprise that makes lots of money, increases power and makes corporate heads happy while the rest of us are crying. Corporate spokesmen call it "free enterprise," while sane citizens call it heartless treachery. There's a fortune to be made every day in sick care and medical care, so the chemicals keep coming.

Through our gullible and compliant major media, we are fed continuous warnings about risk factors and genetic predispositions, along with theories about mysterious viruses, and false hopes by corporations denying that they are producing cancer-causing chemicals. Regarding breast cancer, one consumer advocate explains, "We are told that getting older and being female are the major risk factors for breast cancer. Yet these 'risk factors' do not cause cancer. Many of the same corporations that sponsor Breast Cancer Awareness Month events either profit off of cancer or produce cancer-causing toxic chemicals which is why they never mention cancer prevention or the environmental causes of cancer."[3]

Bradley Angel, executive director of Greenaction, says, "It's time to stop cancer where it starts, at the chemical plants, refineries and incinerators that spew deadly cancer-causing chemicals into our air and water."[4]

1. Simmons, Ashley Hotz, "Poison for Profit—What A Business Plan! creativehealth.netfirms.com, 2002

2. Simmons, Ashley Hotz, "Poison for Profit—What a Business Plan!, May 2002; redflagsweekly.com

3. San Francisco Mayoral Proclamation Declares October "Stop Cancer Where it Starts Month," www.greenaction.org/cancer/pr101900.shtml, 2002

4. ibid

## CHILDREN AS VICTIMS

One of the biggest concerns in the area of cancer is the issue of our children who are more and more becoming the victims. Samuel Epstein, M.D., Chairman of the Cancer Prevention Coalition and Professor Emeritus of Environmental and Occupational Medicine, University of Illinois School of Public Health, Chicago, writes, "Since passage of the 1971 National Cancer Act, launching the 'War Against Cancer,' the incidence of childhood cancer has steadily escalated to alarming levels. Childhood cancers have increased by 26% overall, while the incidence of particular cancers has increased still more: acute lymphocytic leukemia, 62%; brain cancer, 50%; and bone cancer, 40%. The federal National Cancer Institute (NCI) and the 'charitable' American Cancer Society (ACS), the cancer establishment, have failed to inform the public, let alone Congress and regulatory agencies, of this alarming information. As importantly, they have failed to publicize well-documented scientific information on avoidable causes responsible for the increased incidence of childhood cancer."[5]

Is cancer caused by bad genes and invisible germs? This would make it our fault, wouldn't it? But we can't let the chemical polluters—the giant industries so fond of defaming environmentalists and consumer advocacy—off the hook so easily. Dr. Epstein shows:

- Over 20 U.S. and international studies have incriminated paternal and maternal exposures (preconception, during conception and post-conception) to a wide range of occupational carcinogens as major causes of childhood cancer.

- There is substantial evidence on the risks of brain cancer and leukemia in children from frequent consumption of nitrite-dyed hot dogs; consumption during pregnancy has been similarly incriminated. Nitrites, added to meat for coloring purposes, have been shown to react with natural chemicals in meat (amines) to form a potent carcinogenic nitrosamine.

- Consumption of non-organic fruits and vegetables, particularly in baby food, contaminated with high concentrations of multiple residues of carcinogenic pesticides, poses major risks of childhood cancer, besides delayed cancers in adult life.

---

5.    Epstein, M.D., Samuel S. and Quentin Young, M.D.: "What War Against Cancer?, Escalating Incidence of Childhood Cancer Ignored," Cancer Prevention Coalition, May 9, 2002

- Numerous studies have shown strong associations between childhood cancers, particularly brain cancer, non-Hodgkin's lymphoma and leukemia, and domestic exposure to pesticides from uses in the home, including pet flea collars, lawn and garden; another major source of exposure is commonplace use in schools.

- Use of lindane, a potent carcinogen in shampoos for treating lice and scabies, infesting about six million children annually, is associated with major risks of brain cancer; lindane is readily absorbed through the skin.[6]

It cannot be reasonably argued that the National Cancer Institute fails to study prevention and environmental toxins as causative factors due to a lack of funding. To the contrary, they've got plenty of money in their escalating bank accounts. Dr. Epstein writes, "The minimal priorities of the cancer establishment for prevention reflects mindsets and policies and not lack of resources. NCI's annual budget has increased some 20-fold since passage of the 1971 Act, from $220 million to $4.2 billion, while revenues of the ACS are now about $800 million. NCI expenditures on primary prevention have been estimated as under 4% of its budget, while ACS allocates less than 0.1% of its revenues to primary prevention and 'environmental carcinogenesis.'"[7]

## BREAST CANCER: GENETIC OR ENVIRONMENTAL CAUSES?

Perhaps one of the most frightening forms of cancer in this world is breast cancer. Breast cancer strikes more women than any other type of cancer, and it kills more women between the ages of 40 and 55 than any other cancer. The incidence of breast cancer in the United States has been steadily increasing since 1940. According to the National Cancer Institute, the lifetime risk of breast cancer is now 1 in 8.[8] The physical and emotional trauma associated with this relative newcomer to modern society is incalculable. Sadly and sickly, breast cancer is making several industries wealthy. Treatment facilities, hospitals, surgeons, drug companies, diagnostics equipment manufacturers and other affiliates of this horrific disease are making millions while buying into the ridiculous claims that breast cancer is simply a genetic problem.

Even as wave after wave of off-base studies broadcast by slick news anchors—reading industry propaganda over the air—report that breast cancer is

---

6.   ibid

7.   ibid

8.   "Breast Cancer and the Environment," Stony Brook State University of New York, 2002

caused by genetics, the truth remains hard to suppress. More than 184,000 women are annually diagnosed with breast cancer, yet 70% of these women have none of the known risk factors (radiation exposure at a young age, early menarche [first menstrual period during puberty], late menopause, or giving birth to a first child after age thirty) identified by the medical community as causative factors.

The proof is mounting that there is a connection between breast cancer, toxins and the environment—evidence that chemical manufacturers and pollution-creators are attempting to hide and discredit. But the reality of the connection is hard to ignore. Here are some examples: Women working in industries with high levels of chemical exposure—including exposure to dioxin—have very high rates of breast cancer:

> A study among 24,000 blue-collar workers in New Jersey found significant association between breast cancer among African-American women and employment in several chemical-intensive industries. Breast cancer mortality was 1.64 times higher among pharmaceutical workers and 1.51 times higher among electrical equipment manufacturing workers who, it was noted, are often exposed to high levels of solvents. *(1991, American Journal of Industrial, Medicine)*
>
> Similar results were found in New York state where high breast cancer rates were seen in women in the electrical and printing industry. *(1986, New York Department of Health Monograph #21)*
>
> Women chemical workers exposed to high levels of dioxin in a German pesticide plant had higher rates of breast cancer and twice the mortality rate of the German population as a whole. *(1991, Lancet 338)*
>
> **Concentrations in humans:** A New York University study on women's health reported that women with the highest concentration of chlorine based pesticides and other organochlorines in their blood and fat had breast cancer risks 4–10 times higher than women with lower concentrations. *(1993, Journal of the National Cancer Institute)*
>
> **Hazardous waste sites:** A study by the U.S. Environmental Protection Agency found that people who live in counties with hazardous waste sites are 6.5 times more likely to have elevated cancer rates than those living in counties without those sites. Santa Clara County has 29 Superfund sites—more than any other county in the U.S. Chlorinated solvents, pesticides and manufacturing waste are the most common contaminants at Superfund sites. Trichloroethylene (TCE) is the second most common material found in Superfund sites after lead *(Rachel's Hazard Waste News #370)*
>
> **Long Island, New York:** A report by New York's Department of Health found that women who once lived near large chemical plants on Long Island had a greater chance of developing breast cancer after menopause. The report, "Residences Near Industry and High Traffic Areas and the Risk of Breast

Cancer on Long Island," found that 14.5% of the women who developed breast cancer after menopause lived less than a mile from plants producing chemicals, rubber and plastic. While the report did not establish conclusively that chemical pollutants caused the higher rates of breast cancer, according to Dr. Mary Wolff, professor of Community Medicine at Mt. Sinai Medical Center in Manhattan, it is considered the first credible study done to suggest a link between industrial pollution and breast cancer. (Coalition for Environmental Concerns, Albany, NY)[9]

The rise in the breast cancer rate is concurrent with the rise in chemical waste and toxic chemical production in the modern world. Researcher Megan Williams concurs, "The worldwide increase in breast cancer rates has occurred during the same period in which the global environment has become contaminated with industrial synthetic chemicals, including the toxic and persistent 'organochlorines.'"[10] Nancy Evans, the Breast Cancer Fund, writes,

> Breast cancer rates have been climbing steadily in the United States and other industrialized countries since the 1940s. Billions of dollars have been spent in an effort to stem this unrelenting tide, yet more than 50 percent of breast cancer cases remain unexplained by the characteristics and risk factors associated with the disease.
>
> Ionizing radiation is the only proven environmental cause of human breast cancer. But powerful circumstantial evidence indicates that some of the 85,000 synthetic chemicals in use today are responsible for many of the unexplained cases of the disease.
>
> The strongest evidence linking chemicals to breast cancer—based on the fact that lifetime exposure to natural estrogens increases the risk of breast cancer—concerns natural and synthetic estrogens, including drugs like diethylstilbestrol (DES), plastic additives like bisphenol-A (BPA), polyvinyl chloride (PVC) (found in many consumer products), dieldrin and some pesticides. Other synthetic substances strongly linked to breast cancer through experimental evidence are: organic solvents (used in many manufacturing processes, including the manufacture of computer components), polycyclic aromatic hydrocarbons (PAHs) (created in soot and fumes from burning diesel, fuels or cigarettes) and 1,3 butadiene (a byproduct of internal combustion engines).
>
> There are also chemicals for which the evidence indicates a probable but less certain link to breast cancer. These chemicals include dioxin (created when plastics or other materials containing chlorine are burned), the pesticide

9.   Breast Cancer Action, bcaction.org, "Breast Cancer and the Environment: The Toxic Connection," Newsletter #29, April 1995

10.  Williams, Megan, "Breast Cancer and the Environment: The Chlorine Connection," Toronto Now, 1992

DDT (dichloro-diphenyl-trichloroethane) and its metabolite, DDE and PCBs (polychlorinated biphenyls), previously used in the manufacture of electrical equipment and other industrial and consumer products.

Finally, there is evidence of chemicals that affect how the body functions in ways that suggest a possible link between these substances and breast cancer. These chemicals include the insecticide heptachlor and phthalates, used to make plastic soft and flexible.[11]

## HERE'S HOW TO REDUCE YOUR CHANCES OF GETTING BREAST CANCER:

For more great information on the link between environmental toxins and breast cancer, visit the website www.breastcancerfund.org. This website advise:

The following 5-point plan will help us reduce the risk of breast cancer and ultimately end the epidemic:

1.  PHASE OUT TOXIC CHEMICALS that are omnipresent in the lives of so many people.

2.  ENACT "SUNSHINE" LAWS AND ENFORCE EXISTING ENVIRONMENTAL PROTECTION LAWS to reduce the use of toxins by requiring companies to report how many tons of chemicals they use.

3.  PRACTICE HEALTHY PURCHASING, with local, state and federal governments [that should be] leading the way in purchasing environmentally preferable products, thereby creating an example for individuals to follow.

4.  OFFER CORPORATE INCENTIVES that encourage businesses to eliminate the use of harmful chemicals in their products and processes.

5.  MONITOR BREAST MILK, through a comprehensive community program that identifies the chemicals present in breast milk, establishes links to geographic areas and initiates a plan to eliminate these contaminants.[12]

---

11.  Evans, Nancy, "State of the Evidence: What is the Connection between Chemicals & Breast Cancer?", The Breast Cancer Fund & Breast Cancer Action, breastcancerfund.org, 2002

12.  ibid

## DIETARY FACTORS

- Eat whole, raw foods that are organically grown to avoid large amounts of pesticides and synthetic fertilizers in your daily diet.

- Switch to organic foods and ingredients of all sorts, being aware that all artificial ingredients are bad for your health. These include, but are not limited to, chemical additives, preservatives, food dyes, artificial colorings, emulsifiers, separators, MSG, artificial sweeteners, aluminum compounds, and more.

- Be sure to take omega 3 fatty acids which are available in cod liver oil, fish oils and flaxseed oil.

- Eliminate bad fats and oils from your diet, including foods that are fried, contain hydrogenated and/or partially hydrogenated oils, margarine, fake fats, fake butters and snack/junk foods.

- Do not eat genetically engineered food.

Conduct your own research on mammograms, drugs, therapies, foods, chemicals, corporate behavior, corporate ownership (in treatment facilities, drug companies and diagnostic equipment) and toxicity of the environment. Do not rely solely on any single doctor—medical, natural or otherwise—as your only source of health advice.

# How Evil is
# Environmentalism?

Since when is environmentalism evil? The answer: Since certain awakened individuals began to find out that industrial toxins are killing people, causing cancer and destroying the food chain, they started to expose big polluting industries for their greed, irresponsibility and destruction of life and health on this planet. This, of course, started a war. The industrial giants rolled out their cannon, because, before environmentalists began to speak out against them, they were the spoiled rich kids who did whatever they wanted with no opposition, no control and no responsibility. Environmentalists, providing a sense of conscience, became the enemy and the eternal target of corporate defamation, much the way a spoiled child lashes out at his playmate who just wants an equal share in the fun.

Environmentalists are mothers, wives, businesswomen, grandmothers, professors, independent scientists, writers, journalists, inventors, construction workers, engineers, college girls, actors, film makers, scientists and other outraged citizens who are sick and tired of being poisoned by chemical-makers and polluters. They are trying to protect their nation, other nations, national parks, waterways, oceans, children, grandchildren, husbands, wives and neighbors. For this they are labeled tree-huggers, junk-scientists, paranoids, fear-mongers, crack-pots, anti-Americans, Communists, Boulder-sandal-wearing-left-wing hippy dippies and party poopers. Out of all of these only the first two are accurate: Trees deserved to be hugged and thanked for giving us shade, fruit, shelter, soil and oxygen, and we ought not let corporations kill them off with chemicals. Environmentalists are also party poopers, telling the corporate polluters that their little private, exclusive parties are over, because it's wrong to celebrate and laugh at the expense of the rest of us who are forced to breathe and drink their toxic effluent.

The world can thank Rachel Carson, author of *Silent Spring*, for kicking off the environmental movement. She exposed the dangers of the pesticide DDT and how it found its way into our food chain and has been causing suffering ever since it was first carelessly applied to wipe out insects.

## WOULD YOU DRINK BUG SPRAY?

Think about this for a quick moment (or longer): Pesticides, including bug sprays in your can of Raid, plus those used for fruitfly spraying, crop-dusting, mosquito-dusting, house-fogging, termite tenting, as well as the kind MegaFarm, Inc. sprays on non-organic food crops, are meant to do one thing—**kill living creatures**. Sure, you may say they are meant to kill bugs, not people. Unfortunately, when Dr. Frankenstein created his monster, he couldn't control it. He didn't mean for it to get out of hand, but it did, and that was bad for everybody. Pesticides are meant to kill bugs, but since they are toxic chemicals, they don't stop at killing bugs—they kill people too, as well as animals on the land, fish in the sea and birds in the air. In the least they make us all sick. Still, chemical producers won't admit to causing cancer in your family. Hey, it's nothing personal, just business.

### Taste Test

How appetizing would it be if you had a bunch of ripe, shiny grapes, and, right before you ate them, you took them outside and sprayed them down with a can of your favorite bug spray? Let them sit, drenched in pesticidal chemicals for a little while. Then, *still* dripping with bug spray dripping with bug spray, take the grapes to the sink and give them a quick rinse under the tap water, then begin popping them in your mouth. Sound delicious? No? Yuck? Well, whether you see it or not, most farmers spray chemicals far more dangerous than household bug spray onto all of the foods they grow. Pesticides meant to kill bugs are coating your fruits, vegetables, nuts and seeds. Amazingly, pesticide residues can also be found on foods that you wouldn't think of as containing them—from chocolate chip cookies to pasta sauce. Pesticides do not just wash off under your faucet. They stick to your foods, they are INSIDE your foods, and they contaminate other foods. Developed by scientists to kill crop pests, pesticides—manufactured by big chemical manufacturers—are killing people and causing diseases from cancer to swollen gums, and from nerve damage to respiratory illnesses and from infertility to birth defects. All the while, chemical companies and their lackey scientists are telling you that there's no danger from eating bug spray. Funny, but they said the same thing about DDT in the 1950s as well. In fact, you can still procure some old film footage showing teachers dusting their little students until they are lost in a cloud of poison while trying to eat their lunch at a community picnic table.

Scientists working for the big chemical companies used to tell us that DDT was safe and beneficial. Now it's a banned substance in the U.S. However, since it is not banned everywhere else, chemical manufacturers can sell DDT out of the country where it is used as a pesticide on plant foods that eventually are imported back into the U.S.

Pesticides, fertilizers and herbicides do not only attack your body from the foods you eat. Many of these toxic chemicals are sprayed at home, on the lawn and in the garden where they can enter the atmosphere, the ground water, the earth, your skin, your lungs and can even be tracked into your house on the bottoms of your shoes or through the air.

> In October, 1996 CNN broadcast a news feature about the results of a study conducted by the U.S. Environmental Protection Agency. This study has documented that the level of lawn and garden herbicides, fungicides and insecticides in indoor carpets are from 10 to 100 times higher than they are outdoors.
>
> These herbicides and insecticides are carried inside on shoes and on pets, and readily accumulate in carpets. The CNN news documentary report was accompanied by a video reportage of four babies crawling around on a carpet—and mouthing every available toy.
>
> A substantial contributing factor to the excessively high levels of herbicides and pesticides in carpets is that these pesticides are not degraded by sunlight, ultraviolet light and rain, and therefore persist in indoor carpets far longer than they do outdoors.
>
> Exposure to home gardening pesticides has been strongly associated with hyperactivity, leukemia, and damage to the blood/brain barrier in children, and with birth defects in newborns due to maternal exposure. And due to the much smaller body mass of babies, toddlers and small children, any given pesticide level is a far larger factor—and threat to their health—than to the far larger body mass of an adult. For greater detail on many more studies, effects and formal references, go to this web site (www.chem-tox.com).[1]

As of this writing, several Hollywood celebrities have become outspoken critics of the imminent dangers of household chemicals. Among the more vocal are actors Olivia Newton John and the married couple Kelly Preston and John Travolta. Almost losing their baby to chemical poisoning, Preston and Travolta have taken their personal story to the mainstream press.

---

1.    http://www.truehealth.org/ahealt04.html Vancouver, Canada 2002

Like many celebrity advocates, Kelly Preston's road to activism began with personal experience when her 2-year old son was hospitalized for inhaling fumes from carpet cleaning agents in 1994. Soon after, the actress...took on the role of spokesperson and board member of the Children's Health Environmental Coalition (CHEC), a non-profit organization whose mission is raising awareness about environmental toxins affecting children's health.

"It's not like 30 years ago, when the only way you'd get poisoned is if you accidentally swallowed something from under the sink," says the actress, who is married to actor John Travolta. "Now it's as simple as breathing the air or eating certain foods."

Unlike numerous celebrities, who commit to a cause-of-the-month and then move on, Preston has stayed the course, addressing the National Press Club on the hazards of household toxins last year, and making a CHEC educational video, "Not Under My Roof: Protecting Your Baby From Toxins at Home", with Olivia Newton-John.

[Practical health advice on] the website www.checnet.org/healthehouse and in a recent CHEC-funded report, "The State of Children's Health and Environment"—which documents rising rates in asthma, childhood cancer and ADD/ADHD, and their link to environmental causes—is frightening.

...[S]everal common sense strategies...are as simple as removing shoes before entering the home, or using water/vinegar solutions instead of extra-strength cleaners. Other strategies, such as replacing particleboard furniture (manufactured wood can release volatile organic compounds/VOCs that can pollute indoor air), or getting your kids to eat organic produce, is a bit more problematic.

..."Start in your own home," advises Preston. "Do whatever you can, even if you only do it for your family, friends and the people you come in contact with, and then start to branch out. The more you learn, the more you'll want to do to help the environment and others."[2]

## WHAT YOU CAN DO TO KEEP PESTICIDES & SYNTHETIC FERTILIZERS OUT OF YOUR FOODS:

- Eat only organically grown foods, whether raw or packaged. Organically grown foods do not contain deadly chemicals. "A comparison of organic with industrial farming reveals that organic agriculture is significantly better for the environment than its industrial counterpart. Case studies show improvements in a wide range of factors, including nutrient leaching, pesticide pollution, energy use, and diversity of wildlife. Studies also show that organic types of agriculture are technically and economically viable, and that they can produce sufficient food to meet people's needs."[3] Further,

2.   *Tavlin, Cynthia*, "Kelly Preston: on Protecting Your Baby from Toxins," parentsknow.com, April 2002

organically grown foods contain far more nutrients than non-organic counterparts. Primarily this is because organic farming does not function on damaged, depleted and chemicalized soils. Richer soils yield healthier, more nutritious plant foods.

- Since big corporate processed food manufacturers and farming concerns are always trying to find a loophole in the organic standards laws, buy only from those companies who truly embrace the organic philosophy. Big, greedy, dishonest corporations are forever trying to crash the organic party and lower the standards set by those who really care about health.

- Send your money and support to Greenpeace. This organization has been often defamed by big corporations because Greenpeace is extremely active in blocking the dumping, transport and manufacturing of toxic substances worldwide. This organization is not afraid to take on the powerful corporations or challenge them at sea where much of the toxic dumping takes place worldwide. Greenpeace is involved in fighting many fronts at once, including genetic engineering, use of dangerous pesticides, transport of chemical wastes across national boundaries and legal threats by transnational corporations who try to bully local towns, individuals and businesses.

---

3.    http://archive.greenpeace.org/search.shtml

# Sustainability is the Answer: The Sweet Smell of Success

Dwelling on environmental issues can be daunting and depressing. If you do enough research, as I have, especially for this book, after a while it looks like the earth and all of its inhabitants are doomed. We have to hang on to hope so we don't lose our minds over the insanity that causes corporate leaders, politicians and other ignoramuses, large and small, to destroy the air, water and land that we all need as biological beings for survival. There are two sides to every coin. On the one side are the institutions and individuals contributing to the toxicity and diseases plaguing this world unnecessarily. On the other side are those fighting for cleaner air, water and land, and occupying their time with activities ranging from recycling to intercepting oil tankers trying to do their dirty deeds in the middle of the North Atlantic.

We have glimpsed at the ugly side of pollution, but there is so much more to tell—so many more misdeeds and horror stories and corporate ugliness and treachery. The books and magazine articles exposing the inhumanity come to us like an endless outflow of steam rising up from the depths of the earth. We have only touched on a few examples of what evil genius is capable of when their irresponsible behavior is unrestrained by public outcry; censored, self-serving national media; and common decency. But now it's time to look on the bright side of life with a few examples of good news.

If you had the chance to see the movie "A Beautiful Mind," you may remember a profound concept that was all but trivialized and lost in the rest of the plot—It is more rewarding to work together in pursuit of enrichment than it is to work as individuals. In more simplistic terms, there is a way we can all "win" in our attempts to improve our lot in life. You don't need to destroy the environment in order to be wealthy and enjoy the richness of life. We don't need fossil fuels to run our cars, trucks, planes and trains—we do not need to destroy our air to be able to transport ourselves from place to place. We do not have to destroy our forests to build our homes and buildings. We can manufacture goods without ruining our drinking water. We do not have to use deadly pesticides and synthetic fertilizers to grow our food and feed our people. We can even treat illness without the use of unnatural, laboratory-made chemicals. Human suffering and death and wasting does not have to be the "down side" of modern health care, manufacturing, transportation, economics, education, religion, or agriculture.

## CORPORATE CONSUMERS CAN
## MAKE A DIFFERENCE

Much of this book has concentrated on what individual consumers can do to reverse world—and personal—toxicity. But now let's consider institutions themselves as consumers who can stem the tide of disaster with their purchasing decisions. "In some industrial countries, government purchasing accounts for as much as 25 percent of GDP. Government procurement in the European Union alone totaled more than $1 trillion in 2001, or 14 percent of GDP. In North America, it reached $2 trillion, or about 18 percent of GDP. Universities, too, spend billions of dollars each year on everything from campus buildings to cafeteria food. In the United States, colleges bought some $25 billion in goods and services in 1999—equivalent to nearly 3 percent of U.S. GDP. And the United Nations spent nearly $14 billion on goods and services in 2000."[1]

> Because of the large-scale, systematic approach that most institutions take in their purchasing, a single decision made by one professional buyer or purchasing department can have a tremendous ripple effect, influencing the products used by hundreds or even thousands of individuals.
>
> ...By investing in everything from energy-efficient lighting to organic food, growing numbers of businesses, government agencies, hospitals, and other organizations are not only creating safer and healthier workplaces, but are also saving money." [Worldwatch Research Associate Lisa Mastny, author of *Purchasing Power*]
>
> If enough demand for green products is generated, entire markets can shift. A few notable successes point to the tremendous power of green purchasing:
>
> When the world's single largest computer buyer, the United States government, was directed by President Clinton in 1993 to buy only computer equipment that met energy-efficiency standards described under the government's Energy Star program, it set into motion a massive overhaul of the consumer

---

1.    worldwatch.org, World's Biggest Consumers Hold New Hope For Environment: Worldwatch Study Documents How Green Purchasing is Helping Institutions Save the Planet and Their Own Bottom Lines, Washington, D.C., July 24, 2003

market. Today, largely as a result of this increased demand, 95 percent of all monitors, 80 percent of computers, and 99 percent of printers sold in North America meet Energy Star standards.

…Government purchasing is credited with spurring the rise of recycled paper to the level of standard office supply in many European countries. And analysts link a jump in the environmental performance of Japanese electronics to that country's preeminence in the green purchasing of computers and other high tech products.

Mastny says that one way institutions can help spread green purchasing in developing countries is by using their own procurements to strengthen local green markets. By seeking to buy a greater portion of their goods and services from local green suppliers, leading international players like the United Nations, the World Bank, and multinational corporations can not only stimulate green markets, but also combat mounting criticism about the environmental impacts of their activities.

"Green purchasing will never be a magic solution to the world's rampant resource consumption, but it does offer tremendous opportunities for lessening the impacts," says Mastny. "And as more and more institutions realize the benefits of buying green—in terms of employee health, the environment, and their own bottom-lines—groups that disregard environmental factors risk being left behind."

## *SUSTAINABILITY*

The use of earth-friendly/human-friendly means of manufacturing and doing business is called **sustainability**. Sustainability represents a win-win relationship between human beings, the plant and animal kingdom and the rest of our environment. The idea is that, if we are kind to our environment then our environment will return the favor by letting us live without undue pain and suffering. The concept of sustainability, however, encompasses much more than environmentalism. It is an understanding of how to live in cooperation with other forms of life and the environment in all that we do—in education, politics, religion, entertainment, manufacturing, finance, sports, the arts, industry, health care and government. Rich or poor, conservative or liberal, male or female, black or white, European or Mongolian, fat or skinny, sustainability is our only hope for survival as a worldwide community and a biological species that is undeniably dependent on basic biological necessities:

It's a law of nature that living organisms must exchange raw materials and wastes with the surrounding environment in order to survive. But there are limits to the rates at which the human population can use natural resources without overwhelming the Earth's processes of absorption, regeneration and regulation.

### Sustainability Is Balance

Sustainability is a balanced state of "give and take" between human beings and the Earth. By only taking the amount of natural resources the Earth can regenerate and disposing of only the amount of pollution it can assimilate, we approach sustainability.

### Sustainability Is Responsibility

Sustainability goes a step further than conservation, which seeks to protect natural resources by eliminating the influence of human life. Central to the concept of sustainability is the acknowledgment that humans live within the ecosystems of the Earth—not outside or "on top" of them—and therefore share a responsibility for their care.[2]

Under the umbrella of sustainability are activities that adhere to the basic principle that life is designed to follow a circular flow. For instance, we can make a product from natural substances, utilize the product, then, when we discard it, it returns back to nature without causing unnatural toxicity. Of course, all plants, animals and humans impact the environment; and of course the environment impacts us. This is the way of life. But, with sustainability, we act responsibly by minimizing the damage we do to the world around us—the world that we rely upon to survive in health now and in the future.

In the past 100 years or so, the human race has moved rapidly further away from sustainable practices with the advent of scientific inventions, industrialization, urbanization, consumerism. Some of our inventions are fantastic, while others have been devastating, causing millions of deaths and untold cases of disease and human and animal suffering. Now that science has evolved to the point where sustainability is possible, the only reason not to go down this path is selfishness, greed, ignorance and carelessness. How else could we explain choosing fossil fuels over hydrogen, wind, solar or hydroelectric power? Why opt for a fuel that is a known cause of global warming, smog, carbon monoxide poisoning and cancer? Once oil is burned as fuel it is an environmental hazard. It is not sustainable, not to mention the destruction caused by the process of getting it out of the ground, refining it and transporting it. There's also a matter of loss of life, human

---

2.    worldwise.com, 2002

suffering and environmental catastrophe borne of going to war to seize oil and other resources from nation to nation.

## THE 2002 WORLD SUMMIT

On the day I wrote these particular words, I turned on the television to watch the news—a rare event for me, for reasons already explained. I was intent on finding out which stories were going to make it to the headlines. Each major network began with the same lead—the fact that a Major League Baseball strike had been averted and that professional baseball games would continue as scheduled. This was the most important bit of information the media could deliver to the nation! The baseball story even won out over the president's impending push to bomb Iraq, possibly killing thousands of people in the conflict. At a time when 1.2 billion people in this world do not have sufficient amounts of water to drink, baseball news was determined most important. Events unfolding at the World Summit didn't make the nightly national or local news.

In Johannesburg, South Africa, the World Summit on Sustainable Development came to a close with almost no media attention in the United States. Out of curiosity, I asked everyone with whom I came into contact if they knew what the World Summit was and if they were aware that it had just taken place. The general answer was "No, what is it? I didn't hear about it on the news."

The World Summit was a huge meeting created by consensus of the world's leaders to adopt a meaningful, practical and definitive plan to design national and global policies to address the myriad actions that are destroying our planet. It's serious business, on a global scale, for many reasons, least of which is the fact that even baseball players need air to breathe if they want to run the bases. The 2002 meeting was also being called Earth Summit II and Rio+10, because it came on the heels of the first Earth Summit—officially called the UN Conference on Environment and Development—held in Rio de Janeiro in 1992. The first international gathering to discuss the global environment was the Stockholm Summit held in Sweden in 1972. In 2002, between 20,000 and 60,000 attendees showed up for the World Summit, more or less, counting protesters, party crashers, dignitaries and ambassadors. More than 100 presidents from nations around the world were in attendance to show their sincerity and interest in halting the rapid and uncurbed destruction of the environment and world hunger, and to move forward with more progressive ideas and actions in favor of sustainability. The overriding theme of this event was for nations to join together and act as a global community to end human suffering, environmental destruction and corporate irresponsibility.

The importance of the World Summit cannot be overstated because of its magnitude, involvement of so many nations and its formal, public recognition of the problems facing every living being on this planet. It's big news. Amazingly, the leader of the world's most powerful nation was absent from this historical event. President George W. Bush, to the chagrin, disappointment and amazement of detractors and supporters alike, stands out like a sore thumb, saying to the rest of the world with his actions, "I have no commitment to this meeting because of my investment in, and undying support for, those practices that are contributing to world environmental disaster and human suffering."

The nation (United States of America, home to the corporations and policies causing the most destruction to our planet, was a virtual no-show, giving the rest of the world "the finger." Certainly, a few U.S. delegates attended the World Summit, making excuses for a president who openly earns fortunes in the oil and gas business. But the absence of George W. Bush in person has been taken as a statement of mockery, defiance, smugness and guilt to the rest of the world working to save this reeling planet. This is the same man who stated during his debate with Vice President Al Gore in 2000 that there was not enough proof that global warming exists. Since he took office, Bush has continued his position, through alteration of public records and lying to the American public, that global warming does not exist and therefore presents no danger.[3] This kind of Dark Ages mentality is antiquated and deadly in these modern times when the world's polluters and abusers should be stopped in their tracks before it is too late for the rest of us who care about the futures of our children and grandchildren.

We are at a crossroads in our history as a human race, and our leadership has thus far proven that money and power is more important than health, resulting in a major set back for humankind. Need we remind these kinds of small thinkers that "if you don't have your health, you don't have anything"?

---

3.    "In September 2002, administration censors released the annual EPA report on air pollution without the agency's usual update on global warming, that section having been deleted by Bush appointees at the White House. On June 19th, 2003, a "State of the Environment" report commissioned by the EPA in 2001 was released after language about global warming was excised by flat-earthers in the White House. The redacted studies had included a 2001 report by the National Research Council, commissioned by the White House. In their place was a piece of propaganda financed by the American Petroleum Institute challenging these conclusions."—Robert F. Kennedy, Jr., "Crimes Against Nature," *Rolling Stone*, December 11, 2003, p.187-188

And so, instead of leading the world into sustainable practices, reduction of pollution, obliteration of gas guzzling vehicles and cessation of nuclear power production, the lasting memory of the U.S.'s participation at the world summit is of General Colin Powell being booed completely off stage after suggesting that Africa's starving people were "crazy" not to accept genetically engineered food gifts from the United States. Let 'em eat cake even if the cake isn't really cake, genetically speaking.

For the still-sane among us in the world community, global meetings such as the World Summit are evidence to millions of people and their governmental, religious and educational leaders (excepting the U.S. president, vice president and other such members of this elite club of energy millionaires and industry pawns) that steps can, and must, be taken to ensure safety, happiness, freedom, peace, sustainability and good health throughout the world.

On the 2002 World Summit, environment columnist Stephen Hesse wrote:

> From the depths of our oceans to our atmosphere's ozone layer, there is little doubt that the global environment is taking a beating. Even so, most of us are still waiting for someone else to take action, which is why the United Nations World Summit on Sustainable Development starting this week in Johannesburg, South Africa, is good news.
>
> If all goes as the organizers plan, the WSSD will kick-start worldwide efforts to help millions out of poverty while conserving our planet. The problems, of course, are daunting—and drummed into us daily. So often, in fact, that we have grown inured to them.
>
> But in case you have been daydreaming for several years, and missed the bad news, here are a few examples:
>
> • The Earth now supports more than 6 billion people, but 1.1 billion have no safe drinking water.
>
> • Some 1.2 billion people live on $1 or less a day, while the richest 1 billion receive 78 percent of world income.
>
> • For every single ton of waste, five more tons are produced in the manufacturing stage of the product stream, and 20 more tons at the resource-extraction stage.
>
> • Every day, three to five new chemicals enter the marketplace, though about 80 percent are not tested for toxicity, and toxicology data is not available for 99 percent of the more than 70,000 industrial chemicals now in regular use.

- Of the world's adults, 20.6 percent cannot read or write, and the number of illiterate women has increased over the past decade.

The list goes on, and on—but you get the idea.[4]

Now that the World Summit 2002 has come and gone, we can see what, if anything, has been accomplished. The British Broadcasting System sums up the proclamations and findings of the meeting in Johannesburg:[5]

### Water and sanitation:

- Governments agreed to halve the number of people lacking clean drinking water and basic sanitation by 2015. The deal was welcomed by development charities as an important step towards preventing millions of deaths from preventable diseases.

- Around the world, about 1.1 billion people lack access to adequate drinking water, according to the United Nations. Clean water will save millions of lives It is estimated that half the people in 25 countries in sub-Saharan Africa will not have access to drinkable water by 2025.

- Bringing proper sanitation would significantly reduce diseases such as cholera.

### Energy:

- Governments agreed to take action to help the poor gain access to affordable energy but failed to agree on specific targets to boost the share of global energy produced from renewable "green" sources such as solar or wind power.

- **The European Union wanted targets, but the United States and some other oil-producing countries opposed them.**

- Some want 10% of energy to come from renewable sources such as the sun.

- The summit's action plan calls on countries to "substantially increase" the global share of renewable energy.

---

4.    Hesse, Stephen, "Your planet needs you!," Japan Times, August 25, 2002

5.    BBC News, "Summit conclusions at a glance," news.bbc.co.uk/1/hi/world/africa/ 2230670.stm, 2002

- Environmental groups accused the EU [European Union] of capitulating to American demands. A spokesman for Greenpeace said the agreement was "worse than we could have imagined".

- The summit also saw wrangling over the meaning of the term "renewable," with some countries arguing that nuclear power and lucrative hydroelectric schemes should be included under this banner.

Several smaller proposals on energy were agreed:

- Promotion of energy-efficient technologies

- Removal of lead from petrol

- Reduction in the practice of flaring and venting of gas during crude oil production

- Improving the competitiveness of clean energy sources by creating a level playing field in the market.

### Global warming:

- The Kyoto treaty on global warming got a new lease of life at the summit when Russia announced that it would ratify the treaty. Russia's backing means that enough big producers of greenhouse gases have signed up to bring the treaty into effect. **The treaty received a massive blow when the US said it would not ratify it**.

### Natural resources and biodiversity:

- Governments agreed to cut significantly by 2010 the rate at which rare animals and plants are becoming extinct. Environmentalists fear a retreat from promises to protect species.

- The plan does not set specific targets and the wording does not inhibit countries from pursuing development projects.

- The Worldwide Fund for Nature said the plan "will not provide significant movement forwards…in some cases it actually constitutes a step backwards".

While the list of agreements at the World Summit looks like a progressive start on the face, too many insiders were left feeling emptier than the proposals made. Many nations agree on public recognition of problems ranging from lack of drinking water to environmental concerns, yet it seems no real, binding and enforceable terms were defined before the Summit came to an end.

The United Nations World Summit on Sustainable Development, it has been said, "produced little more than meaningless platitudes in terms of improving access to clean water and sanitation, experts say. The summit's final action plan had a destination without a map."[6] "Michael De Alessi, director of natural resource policy for the Reason Foundation, said the summit succeeded in agreeing to goals everyone approves of such as delivering more clean water to the poor, but because they're not binding, they probably won't have much of an effect. "It sounds great, but I'm waiting for the results," he said. "Targets are meaningless without a program to implement them."[7]

## WHAT CAN WE DO TO HELP?

It is clear that we have very little leadership in this world, and that our own national leadership more often than not represents selfish interests in the guise of democracy. Historically, going back to kings and queens who used to assassinate their own relatives to antagonize the populace enough to take up arms in battle, using live human beings as sacrifices for the acquisition of power and money is nothing new. However, nowadays at least we have an opportunity to be more proactive at the lower levels. We obviously cannot rely on our leaders to care about our environment or human suffering either globally or for our own families, so we should take matters into our own hands. Blaming world leaders for coming up short on their commitments at the World Summit or Kyoto is like blaming wolves for salivating at the sight of chickens. We wish they wouldn't do it, but what more can we expect from animal instincts?

Stephen Tindale of Greenpeace writes, "People have rightly identified that the earth summit achieved very little. However, it's deeply depressing that they're not doing more in their own lives."[8] This is it in a nutshell. We need to become personally involved in making this world a better place. You can do this by buying electric vehicles and hybrid automobiles, supporting solar electricity, refusing to own gas guzzling cars, stop using toxins such as chlorine bleach, fluoride, pesticides and chemical solvents, and eating organic foods. You can buy your goods at family-owned stores rather than supporting corporate giants and chain stores that don't think twice about poisoning your neighborhood, driving your neighbor out

---

6.    Natural Resources Defense Council, "Many Disappointed in World Summit's Results," Sept. 12, 2002, E&E Publishing

7.    ibid.

8.    "World Summit fails to set renewable targets," www.sparkingreaction.info/news, Sept 19, 2002

of business with artificially low prices, using slave labor or impoverishing entire villages to produce their goods, or feeding your family chemicals that pretend to taste like food. Make it personal and spend your money accordingly. It's called socially responsible spending, and it's the wave of the future. Try it, you'll feel good about yourself!

The 1992 World Scientists' Warning to Humanity advised: "A new ethic is required—a new attitude towards discharging our responsibility for caring for ourselves and for the earth. We must recognize the earth's limited capacity to provide for us. We must recognize its fragility. We must no longer allow it to be ravaged. This ethic must motivate a great movement, convincing reluctant leaders and reluctant governments and reluctant peoples themselves to effect the needed changes."[9] We must—as individuals, neighbors, communities, states, families, nations and businesspeople—take responsibility for our actions. Most of all, we need to take things personally.

## ENVIRONMENTAL REVOLUTION, OR ELSE?

Environmentalist Lester Brown, author of *Eco-Economy: Building an Economy for the Earth*, stated that the modern world must either bring its economy into line with the demands of the environment or prepare for decline and eventual collapse. In a statement on Radio Free Europe (Brussels, February 2002), Brown said the rate at which the world's economy grows and its population expands will simply soon exhaust most of the natural resources on which they vitally depend.

> "Our current economy is slowly destroying its support systems. We know from earlier civilizations, whose archeological sites we now study, that when they got on an economic path that was economically unsustainable, they eventually declined—whether that's the Sumerians in what's now southern Iraq or the Mayans in what's now the coastal lowlands of Guatemala or the Eastern Islanders," Brown says. "One can go through a long list of early civilizations whose economies were undermined by environmental degradation and disruption."
>
> In "Eco-Economy," Brown explains how despite all its innovative ingenuity, the ancient Sumerian civilization was eventually brought down by a fatal ecological design flaw. When diverting river water for irrigation, the Sumerians did not take into account what happens when some of the water inevitably "percolates" downward from the fields. Over the years, underground water tables rose gradually. When it got to within a few feet of the surface, the water started affecting the development of root systems. The Sumerians then intro-

---

9.    Union of Concerned Scientists

duced different, more water-resistant crops, but over time water got closer still to the surface and started evaporating, leaving behind salt deposits. This made further agricultural activity impossible, and, as Brown notes, many of the original Sumerian sites in southern Iraq are barren to this day.

Brown often uses the example of China to demonstrate how close today's global economy is to the limits of what is ecologically possible.

Brown says China, with its rapid economic growth in recent decades, "telescopes history"—letting us see what happens if large numbers of poor people become more affluent. He cites in particular the decision of the Chinese government in 1994 to develop a car-centered transportation system. Brown says that to have a car—or two, in traditional U.S.-style—in every garage, China will need more oil than the world currently produces. Or, if paper consumption in China reached U.S. levels, it would need more paper than the world currently produces.

Brown says the "throwaway" approach to the global economy will fail not only in countries with rapidly expanding populations like China and India, but eventually in the rest of the developing and developed world.[10]

---

10.   Lobjakas, Ahto, "World: Environmentalist Predicts Economic Collapse If Trends Continue," Radio Free Europe, www.rferl.org/nca/features, 2002

# People & Nations
## Making A Difference

Enough of the scary, sickening, bad news about our environment, poisoned food supply and toxic habits. To keep us from hanging our heads and jumping off the nearest bridge, there is good news for a change—about people creating sustainable businesses, governments and nations; making wise decisions on energy; and a handful of corporations acting responsibly. Certainly the good ole U.S. of A. is officially far behind the rest of the world in embracing sustainability and healthier energy and lifestyle choices, but maybe if the US government, the media and corporate powers-that-be recognize the ever-growing numbers of Americans welcoming cleaner air and less waste, we have some hope. Sanity, invention, ingenuity (the good kind) and insight are alive and kicking across the U.S. Individuals are on the (progressive) move.

Much credit needs to be given to our neighbors, socially responsible companies and vision-oriented communities who are forging ahead with sustainable business and progress even when the U.S. government and politicians are dragging their feet or putting up roadblocks. Worldwatch Institute writes, "Around the world, businesses, governments, educational bodies and other large institutions are working for a better environment by making responsible purchasing decisions. With each network they form or buying decision they make, these groups are proving that environmentally friendly choices are not only good for the Earth, but are also sound business." Here's some good that should make you think we have a fighting chance to pull ourselves out of the corporate muck…

Worldwatch Institute (July 22, 2003, "Green Purchasing Success Stories," www.worldwatch.org/press/news/2003/07/22/) reports that more than 50 cities and other local governments in 20 countries now belong to the International Council for Local Environmental Initiatives' Buy-It-Green Network (www.iclei.org), which helps members exchange information and experiences, join forces, and make joint green purchases. (p. 44). More than 275 university presidents and chancellors in over 40 countries have signed on to the 1990 Talloires Declaration (www.ulsf.org/programs_talloires.html), a 10-point action plan that, among other things, encourages universities to establish policies and practices of resource conservation, recycling, waste reduction, and environmentally sound operations. (p. 46)

In the hospitality industry, the International Hotels Environment Initiative, a global nonprofit network of more than 8,000 hotels in 11 countries, sponsors a web-based tool (benchmarkhotel.com) to help hotels improve their environmental performance (and save money) through purchases of items from energy-efficient lighting to environmentally preferable flooring materials, refrigerators, and minibars. (p. 46)

The World Resources Institute is recruiting leading companies (thegreenpowergroup.org) to help meet its goal of developing corporate markets for 1,000 megawatts of new green power by 2010—enough capacity to power 750,000 American homes. (p.29)

In 2001, more than a third of the cotton garments Nike produced contained a minimum of three percent certified organic cotton. In 2001, the company helped launch Organic Exchange (organicexchange.org), a network of 55 businesses that intends to significantly expand the use of organic cotton in manufacturing over the next 10 years. (p. 21)

## Europe

In 2002, the Swiss supermarket Migros (migros.ch) became the first European retailer to stop buying palm oil supplies from ecologically unsound sources in Malaysia and Indonesia. The company audits its suppliers for compliance with environmental criteria and labels products that "protect tropical forests." (p. 19)

In Europe, 250 municipal leaders from 36 countries pledged in the Hannover Call (sustainable-cities.org/cevent.html) of 2000 to use their purchasing power "to direct development toward socially and environmentally sound solutions." (p. 25)

## Dunkerque, France

Municipal purchasers in Dunkerque, France, have found that they now save about $.50 per ream (about 16 percent) by buying recycled paper. (p.17)

## Denmark Thinks Green

Kolding, Denmark set an ambitious goal in 1998 of incorporating environmental considerations into 100 percent of its framework purchasing by 2002. By May 2001, roughly 70 percent of its purchasing requests had specified and integrated environmental demands, primarily in the areas of food, office equipment, cleaning products, IT equipment, and health care supplies. (p. 25)

**Japan's Green Purchasing Network** (eco.goo.ne.jp/gpn/index.html) now boasts some 2,730 member organizations, including more than 2,100 businesses (among them Panasonic, Sony, Fuji, Xerox, Toyota, Honda, Canon, Nissan, and Mitsubishi); 360 local authorities in places like Tokyo, Osaka, Yokohama, Kobe, Sapporo, and Kyoto; and 270 consumer groups, co-ops, and other nongovernmental groups. (pp. 45–46)

In 2001, **Toyota** (toyota.co.jp) switched some 1,400 office supply items and 300 computers and other equipment to green alternatives. It achieved 100 percent green purchasing in these areas in 2002. (p. 20)

## United States

The city of **Santa Monica, California** (pen.ci.santa-monica.ca.us), kicked off its green purchasing effort in 1994 with less-toxic cleaning products because a large body of knowledge about product alternatives already existed. Without doing too much additional research, buyers were able to replace traditional cleaners with less-toxic options in 15 of 17 product categories, saving 5 percent on annual costs and avoiding the purchase of 1.5 tons of hazardous materials per year.

In 1999, Santa Monica, California, became the first U.S. city to buy 100 percent of its municipal power from renewable sources, including geothermal and wind energy. The state of Minnesota (moea.state.mn.us) now has some 110 different contracts for green products and services, including alternatively fueled vehicles, low-toxicity cleaning supplies, energy-efficient computers, and solvent-free paint.

## Green Angels

In 2002, the U.S. Archdiocese of Los Angeles received thousands of dollars in local rebates when the Cathedral of Our Lady of the Angels became the city's first religious edifice to install solar panels on its roof, generating enough energy to power both the building and more than 60 additional residences.

## All That Jazz

In 2001, the city of Chicago and 48 suburbs pooled their jurisdictional resources to buy a larger block of electricity at a reduced rate, and will use the savings to meet at least 20 percent of group power needs with renewable sources by 2006.

### *Kansas City & Jackson County in Missouri*

...have agreed to pay a premium of 15 percent more for alternative fuels, cleaning products, and other products they consider environmentally preferable.

### *Holy Coffee Beans!*

Catholic Relief Services (CRS) is working to get U.S. churches and parishioners into the practice of buying "fair trade" coffee (a certified product that guarantees farmers a fair price for their crops). "There's a lot of coffee being moved through faith communities," says Karen Smith, director of CRS' coffee program. "It's tying into people's values, and they're making conscious decisions based on their values." Americans spend $19 billion on coffee each year. With 65 million Catholics in the U.S., CRS is hopeful this new initiative can have a positive impact on coffee farmers everywhere.[1]

### *Smart College*

In 2001, more than three-quarters of students at Connecticut College (connecticutcollege.edu) agreed to a voluntary $25 increase in their activity fees to fund the school's transition to renewable energy. By January 2003, the school was supplying 22 percent of its annual electricity consumption from new wind energy, the largest share purchased by any U.S. college or university. (p. 38)

In November 2002, a group of 56 environmental groups across North America adopted a set of common environmental criteria for environmentally preferable paper and released detailed guidance to advise paper buyers about their choices. (conservatree.com/paper/Choose/commonvision.shtml) (p. 39)

### *Delighted With Denmark*

In Denmark, construction worker David Gibson, head of the Copenhagen local of the waste and power workers' union, began to look deeply into alternative energy.[2] His first fear was that new environmental measures could create a loss of jobs at coal plants, but this was overcome with the thought that the newer energy industry would create even more jobs. He was right, because the Danish wind power industry bloomed "overnight into 10,000 good-paying jobs." This encour-

---

1.    organicconsumers.org, Yoo, In Sung, Faith organizations throw weight behind 'fair trade' coffee movement, *USA TODAY*, December, 2003

2.    Walljasper, Jay, "The Next Revolution: The emerging eco-economy will transform society," Tune Reader, Sept.-Oct. 2002

aged people to begin working to clean up the environment. Gibson put his union members to work for the common good by expanding recycling programs, installing energy and water conservation systems and more.

Writer Jay Walljasper, in his article on Gibson and the Danish success story, wrote:

> A study commissioned by the General Workers Union, Denmark's second-largest trade confederation, identified thousands of potential green jobs. Ole Busck, health and environment director for the largely blue-collar union, told me, "We looked at proposed plans for cleaning water pollution for reducing traffic, and greening cities and calculated that 40,000 new jobs could be created...Danish unions now use their political clout to push for vigorous environmental measures along with green taxes to help fund ecological cleanups. "Rather than dragging our feet on environmental regulation, we found that there are great economic opportunities in being ahead of the rest of the world in pioneering new environmental technology, Busck said.[3]

Denmark is a model world citizen, having stabilized its population growth, done away with coal-fired power plants, banned non-refillable beverage containers, and established wind powered electricity. Thirty-two percent of all trips in Copenhagen are now made on bicycles.

### Other Countries On the Mend

South Korea has instituted a massive reforestation campaign, the Netherlands has aggressively been promoting bicycle and pedestrian transportation, China has begun to stabilize its population, and Singapore and Norway have limited urban automobile traffic. Costa Rica has committed to all renewable power by the year 2025.[4]

### More Progress in the USA

Alternative energy is now a reality in the United States, thanks to the ingenuity and support from the private sector—and no thanks to the mainstream media, politicians or oil billionaires meeting our crisis with their brakes on and their heads perpetually shaking "no." (Total private investment in wind energy in California alone, for example, amounted to $3.2 billion through 1991). Here's a progress report:

---

3.  ibid
4.  ibid

## Wind Power

Lake Benton, MN, is proud to be known as the "Wind Power Capital" of the American midwest. Presently the home to over 200 wind turbines—with more currently under construction—Lake Benton is emerging as an important source of alternative, wind-generated electricity.

A 1990 study of Minnesota's wind energy potential by the Department of Public Service found that the area around Lake Benton—the "Buffalo Ridge"—has enough wind to produce electricity well in excess of a full year's net electrical consumption in Minnesota. The Buffalo Ridge provides more high-grade wind resources than the entire state of California.[5]

Fort Collins, CO, government officials, following this city's adoption of a wind energy program, show that each 660 kW wind turbine reduces the amount of coal burned by more than 980 tons per year and eliminates more than four million pounds of carbon dioxide emissions annually. Besides carbon dioxide, every kilowatt-hour of wind energy offsets emissions of sulfur oxide, nitrogen oxide, particulates and other pollutants and reduces the accumulation of toxic materials found in coal.

## Power From the Sun

In Philadelphia, solar energy is working out just fine...The Cooperative, a Phila-delphia-based competitive energy supplier, agreed to buy the electricity produced by Andy Rudin's residential solar energy system in Melrose Park, PA. Under this landmark program, the Energy Cooperative will pay its members who have a photovoltaic solar system twenty cents per kilowatt hour for the output from their system. The Energy Cooperative of Pennsylvania is the first non-utility competitive supplier in the country to institute a residential solar energy purchase program with its customers.

> "Our goal is to change the economics of solar power," said Nadia Adawi, Director of Operations for the Energy Cooperative and author of the program. "The Cooperative's financial support can reduce the payback for a typical photovoltaic system by as much as 30%. We want all of our members to consider putting a system on their roof."
>
> Glen Thomas, Chair of the Pennsylvania Public Utility Commission, said "Pennsylvania has become a national leader when it comes to renewable energy—thanks to electric competition and to the spirit of innovation we have fostered here. We applaud this kind of market innovation."

---

5.    American Wind Energy Association, 2002

Solar power is widely recognized as one of the cleanest ways to generate electricity. And contrary to popular belief, solar power works quite well in the Philadelphia area, which gets as much as 70% of the solar radiation as extremely sunny places like Tucson (AZ). Also, solar works best just when electricity is in highest demand—during hot, sunny weather.[6]

## Reducing Vehicle Pollution in Portland

The city of Portland, OR, has "launched the first comprehensive citizen carbon dioxide reduction program in the nation. By embarking on a 30-day low carb diet, Portland residents can lose 5,000 pounds—of household carbon dioxide emissions. In the campaign's initial phase, 50 households racked up CO2 savings of some 200,000 pounds."[7]

Also from Portland—the American Automobile Association now has a green counterpart, thanks to two entrepreneurs from Portland, OR, who created Better World Travel Club (BWTC) which will designate a portion of each airline ticket purchased through the club for energy conservation programs. "The club also offers discounts on electric and hybrid car rentals as well as on bicycle and electric car purchases.[8]

## Clean, Healthy Organic Dining

Restauranteurs Jon and Yvonne Pell operate a very successful organic restaurant in Boulder, CO, called Sunflower. As an award-winning chef, Jon is a stickler for clean, healthy food, from the oils he uses to his organic salad bar, and from his filtered water to his organic wine selection. Jon's ingredients include certified organic vegetables, free-range poultry, fresh seafood and an all-organic salad bar. He also offers organic wine, organic beer, organic coffees and raw, organic cheeses. He uses no refined sugar, and you won't ever find a packet of artificial sweetener for your tea or coffee. Instead, he offers agave or honey. A large part of Jon's success is that he is personally committed to his family's health, having adhered to an organic diet for the last thirty years. In this day and age when organic eating is just another fad for too many restaurants, for the Pells this is a lifetime enterprise. Sunflower is a fine dining restaurant, unique not only for the

6.  The Energy Cooperative: Sun Provides Electricity; Local Company Provides Financial Incentive: Energy Supplier Kicks Off Summer Season With Innovative Program, "Purchases Solar Power at a Premium," Philadelphia, PA, June 2002
7.  Tune Reader, New Planet, Sept/Oct 2002
8.  Tune Reader, New Planet, Sept/Oct 2002

quality of food, but also the upscale ambiance, showing that it *is* possible to eat out at a fine restaurant while nurturing your health at the same time. The Pells' restaurant is a favorite among visiting celebrities, locals and tourists, and is the perpetual winner of Boulder's best natural foods restaurant award.

Jon Pell advises, "I hope that some time soon we all begin to realize that it would be best to support our local, organic and biodynamic farms for most of our food and let the huge, petrochemical based factory farms fade away for good. We then can return to eating the truly delicious and health promoting foods that our families consumed for millennia, and some day those environmentally destructive agribusinesses will simply be viewed as a passing fad. As usual, let common sense prevail, and if you cannot pronounce an ingredient in what you're eating, it is probably not good for you or, ultimately, the health of the planet."

### *Celebrities For A Better World*
### *—Actor Ed Begley, Jr. Raises the Bar*

Television and screen actor Ed Begley, Jr., ("St. Elsewhere," "Best in Show," "A Mighty Wind") a longtime environmentalist, was the first retail customer to purchase Toyota's RAV4-EV electric vehicle in 2002. In addition to his new RAV4-EV, he is also the owner of a Toyota Prius gas/electric hybrid vehicle. "The RAV4-EV demonstrates Toyota's commitment to the environment, the EV market and consumers like myself who are looking for a functional zero-emissions vehicle to meet their everyday needs," said Begley, Jr. "I'm very excited and honored to be the first retail owner of a RAV4-EV in California."[9] One interviewer said, "Ed's commitment is more than just lip service. He grows his own vegetables and commutes across the country via AmTrack passenger train which he regards as more environmentally benign than jet travel. If he has to go any distance by road, he relies on his second car which uses compressed natural gas. Ed's solar home, which was built in 1936, provides him with nearly all his electric power, all but about $40 worth a year which he buys from his local power company. His photovoltaic system generates nearly 7 kW of energy, enough for him to also recharge his EV1 [electric vehicle].[10]

Other celebrities have started to purchase environmentally friendly gasoline electric hybrids. One such popular automobile is the Toyota Prius, which has been honored as The Greenest Car in America by the American Council For

---

9.    www.canadiandriver.com/news/020305-6, 2002

10.   "Confessions of an EV Purist: An Interview with Ed Begley, Jr., Omaha, NE, May 31, 1998, www.evworld.com

Energy Efficiency. Celebrities from the entertainment, political, environmental and technology areas include Larry David (Seinfeld, Curb Your Enthusiasm), Brad Pitt, Donna Mills, Donny Osmond, and Leonardo DiCaprio.[11] During the 2003 Academy Awards, several celebrities, including Cameron Diaz and Harrison Ford, pulled up to the red carpet in Hybrid automobiles. Director Rob Reiner traded in his BMW for a Toyota Prius, and Larry David traded in his Lexus.

A recent article in EV World stated:

> The list of Hollywood's hybrid-come-lately car owners reads like the table of contents of People magazine: Cameron Diaz, Leonardo DiCaprio, Carole King, Billy Joel, David Duchovny and Bill Maher, to name-drop a few. Patricia Arquette bought one recently; so did rocker Jackson Browne. Larry David bought three, including one so that his character, "Larry David," could drive one on his HBO series, "Curb Your Enthusiasm."
>
> "It works on every level," says David, who is married to a staunch environmentalist. "I'm doing something good, and my wife has sex with me more often."
>
> Asked about his car, DiCaprio responded with an e-mail, writing, "This is the most radical mass-produced car in the world and I can't find any downside. My family and I own a total of four, and we drive them all over Los Angeles."
>
> The Prius (pronounced PREE-us) isn't the only hybrid car on the market. Honda makes the two-seater Insight, which gets 68 miles per gallon, and just started mass-producing a hybrid Civic. But Toyota's version, with its computerized display showing fuel consumption, has captured the imagination of Hollywood buzzmakers.
>
> Larry David first got a hybrid because his wife, Laurie, has strong views about big, gas-guzzling SUVs, which are hugely popular in Los Angeles and hugely annoying to her.
>
> "Those cars should just have 'pig' spray-painted on them," says Laurie David, apparently not one for understatement. The Prius, she says, is the antidote. "I got involved because of global warming, but hello! It's national security now. Shouldn't we be reducing our dependence on foreign oil?"
>
> The Davids started something of a chain reaction among their friends. "I have one because I found out they existed," says Reiner. "Larry David had one; he told me there's this hybrid car...I thought, 'Here's something I could actually do that would save on gas, save the environment, protect us from global warming.'"
>
> Commentator Arianna Huffington bought one last week. "I got a little tired of hearing how we're at war, and we're being asked to do nothing about

---

11.  ibid

it but go shopping, go to Disneyland and the mall," she says. Huffington gave up her SUV in November, then sold her Lexus when she recently saw the Davids' hybrid. "It is very much a little peer pressure," she says. "Positive peer pressure." And it's a conversation piece. The day Huffington got the car, she drove it to lunch at the Bel Air mansion of Selim Zilka, a former oil baron who is now a leading proponent of wind power. Within minutes a dozen people had filed out to gawk at the little motor that could run on gas or electrical power.

"The parking lot was full of Jaguars and Bentleys," she recalls, "and my host...brought everyone out to the driveway to look at Arianna's car. It became this point of attraction."[12]

## More Celebrity Support

Many celebrities have shown their support of environmental issues by attending the Earth Summit at the United Nations. Among these stars were Susan Sarandon, Alicia Silverstone, Kevin Bacon, Patrick Stewart and Joe Pantoliano. Hollywood also has its own voice for the environment in an organization called The Earth Communications Office (ECO). It uses the power of the entertainment industry to deliver messages about the earth to the general public. The board of ECO is comprised of talent in the film, television, music, advertising and public relations industries.[13]

Actor Kevin Bacon commented, "From the day my son was born, I've been concerned about leaving a legacy of an unhealthy planet and I continue to be concerned about my children's future."[14]

Concerns over dangerous nuclear dumping have prompted Mike Farrell, well known for his role in M*A*S*H, to deliver a letter to Congress signed by more than 50 celebrities, urging politicians to reject two nuclear dump proposals. Those signing the letter included: Harry Belafonte, Ossie Davis, Jamie Farr (Klinger on M*A*S*H), Ken Howard, Melissa Gilbert (Little House on the Prairie), Danny Glover, Tess Harper, Marilu Henner (Taxi), Judd Hirsch (Taxi), Norman Lear, Bonnie Raitt, Rob Reiner, Tim Robbins, Loretta Swit (M*A*S*H's Margaret Houlihan), Ed Asner and Alec Baldwin.[15]

---

12. EV World, "Half Gas, Half Electric, Total California Cool," *Prius becomes politically correct in Hollywood,* Source: Washington Post, June 06, 2002

13. Shaw, Sue, "Celebrities Who Care: Actors, Singers, Musicians step forward to save the planet and animals," SORT, 7-01-2002

14. http://www.hollywoodplayersnetwork.homestead.com/celebsenvironment.html, Hollywood Byline, 2002

15. Shaw

## *Sensible & Sustainable Transportation:*
## *Evolved Mobility: King of the Hill*

Advanced transportation specialist Graham Hill, Boulder, CO, www.21wheels. com, has put his engineering and mechanical skills to use by converting vehicles to electric power. Hill is a leading-edge advocate of alternative energy solutions, an environmentalist and industry consultant who is focused on urban livability conditions. He uses a solar-powered lawnmower at home, owns a Daimler Chrysler GEM, hosts lectures and author appearances on environmental issues and alternative energy, organizes his neighborhood transit program and works as a lobbyist for a cleaner environment, electric vehicles and sensible mass transit systems.

Graham started his company, 21 Wheels, in 1997 with an emphasis on consulting transit agencies and developments on smart mobility strategies. His company is fully engaged in air pollution remedies, shared vehicle systems, intermodalism, mass transit, bikes, electric bikes, pedicabs, small electric vehicles and renewable energy. He presides over the Boulder County (Colorado) Clean Air Consortium and the Denver Electric Vehicle Council. Between 1997 and 2001 he lobbied and helped successfully pass legislation for electric vehicle incentives in several states.

Graham Hill tells us, "The current U.S. transportation system, corporate politics and the American mindset (affected by marketing)—must evolve sensibly to enable us to move into a more realistic, sustainable energy paradigm." He candidly explains both the problem and solution facing the stressed-out U.S. transportation system:

> Perhaps one of the greatest issues we must overcome in the United States is our thirst for more and more cars that dictate our embarrassing and lazy lifestyles. The quest and ever-misleading campaign put on by Detroit and other large auto makers, continues to drive the point home that Americans need an open road to satisfy our need to "get away from it all." Well, with 40 million cars sold worldwide, there just isn't a lot of room for this type of campaign to continue. With Americans' thirst for 25% of the world's oil, represented by only 5% of the population, it is no wonder our destructive, out-of-balance approach to transportation and fuel consumption is beginning to take its toll on the world's stage. The Center for Disease Control attributes some of our increasing obesity statistics to poorly designed, sprawling neighborhoods and our car-first attitude.
>
> Could there be a better time for our bureaucrats to commit the billions needed to build an effective national rail system? Our aviation system came

under attack in 2001, and much of it is because of our head-in-the-sand attitude toward protecting our Almighty lifestyle. The world is not envious of us, they are fed up with us! It is now time to accept that we need to humble ourselves and understand the attitude that exists about the United States outside of our borders before the whole world turns against us. We are addicted to having and owning more. It is no wonder that the U.S. is experiencing these problems. We pay $2 less at the pump for each gallon of gasoline we purchase compared to other western countries. Can you imagine if we just added an additional dollar to the price of a gallon of gas, what kind of rail system we could build?

Our insistence to demonstrate to the world that the private auto is the cats meow has caught the eye of the Chinese. They now are busily planning to build massive quantities of their own cars to satisfy their desire to look like the west. This could be very scary if indeed it does happen. What we need to do is begin to model the new American household!

We need to demonstrate the new American heartbeat. One that is conscientious towards our environment, our resources and our community. We need to build neighborhoods that provide transit, close proximity to our groceries, schools and other services that we typically frequent in a car. We need to build green homes, using recycled products and renewable energy to heat and cool them. It is our turn to show everyone that we care and we can change our desire to always have the best. We can spend our money on things that matter, and curtail our ownership of hardly used second and third vehicles that sit on average of 22 hours a day, with no positive long term effect on our society. We need to explore with vigor shared vehicle systems, electric bikes, advanced appropriate sized vehicles operating on batteries and fuel cells. We need to raise the driving age to 18 and we need to vote for policy makers who can make these things happen. Tax breaks and other incentives are vital to this notion of evolved mobility.

We no longer can afford to allow corporate America to dictate our lifestyle! We must become sustainable yesterday. We need to applaud those individual oil sippers who have respect for what we have, and follow their leads. Let them do the modeling and the policymaking that can help us gain the needed respect we need before thousands of more people die of wasteful air pollution due to our unbalanced mobile lifestyle. Let's not forget that General Motors, Firestone Tire, and Standard Oil conspired to eliminate our fabulous street car system. We must change the direction in which we are going—fast!

# Removing Toxins
# From Your Body

It's true that a bubbling, festering, poisonous soup exists in our world—in our food supply, land, water, air and personal care products. The question is: While we're trying to rid our environment of these toxins, how do we get them out of our bodies, or at least minimize their accumulation and deleterious effects on our health? First, we have to stop denying the problem...

Let's put forth a very clear and explosively direct accusation of all scientists, corporations, politicians, PR execs, processed food manufacturers, fast food chains and chemical companies who proclaim that chemicals and industrial waste do not make people sick and die. These people lie and deceive us so that they can make billions of dollars a year. They hire scientists who lie and bend the truth and forge inaccurate, misleading "research" findings. They cover up deadly practices. They defame and ruin the credibility of consumer advocate groups and individuals trying to save our lives, suffering of all life forms, human and financial resources, and precious health. And they are concerned with making huge profits despite the fact that our relatives (and theirs) are dying of cancer, tuberculosis, heart disease and diabetes. We cannot listen to anyone who tells us that any amount of pollution, industrial waste or chemical that we eat or in any other way come into contact with, is at all safe. Artificial chemicals are deadly. Period.

We as human beings are not biologically equipped to ingest chlorine, fluoride, gasoline, automobile and truck exhaust, plastic gases, artificial ingredients, refined sugars, drug compounds, nuclear waste, radioactive materials, processed foods in cartoon-crafted boxes, aspirin, mercury, lead, MSG, paint fumes or any other unnatural chemical through our mouths, lungs or skin. Whether we notice today, tomorrow, or 20 years in the future, the fact is that all of the chemical creations of scientists take their toll on our health. Anyone who says otherwise is either lying or deluded, either because he/she has been deceived by corporate science, or because he/she is working for corporations. Ignorance of the laws of nature is no excuse.

## *DETOXIFY YOURSELF*

One of the finest books written on diet and toxicity is *Natural Detoxification* by Jacqueline Krohn, MD and Frances Taylor. There is no simpler textbook for understanding and acting upon the toxic problems we face through our daily diet and lifestyles. The authors explain, "Our bodies act like sponges, absorbing the chemicals to which we are exposed. Water-soluble chemicals are absorbed and then excreted. However, fat-soluble chemicals accumulate in our fat cells and cell membranes, becoming internal toxins. When the body is under stress, it releases these chemicals from the fat to circulate in the bloodstream. Later, these chemicals will return to the fat cells and cell membranes, to be released another time. The release and return cycle of these chemicals continue indefinitely unless we help our bodies rid themselves of toxins."[1]

One of the ways to eliminate these toxins is through reduction of exposure, which may mean moving away from a contaminated neighborhood or workplace; or to change your diet to include only organically grown foods. An additional means of elimination is through the process of bodily detoxification.

If you eat the typical, modern, Western, daily diet, you need to detoxify yourself at least periodically. The modern diet of commercial grocery store and restaurant food consists of what has been termed "foul nutrition," meaning that the foods in the diet are health-defying, disease-causing; and failing to support the health, maintenance, repair and recovery mechanisms of the body. The diet has also been referred to as of late as SAD (Standard American Diet).

There is a range of troublesome foods consumed in the "typical" modern diet, including fast foods, French fries, ice cream, burgers, potato chips, iceberg lettuce salads, sauces, frozen dinners, frozen foods, crackers, cheese spreads, fake butters, mayonnaise, soft drinks, beer, soft drinks in aluminum cans, instant tea, candy and pastries. This is only a small sampling of the modern fare, but it gives you an idea of whether you are personally partaking in a health-defying diet. If you didn't even know that such non-foods were bad for you, you are in good company, because I used to be the king of the Sad Food Diet before eventually discovering the difference between junk food and healthy food. Even worse than getting relatively no nutritional value from the SAD diet, is the fact that these foods actually rob you of health, causing nutritional deficiencies, building diseases, manifesting in symptoms and resulting in lowered immune systems. Depending on the constituents of these foods, they have the ability to remove

---

1.    Krohn, MD, Jacqueline and Frances Taylor, MA, Natural Detoxification, A Practical Encyclopedia, 2nd Ed, Hartley & Marks Publishers, 2000, p.6

important vitamins and minerals from your cells, break down tissue linings, starve glands and organs of nutrients, create ulcerations in tissues, drain you of energy, disallow your cells from rebuilding and multiplying, and impair your mental/emotional faculties.

Nutritionist/author Dr. Bernard Jensen used to say, "Today's doctors make a living on bad diets." The problem is, however, that only a handful of medical doctors are only now just beginning to recognize "disease" as toxic overload. A human being is not biologically designed to survive on a diet of burgers, fries, milk shakes, artificial ingredients, fried foods and pies. None of these types of commonly accepted foods can be found in nature. They are convenient to eat, but destroy us in the long run if you think about how much time, money and health is lost once they cause the demise of your health and your children's health.

Perhaps more startling than the fact that the modern, processed-foods diet is devoid of the building blocks of health is that these foods actually contribute to your storage of toxins. Why? Because they are full of chemicals such as pesticide residues, dyes, chemical flavorings, MSG, refined sugars, altered fats, hydrogenated and partially hydrogenated oils, emulsifiers, separators, texturizers and preservatives—many of which are not even listed on the label. Soup is good for you, but not CHEMICAL soup!

## *HERE'S HOW TO SAVE YOUR FAMILY FROM POOR HEALTH FROM EATING TOXIC CHEMICALS*

Go on a "detox diet" to eliminate chemicals from your daily eating regime. This diet is suggested in the book just noted, as well as in several other sources. Sure, your kids may still eat peanut butter (if they can tolerate it), but you just need to know what kind is the healthiest choice—the kind that contains only three ingredients: 1. organically grown peanuts, 2. salt 3. honey. There should be no other ingredients. If there are names of chemicals on the label, then don't eat it.

And you can still eat burgers when you learn how to buy meat without steroid, hormone and pesticide residues (all of these toxins are contained in USDA beef, despite how the beef industry may rave about the value and quality of beef).

You can also drink milk and orange juice, but without the pesticides and other chemicals that are contained in the commercial brands. Horizon brand is one great example of a healthful, organic juice and milk company.

## THE DETOX DIET

Biochemical researchers tell us that toxins—particularly heavy metals and metal compounds—entering through our diet, drugs (prescription, over-the-counter and otherwise) and the environment are not all eliminated (as are natural food wastes) from our bodies through digestion, respiration or perspiration. Instead, they are stored in certain tissues for which they have an affinity. Some toxic metals are stored in bone, such as aluminum and fluoride, while others are stored in fat, such as dioxins, etc. These toxic substances, more often than realized, lead to nerve damage, disease, birth defects and premature death.

The idea behind the detox diet is to eat real, natural, whole foods that supply the body with the nutrients and energies to help pull toxins out of the tissues wherein they are stored. If someone is particularly "toxic"—sick from toxins stored in their body tissues—in addition to the detox diet, there are specific herbs and foods that can be used to help detoxify the body. Some of these include olive leaf, cat's claw, pau d'arco, kelp, grape leaf, burdock root, dandelion root, red clover, echinacea, milk thistle and others.

NutriPlex Formulas, a whole food concentrate company, makes a detoxification supplement tablet (called Detox Formula) that contains a number of the above foods and herbs designed to detoxify the body of toxins. (nutriplexformulas.com)

There are also some non-foods (found in most healthfood stores) that are used for detoxifying, including bentonite clay, charcoal and psyllium seed. The latter work by promoting better digestion and detoxification as they clean out the digestive tract and pull toxins out of the cells.

EDTA, a chemical compound, is administered by certain physicians for more serious cases of toxicity and heavy metal poisoning in a clinical treatment called *chelation* therapy.

But the oldest method of detoxification, mentioned in religious texts the world over, is fasting (refraining from eating anything, and only drinking water or juices). Fasting, lasting a few days or longer, has been used successfully for detoxing for thousands of years.

## HERE'S HOW YOU CAN TELL THE DIFFERENCE BETWEEN HEALTHY FOODS & CHEMICALIZED FOODS

Read labels carefully. Believe it or not, most people do not read the labels on the foods they buy every week at the grocery store. Way back when I started eating a healthy diet, I learned that most foods in the average grocery store contain a host of offensive chemicals,—even ketchup and mustard, baking powder and salt, canned soup and beef stock, and ice cream. It's truly amazing that most Americans eat chemicals by the caseload without knowing it—hundreds of pounds of chemicals a year. The average American eats more than 140 pounds of sugar alone. And the evil geniuses working for processed food manufacturers are laughing all the way to the bank as your children are getting sick from the SAD diet you are feeding them in good faith—faith that our government is protecting us from dangerous chemicals, and faith in the big companies that advertise on television and in magazines while tugging on your heartstrings. Well, guess what—these corporations and their paid-off buddies in our government allow the use dangerous chemicals in foods if they want to because it is not illegal to do so even if it makes us sick. So we have to become proactive, taking matters into our own hands, educating ourselves and policing our own pantries. We cannot rely on government agencies that are influenced by multi-billion-dollar corporations who demand the right to feed us toxic chemicals as they try to trick us with food products that are crisper, longer-lasting, richer, fluffier, brighter or more "flavorful."

To tell the difference between foods and chemicals, here are some names of foods:

- carrots
- beets
- barley
- spinach
- mushrooms
- zucchini
- peanut butter
- grapes
- oranges
- lemons
- strawberries
- whole wheat flour
- tomatoes
- sea salt

- cold-pressed, unrefined olive oil
- raw, unrefined honey
- raw, unrefined maple syrup

Now here are the names of some chemicals that are not foods and are known to cause health problems because the human body recognizes them as "foreign invaders" once they enter your body:

- orange flavoring
- MSG (monosodium glutamate)
- table salt
- sugar, brown sugar, high fructose corn sugar, corn syrup, sorbitol
- grape juice sweetener
- refined maple syrup
- egg substitutes
- seasonings (unspecified)
- butylated hydroxytoluene (BHT)
- dyes such as yellow #5, blue #1
- aluminum (such as aluminum phosphide)
- decanal (synthetic flavoring)
- disodium EDTA
- aspartame
- artificial flavoring

And don't be fooled by the use of the word "natural" on a label. It means very little, and does not protect you from consuming toxic chemicals. When you start to seriously read labels, you'll discover, as I did, that food companies have been poisoning you and your family without remorse. It takes evil genius to get the whole modern world to eat fake, chemical-laden foods then tell us the reason why we are sick is due to a flu or bacteria or viruses or genetics.

## *EAT MORE NATURALLY*

There are literally thousands of artificial ingredients found in today's foods that have no place inside of our bodies. For an extensive list, pick up a copy of Ruth Winter's *Consumer's Dictionary of Food Additives* and have a blast. It is no wonder why unbiased scientists say that people who eat mostly fruits and vegetables have far fewer instances of disease—such people aren't consuming gallons of artificial, synthetic chemical ingredients that take a toll on their health. A recent study from Sweden published in the *International Journal of Cancer*, showed that there is a 30% lower risk of lung cancer in people whose diets are high in fruits and vegetables; and 40% lower in those eating a lot of non-citrus fruits. The study also showed that carrots decreased the risk of lung cancer.[2] Another study, from at Johns Hopkins University in Baltimore, showed that fruit and vegetable consumption increases antioxidant defenses.[3] Still yet another study, in 1999, showed that a diet of fruit and vegetables protects against stroke.[4]

Eating more naturally is the best form of defense we have against disease, even when caused by environmental assaults from automobile emissions, toxic waste and household pollutants. Eating "naturally" means raw fruits, vegetables, seeds, nuts and grains. Eating "unnaturally" means processed foods, foods with chemicals, cooked foods, altered oils and fats, foods in packages and boxes, and synthetic ingredients. Read all labels. If it's not real food, don't eat it.

Many of nature's foods and herbs have the ability to detoxify us. Cilantro, for instance, removes mercury from our bodies. Green tea protects against cancer and tooth decay. Bilberry protects against many eye diseases. Brussels sprouts, cauliflower, broccoli and cabbage prevent certain cancers by flushing fat-soluble toxins out through the kidneys. Milk thistle protects the liver from toxins.

## *ANTIOXIDANT FOODS*
## *& WHAT'S WRONG WITH VITAMIN PILLS*

The term "antioxidant" is relatively new in our vernacular, but it is still not widely understood. In very simple terms, toxic substances rob our bodies' cells of

---

2.   *International Journal of Cancer* 1998;78:430-6
3.   "Fruit and vegetables increase antioxidant defenses," *Circulation* 1998;98:2390-95
4.   Kaumudi J. Joshipura, ScD; Alberto Ascherio, MD; JoAnn E. Manson, MD; Meir J. Stampfer, MD; Eric B. Rimm, ScD; Frank E. Speizer, MD; Charles H. Hennekens, MD; Donna Spiegelman, ScD; Walter C. Willett, MD, "Fruit and Vegetable Intake in Relation to Risk of Ischemic Stroke," *JAMA. 1999;282:1233-1239,* Vol. 282 No. 13, October 6, 1999

oxygen. We all know how important oxygen is to life, because if we don't have enough, or if we are being robbed of what we do have, our bodies cannot perform myriad biochemical and physiological functions like breathing, immunity from disease, digesting foods, creating energy and so forth. Nature's foods contain extra oxygen; some of these antioxidant (food substances that keep us from being robbed of oxygen) foods are those high in vitamins A, C, and E. BUT vitamin pills are not enough because they only contain vitamins and no real food ingredients. We need to eat vitamin-rich whole, natural *foods*, because many food ingredients contain antioxidants other than vitamins. Water, for instance, is an antioxidant. So is the mineral selenium.

### The Difference Between A
### Vitamin & A Food

Although there is a great vitamin craze going on, vitamins are merely chemicals, even if labelled "natural." Vitamins never exist in isolation (alone) in nature. There is no such thing as a vitamin tree. Vitamins naturally exist within real, raw, whole foods. Foods contain vitamins, but vitamins never contain the other very valuable ingredients we need from foods. For instance, not contained in vitamin pills—yet found within real foods—are bioflavonoids, terpenes, minerals, trace minerals, enzymes, coenzymes, fiber, chlorophyll, phytoestrogens, phytonutrients, flavors, aromas, food energies, grass factors, amino acids, whole proteins, essential fatty acids, lipids, pigments, carotenoids, and other valuable food components. These food factors (missing from vitamin pills) exist within a "complex," which means they are all interrelated, interdependent and interconnected. These factors exist and work synergistically—harmonizing as co-ingredients (team workers). When you isolate them (pull them away from their "complex), they do not work the same. Vitamins (in pill and tablet form) are merely isolated chemicals. There's a big difference, which is why we need much more than just vitamins to support life and health. (See the author's book, *Man Cannot Live on Vitamins Alone* for a more complete discussion of this subject).

If you cannot eat all of the right foods you need, the next best thing you can do is to find a good whole food concentrate supplement. This type of supplement contains real, whole, raw foods that have been concentrated into supplement form. And make sure that the brand you buy is not infused, or mixed in, with a bunch of isolated vitamins and minerals. One place you may look for good whole food concentrate supplements (as mentioned above) is online at **nutriplexformulas.com.** Whole food concentrates contain antioxidants and other important food factors, including certain green foods and herbs that, among other things, help nutrify and detoxify the body.

## *THE ULTIMATE DIET —RECIPE FOR HEALTH*

The word diet used here is not the same as a weight loss diet. Instead it is used to mean your daily diet, or what you eat on a regular basis, not for weight control, but for sustenance and promotion of health. It is a lifetime commitment, not a short term, temporary change in eating habits.

The best diet is one that contains only real, whole, natural, raw (or slightly steamed), organically grown foods plus grains and modest amounts of meat (fish, poultry, beef). Since we are all biologically and biochemically different/unique, there is no one perfect diet for everybody. However, none of us are biologically designed to consume, process and eliminate substances that contain toxins and heavy metals, so these should never be part of a healthy diet.

Modern diets fail to deal with the toxins we ingest through our food choices. Our families are not meant, biologically, to thrive on Fruity Loops, pasteurized and fortified (enriched with synthetic vitamins) milk, multiple vitamin pills, mineral toddies and colloidal mineral supplements, prescription drugs, pesticide-sprayed apples, Kool Aid, box drinks, cola, candies, fake butter, cheese wiz, protein powders, body-builder powdered formulas, cheese doodles, power bars, and cookies that contain more chemicals than house paint. These foul foods take their toll on human health so by the time we are in our 40s we "get" cancer and begin to look at all the studies showing us that cancer comes from bad genetics and viruses. Nonsense! We are making ourselves sick; we are not being "attacked" from the outside; the enemy is within. We're not "catching" disease, we're creating it ourselves. When you combine this lifestyle and the SAD eating habits of modern peoples with environmental toxins, you have the recipe for illness. Food manufacturers, power companies, nuclear plants, oil men and car manufacturers may deny this until hell freezes over (which is now a growing possibility), but this is the truth.

**Here's what you can eat to replace the nonfoods/foul foods in your diet:**

- organically grown raw seeds (sunflower, pumpkin, etc.)

- organically grown raw fruits (peaches, pears, apples, nectarines, tomatoes, oranges, lemons, limes, grapefruits, grapes, raisins, kiwi, watermelon, pineapple, etc.)
- organically grown raw or slightly steamed vegetables (cucumber, squash, zucchini, broccoli, spinach, romaine lettuce, beets, carrots, mushrooms, peppers, onions, garlic, Brussels sprouts, cauliflower, etc.)
- organically grown raw nuts (almonds, Brazil nuts, walnuts, pecans, cashews, macadamia nuts, pine nuts, etc.)
- organically grown grains (quinoa, spelt, whole wheat, rye, barley, oats, brown rice, etc.)
- deep sea fish
- organic raw nut butters (almond butter, tahini, sunflower, etc.)
- clean, purified water, and fresh squeezed organic fruit and/or vegetable juices
- minimal amounts of organic meats (chicken, turkey, etc.)

You can actually live off of these healthy foods in great health and happiness. You will feel better and avoid countless trips to the doctor's office. In fact, I know a handful of people who eat this way (including myself and my family) who rarely visit a medical doctor, because this kind of diet is the best kind of ensurance against illness you can have. All of these foods are less expensive than chemicalized, processed foodstuffs, because the savings in health, suffering and lifestyle are priceless, considering the benefits—

- no wasted time traveling to a doctors office
- no cost for doctor's visits
- no cost for deductibles
- no cost of travel to doctors, hospitals and pharmacies
- no cost for prescription and over-the-counter drugs, including aspirin, sleep medicine, stimulants, depressants and pain relievers
- greatly reduced or nonexistent pain and suffering
- no missed work, school or socializing
- no lack of mobility and function

- no other of the thousands of miseries people have needlessly made a part of their daily lives.

## EXERCISE

Lifestyle is also important. Regular exercise helps promote blood flow (circulation), digestion, lymphatic health, bone strength and the elimination of toxins through the skin, lungs and bowels. Some detox doctors claim that one of the best methods of detoxification is by promoting perspiration through exercise (or at least through saunas and steams). (Perspiration carries toxins out of the pores for elimination).

Exercise also engages the mind and provides a release for those stressed-out, pent-up emotions we have from racing by one another at 80mph or waiting 20 minutes on the telephone to straighten out a billing problem on our credit card or with the telephone company. Exercise is as natural as eating an organically grown apple, although both are now rare in the modern world. The best kinds of exercise for detoxification include those that promote an increase in heart rate and perspiration while engaging vigorous movement of the limbs, neck and torso. Examples include running, calisthenics, kickboxing, aerobics, Tae Kwon Do, swimming, climbing, cycling, hiking, full body weight (gym) workouts, basketball, fencing, gymnastics, Judo, Aikido, among others.

## BACK TO NATURE

There is an inherent wisdom and balance to nature and nature's foods beyond the comprehension of modern science. This is what led Thomas Edison to say, "Until man duplicates a blade of grass, nature can laugh at his so-called scientific knowledge." With all his scientific enlightenment, Edison was still in awe of the complexity and dynamism of nature. As time marches on, fewer and fewer people are appreciating this sense of awe, which is what gets us into the toxic, polluted, overcrowded and unhealthy mess we find today. The remedy is so simple because it's right here in the soil under our noses, the wind in our hair and the sun beating down from above. The hope for humankind to reverse the destruction to the environment and life forms on this planet is to once again embrace that which is natural for sustainable solutions to our problems.

# Thwarting the Evil Geniuses

It is most appropriate that we use a farming analogy to illustrate the solution to our problems of toxicity and how it affects our personal and environmental health! To make a change—to save ourselves—we need to sow new seeds and nurture what is natural. Whereas most environmentalists justifiably talk of shifting to alternative energy, less consumption, planting more trees, growing organically and ridding the world of dangerous chemicals, the truth is, to be effective, we have to first replace existing attitudes with more progressive ones. Change must begin with an attitude shift, or all of the ideas and plans for sustainability and environmental progress are moot.

But change in attitude does not come merely by presenting the problem and proposing a solution. No, it is too late to use logic on a brainwashed, mind-altered society. People do not make decisions, choices and changes based on reason alone. Any upper level, covert secret, special marketing ace working for Wal-Mart, GM or Microsoft will tell you this is a non-permutable law of nature. Corporate power brokers and their public relations purveyors of evil genius have beaten us to the punch. They have poisoned more than just our planet. They have poisoned the minds of people to readily accept or ignore the toxins they are force-feeding us through our food, air, land and water.

To truly make a change for the better—to save our dying planet—our environmental strategists need to spend a healthy chunk of their dollars waging a public relations game of their own, because this is where the war against destruction of the environment and health of our families must be fought. For what use is it to tell your neighbor that his SUV is destroying the air that you all must breathe if he does not—on some grander emotional level—feel the urge to contribute to the world's cleanup operation, beginning with his own habits, choices and attitudes? How do you stop your friends from consuming so much gasoline unless they connect the death of their sons at war in the Middle East to their own unquenchable thirst for oil? How can anyone care to give up fast food if they are denied the images of a barren, battered and plundered rain forest?

The first step before we can fully blossom into a sustainable society is to implant new attitudes—new feelings—in people at the most basic level. We have to find a way around our own politicians and corporate controlled-media to do this. This may take an entire overhaul of our national media. And we should use the same sensual, psychological methodologies employed by the evil geniuses who have for so long skewed and diminished our common values and sensibilities. Their success in manipulating the minds of the masses for greed can be the model for "reverse engineering"—taking apart their system of codependent attitude-building and restructuring it for the common good. If they can get consumers to believe that toxic sludge is good for them, or that cancer is caused by bad genes, then there is hope for us who want to instill in our populace the idea that banning pesticides is less painful than watching your sister waste away from cancer day after day in a cold, sterile hospital ward. And using solar power is preferable to having our sons return from the Middle East in body bags.

For physical changes to manifest, seeds must be planted at the spiritual, emotional and mental levels. This is basic psychology and we cannot ignore its power if we want to recapture our wholeness, love for the environment and a society based on mutual respect. Brochures, facts, figures, demonstrations, case studies and pleas are not enough to get the job done. We need to reach people at a basic, emotional level, not merely to get them to recognize our plight, but to embrace our solutions and bear arms against injustices to humanity. We have to have mothers and wives understand, appreciate and be motivated to unravel the connection between their sick children and the incinerator burning a mile away, between beautiful automobiles and cancer from vehicle emissions, between her grocery cart full of genetically engineered food and corporate control over the earth's food sources, between babies with mercury poisoning and those corporations dumping mercury in our oceans, and between helpless, malformed infants and needless drugs prescribed by physicians at the advice of a pharmaceutical salesman looking to make his quota. When these connections can be made, there is nothing that can stop a mother from protecting and defending her children—not even the wall of lies and deception reinforced by the evil geniuses polluting, dismantling and degrading our Garden of Eden.

*When the people of the world all know beauty as beauty,*
*There arises the recognition of ugliness.*
*When they all know the good as good,*
*There arises the recognition of evil.*

—Lao-tzu
(604 BC–531 BC)

# APPENDIX

## *Personal & Environmental Health Resources*

At the time of publication, the websites listed in this section were working just fine. If they no longer are in service, you have my apologies. The environmental listings here are by no means complete, nor the most important. I encourage the reader to continue to search for bigger and better organizations supporting natural and environmental health and sustainability.

### *BOOKS*

Franken, Al, *Lies and the Lying Liars Who Tell Them: A Fair and Balanced Look at the Right*

David Suzuki, *Sacred Balance*

David Suzuki, *Good News For A Change*

John Stauber & Sheldon Rampton, *Trust Us, We're Experts!*

John Stauber & Sheldon Rampton, *Toxic Sludge is Good For You!*

Vic Shayne, *Man Cannot Live on Vitamins Alone*

Vic Shayne, *Illness Isn't Caused by a Drug Deficiency!*

Elson Haas, *The Detox Diet*

Jacqueline Krohn, MD & Frances Taylor, MA, *Natural Detoxification*

Michael Moore, *Stupid White Men*

Michael Moore, *Dude, Where's My Country?*

Peter Phillips, *Censored*

David Steinman, *Safe Shopper's Bible*

Ruth Winter, *Food Additives*

Kim Erickson, *Drop Dead Gorgeous: Protecting Yourself from the Hidden Dangers of Cosmetics*

Martin Teitel & Kimberly Wilson: *Genetically Engineered Food: Changing the Nature of Nature*

Sharon Beder, *Global Spin: The Corporate Assault on Environmentalism*

New Society publishers: newsociety.com

## MAGAZINES & JOURNALS

*The Green Guide: www.thegreenguide.com*

*Tune Reader*

*Earth Island Journal*

*E Environmental News*

*Mother Jones*

*The Nation*

*The Ecologist*

## WEBSITES

*(you may need to add the preface "www." before these addresses)*

Greenpeace: greenpeace.org

Save What's Left: savewhatsleft.org

World Watch Institute: worldwatch.org

Seventh Generation (especially for their *ToxicTimes* online publication): seventhgeneration.com

Clean Car Campaign: cleancarcampaign.org

Environmental Mobility, Alternative Transportation: 21wheels.com

Clean Air & Household: annieappleseedproject.org

Public Citizen: Health, Safety & Democracy: www.citizen.org

Environmental Working Group: ewg.org

Malathion Research: chem-tox.com/malathion/research

Environmental News Network: enn.com

Organic Consumers Association: organicconsumers.org

Healthy Household Products: safe2use.com

Pesticide Action Network: panna.org

Healthier Coffee: sustainableharvest.com

Free Speech: freespeech.org

Earth Island Journal news: earthisland.org

PR Watch: prwatch.org

Censored News: projectcensored.org

Chemical Industry Archives: chemicalindustryarchives.org

Vancouver Electric Vehicle Association: veva.bc.ca

Corporate Watch: Holding Corporations Accountable: corpwatch.org

Rachel's Environmental Health & News: rachel.org

Fluoride Research: nofluoride.com

Breathing & Pollution: psr.org/breathe.htm

Whole Food Concentrate Supplements: nutriplexformulas.com

Sustainability & Environment: David Suzuki Foundation: davidsuzuki.org

scorecard.org

ewg.org

nutritionresearchcenter.org

greenpeace.org

cspinet.org

adbusters.org

prwatch.org

projectcensored.org

21wheels.com

peoplepoweredmachines.com

gristmagazines.com

safe-food.org

nontoxic.com

nottoopretty.org

chemicalbodyburden.org

breastcancerfund.org

chem-tox.com

worldwise.com

emagazine.com

naturalhomeproducts.com

safe2use.com

ecowise.com

saveourenvironment.org

enn.com

earthpolicy.org

cleancarcampaign.org

enviroalternatives.com

chemicalbodyburden.org

worldwatch.org

# Index

0-595-30686-1